G. Wakeling

The Oxford Church Movement

Sketches and Recollections

G. Wakeling

The Oxford Church Movement
Sketches and Recollections

ISBN/EAN: 9783337003937

Printed in Europe, USA, Canada, Australia, Japan

Cover: Foto ©ninafisch / pixelio.de

More available books at **www.hansebooks.com**

ABERDEEN UNIVERSITY PRESS.

THE
OXFORD CHURCH MOVEMENT

SKETCHES AND RECOLLECTIONS

BY THE LATE

G. WAKELING

WITH AN INTRODUCTION

BY

EARL NELSON

"The Church of Christ was intended to cope with human nature in
all its forms, and surely the gifts vouchsafed it are adequate for the
gracious purpose."

—Introduction to Tracts for the Times.

LONDON

SWAN SONNENSCHEIN & CO.

NEW YORK: MACMILLAN & CO.

1895

TO

THE MEMORY OF

THE REV. WILLIAM JOHN BLEW, M.A.

OF WADHAM COLLEGE OXFORD

WHO

WHEN CURATE OF ST. ANNE'S SOHO 1842

SHEWED US

IN LIFE AND PRECEPT

IN DEVOTION REVERENCE AND WORSHIP

WHAT THE MOVEMENT

THEN BEGINNING

IN THE ENGLISH CHURCH

REALLY WAS

THESE SKETCHES AND RECOLLECTIONS

ARE AFFECTIONATELY

AND GRATEFULLY

Dedicated

" For the Catholic Church—
    Its establishment and increase.

For the Eastern—
    Its deliverance and union.

For the Western—
    Its adjustment and peace.

For the British—
    The supply of what is wanting in it ;
    The strengthening of what remains in **it.**"

BISHOP ANDREWES' *Devotions.*

INTRODUCTION

BY

EARL NELSON.

I HAVE much pleasure in writing a short introduction
to Mr. Wakeling's book. To those who, like myself,
were under the influence of the Oxford Movement
from early college days in 1842-43, the remembrance
of the various works and workers must ever be of
great and pleasing interest. But for all there is
much instruction to be gained in seeing how in the
great cause the hearts of men and women, of varying
character and in different walks in life, were drawn
in one by one to sow the good seed ; and in searching
out the way in which the soil in every place had
become prepared for its reception.

Many an earnest soul had felt the deadly torpor
that was surrounding us, but knew not the way of
escape : hence it was that when the trumpet sounded
so many in various classes in life were ready to
answer to the call, and to do their part in raising

the Church from its slough of deadness and de-spondency.

In fact, the very negligences over which we mourned had prepared a soil ready for the good seed, as well as sowers to sow it; the want of properly conducted services and of real pastoral work had created a yearning for something true and real, and had driven our people back upon the study of their Bibles and Prayer-books as the only way in which they could hope to discipline their daily life on sound Church principles. So that in after years it was often remarked that with all our improved teaching and renewed life we had failed to implant among our people that high standard of Church doctrine which shone with a bright ray here and there from truly noble saints in many a neglected parish. The beginning of the evils which had oppressed the Church may be traced to the infidel movement which brought in the French Revolution, and the degraded position of our Church and the Erastianism of it under Walpole's Government. Mr. Wakeling has, therefore, wisely pointed to the great Evangelical revival as the first rising out of the deadly stupor into which the Church had been drugged.

The principal desire of the writers of the *Tracts for the Times* is well foreshadowed in their preface— "The Church of Christ was intended to cope with human nature in all its forms, and surely the gifts vouchsafed it are adequate for that gracious purpose. There are zealous sons and servants of her English branch who **see** with sorrow that she is defrauded **of her** full usefulness **by** particular theories and principles of the **present** age, which interfere with the execution of one portion of her commission ; and while they consider that the revival of this portion **of truth is** especially adapted **to** break **up** existing parties in the Church, and to form **instead a** bond of union among **all who love the Lord Jesus Christ in** sincerity, **they believe that** nothing **but these** neglected doctrines, faithfully preached, **will repress** that extension of popery for which the ever multiply-**ing** divisions of the religious world are **too** clearly preparing the **way."**

It is wonderful **to** see how these desires, written **nearly** sixty years ago, have come so near fulfilment, and have **been** abundantly blessed.

In 1834 the Church's enemies were speculating on her fall : now, **by** God's mercy, she **is** full of life—to which this book **so** wonderfully **bears witness.** But the same life **and vigour have been** imparted to those Christian **bodies who are still,** unhappily, **not in** full communion with her.

The religious zeal which has been **stirred up within her** borders, and taking very **much** the same lines, **has** stimulated life among our Protestant noncon-formists, **while it is** notorious **that the** secessions of our over zealous friends to Rome have imparted new life and spirit to that communion **also.**

NELSON.

P.S.—It has pleased God to call to his rest the author **of these** " Sketches and Recollections ".

Mr. G. Wakeling had himself done much **to sow the seed and** advance **the good cause,** and was a true example of that humble Christian spirit through which the leaven was unostentatiously spread abroad by the daily witness **of** the faithful **followers of our** Lord and **Saviour** Jesus Christ.

N.

TRAFALGAR, 26th *August,* 1895.

NOTE BY THE AUTHOR.

THESE sketches and recollections are simply and truly what their name implies, and do not claim to be a chronological or systematic statement of events. Canon Liddon, in the few words of introduction to his memoir of Bishop Hamilton of Salisbury, has expressed what I would wish to say—" In a mere sketch the reader will not be disappointed at finding neither the exhaustive treatment nor the orderly sequence of events which belong to a biography". Still less would I presume to claim for them a place among the many valuable and historical works now published on the Church revival. They were originally written for the pages of the *Newbery House Magazine,* and it is only in deference to the wishes and opinion of many who read them there that they are now published in a more permanent form. I have endeavoured to recall some few ways in which, from my own personal knowledge, the Tractarian movement spread and made its influence felt in London and other towns and villages, and to describe the persons who were the prime movers and workers, and to whose loyal adherence to the principles of the great leaders we are now indebted for many privileges. Though in these sketches various trials and troubles have been recorded, it may still be objected that they have too much a tone of progress and success. In reply I need hardly say that I write about men and women, and, of course, there were many failures, backslidings and inconsistencies among the people of whom and during the period of which I have written. I have to express my thanks for many valuable suggestions and much information to Earl Nelson, the **Rev. J. L. Fish**, Rector of **St.** Margaret Pattens ; the Rev. Canon Overton, Rector of Epworth ; the Rev. A. Barrington Simeon, Rector of Bigbury, Devon ; Miss Skene, of **Oxford**; Frederick Lambert, Esq. of Garratt's Hall, **Banstead ; and Henry G.** Slade, Esq.

G. WAKELING.

RECOLLECTIONS OF THE OXFORD MOVEMENT.

CHAPTER I.

DEAN CHURCH's volume is the story of the first twelve years of the movement; and there we read of the chief movers in the revival, the great thinkers and writers, the men of learning, energy and perseverance, who set themselves the task of showing that the "trumpet of the Church of England" did not really and truly "give an uncertain sound". He tells us how these leading men laboured and preached and wrote, in spite of all difficulties and opposition. So excellent a record of the source and early work of the movement is invaluable.* We have also Mr. Thomas Mozley's *Reminiscences of Oriel*, which relates what is interesting and amusing about those early workers, though it does not help us much to a knowledge and insight of the one great distinctive mark of the movement,—the extent of its deep religious and devotional aspect. Arch-

---

* Sir John Coleridge's *Life of Mr. Keble* and Mr. Lock's more recent life of him add much to our knowledge.

I

deacon Denison, too, records many of the troubles
and controversies, inseparable from the work, in which
he was ever valiant and staunch; then we have that
brilliant addition to our knowledge in the Letters of
Dr. Newman during his life in the Church of England,
and the story of James B. Mozley's beautiful life as
told by his Letters, both of these being admirably
edited by Anne Mozley, now also called to her rest.
Then we have another very welcome addition to the
history in the autobiography of the Rev. Isaac Williams, Fellow and Tutor of Trinity College, Oxford.
He, although, like Mr. Keble, for the greater part
of his life a simple country parson, was one of the
earliest writers in the cause, the author of some of
the *Tracts for the Times*, of *Sermons and Devotional Commentaries*, and of many exquisite volumes of
poetry, *The Baptistery, The Cathedral, Thoughts in Past
Years*, etc. In this last little volume we learn very
much that will help us to a true estimate of the work
of the movement, and we find what it was that made
John Keble such a wonderful power; and as we look
at the splendid pile of buildings in Oxford raised to his
memory, we no longer marvel that such a memorial
to a simple country vicar came to be erected. Keble's
influence on Isaac Williams was very important; his
description of it is worth recording: "One so overflowing with real genuine love in thought, word, and
deed was quite new to me. I had been used to much

gentleness and kindness in good society, but this was understood to be chiefly on the surface ; but to find a person always endeavouring to do one good, as it were, unknown to one's self, and in secret, and even avoiding that his kindness should be felt and acknowledged as such : this opened upon me quite a new world—religion a reality, and a man wholly made up of love, with charms of conversation, thought, and kindness, beyond what one had experienced,—this broke in upon me all at once."*

The story of the Professorship of Poetry at Oxford is an amusing one. All made sure that Isaac Williams would succeed Mr. Keble ; but it was not to be, and Archdeacon Garbett, who had never written any known poetry, was elected. Years after, on the archdeacon's death, a leading journal of the day really suggested that Isaac Williams' poetry was then not much more remembered than Archdeacon Garbett's *Prælectiones*, although edition after edition of Isaac Williams' poems were still selling and much valued. Dean Burgon, in

---

* Isaac Williams was curate to Dr. Newman at St. Mary's, Oxford, and worked with him and Mr. R. H. Froude, in all the early publications. He was Newman's intimate friend, officiating at the funeral of his mother. Isaac Williams and Newman retained their affectionate friendship through all the years of change and separation. On May 3, 1885, Newman wrote from the Oratory, Birmingham, to a friend : " Have you heard of the death of Mr. Isaac Williams ? I saw him last week, and never saw a person so near death in body, yet apparently so perfectly himself, and with such perfect ordinary command of his mind."

his *Lives of Twelve Good Men*, adds to our store of knowledge the only published lives of two of the most prominent workers in the early days of the revival, Hugh James Rose and Charles Marriott.

From 1825 to 1836, Hugh James Rose, in spite of constant ill-health, was a perfect tower of strength, and "restorer of the old paths". Of Trinity College, Cambridge, 14th Wrangler, he brought all his brilliant talents to help forward the movement. He was curate of Buxted, then vicar of Horsham, and vicar of Hadleigh, then principal of King's College, London, where such famous men as Bishop Selwyn, Bishop Patteson, Bishop Abraham, first heard, knew, and valued him. As editor of the *British Magazine* Mr. Rose was known far and wide, and in America to such as Bishops Hobart, Doane, Whittingham, etc. He was essentially a great teacher, just the man to make a stand ; and at Hadleigh conferences were held in preparation for the literature of the movement, stirring men's minds up, reminding them of ancient truths ; the future Archbishop of Dublin (Trench) was for some time his curate at Hadleigh. In later years Mr. Rose was domestic chaplain to the Archbishop of Canterbury (Howley) ; his early death was a great loss to the movement. He was deeply valued and loved by Newman and Pusey ; the former dedicated the first volume of his *Parochial Sermons* to him, and in Mr. Rose's illness wrote to assure him that he was ever in his prayers morning and evening. **To Dr.** Pusey, when hearts were failing, and friends deserting, such an one **as** Hugh James Rose **would** have been a strong help; **and we may feel sure** his help and advice would have cheered Dr. Pusey in his great labours.

Charles Marriott, the Oxford Fellow, student, **and scholar, spent his life in Oxford,** with **the** exception **of a short time as principal of** the Chichester Theological College, where **he succeeded** that learned divine, Henry **Browne. Marriott was** ordained **priest** at **All** Souls, Regent Street, by Bishop Otter, in **1839,** when Dean Chandler was rector there. He **was** known throughout the University as a man of saintly character, great theological learning and classical attainments, shy and retiring; yet his labours in the **work** of the movement were very great. Fourteen years **he spent in** translating, collating, correcting, or editing **twenty-four volumes of** the *Library of the Fathers.* In **1850 he** succeeded Eden as vicar **of St.** Mary's, Oxford, **and** his work **as a parish** priest **was** well known. **He never** thought of himself **or his own** personal safety, and was fearless **and** faithful, ministering up to the last to the cholera and small-pox patients, 1854, caring afterwards **for** the children of parents who **had** died. All testify to his singleness of purpose, **purity of** heart and heavenly character, from James B. **Mozley,** to his deacon curate, R. E. Sanderson, of **Lincoln College, now Canon** of Chichester, and long

Headmaster of Lancing College. Mr. Upton Richards
said of him, on leaving his grave, " Blessed are the pure
in heart ".   Charles Marriott was the author of two
volumes of sermons, and of *Hints on Private Devotion*,
dedicated to the Bishop of Brechin.   His library was
given to Bradfield College.   He was a power for good
in the University; and the Bishop of Lincoln, Dr. King,
gave the highest testimony to that when he said, " If
there is any good in me I owe it to Charles Marriott ".

With such works we can hardly fail to realise in
some measure the extent and depth of the movement ;
and we now have the most important addition to our
store in the *Life of Dr. Pusey ;* we can hardly over-
estimate its value and importance ; and, besides, it is
the work of the last few years of Canon Liddon, who
gave up all but the duties of St. Paul's Canonry, that he
might devote himself to the biography of his dearest
friend.   In these volumes we have the life and character of one of the chief workers in the great movement,
the one certainly who worked longest and hardest.
His childhood, the care of a good mother, Lady Lucy
Pusey, his boyhood, his pure college life, his marvellous industry and careful scholarship, his Fellowship
of Oriel at twenty-three, his study of languages, his
Canonry of Christ Church, and Regius Professorship of
Hebrew at twenty-eight, his studious habits and energetic unselfishness, his short married life, and the home
at Christ Church with his wife and children, she ever

one with him in **all** his plans and his magnificent and self-denying **gifts are** all detailed; here **we** see **the love and affection of them** all for Newman, and **his love for** them; **the** work and writings **of the** movement, and Pusey's great share in it all: writing, preaching, editing, translating, defending, replying to objections and misunderstanding, **as a** faithful son of the Church of England, with one and only one object in view—to assert and defend **the** true principles and claims of that Church, and this amidst the greatest obloquy and misrepresentation; these volumes clearly show that in his loyalty to Christian antiquity **he** was only taking the Church of England at **her word.** Never was a more critical time for the Church than **that** of 1846; in this crisis **Dr. Pusey's** wonderful power was exercised, and by it **he** rallied round him **the** clergy **and** laity about many of whom I **am** telling **in these sketches.** The death of Mrs. Pusey, and the drifting apart of Newman and Pusey, are most pathetic **as** was said afterwards, " Newman depended on the Bishops, but Pusey looked to God's Providence acting through the Church ".

Lastly, mention must be made of Canon Overton's *Church of England **in the** Nineteenth Century*, a graphic and historical account **of** all the chief workers in the **Church** before 1833, **the** leaders who founded the great **Church** societies, and their progress as the forerunners **of the** Tractarian Movement.

The men we read of in these works were, no doubt, men of very great personal influence, with a wondrous power of imparting their deep convictions, and sound theological learning ; but this influence, great as it was, could only reach a certain number. We do not find what a reviewer of Dean Church's book in the *St. James's Gazette* felt to be still wanting, *viz.,* " a knowledge of how the Church Movement reached the country generally, the gradual trickling of the stream through the quiet drowsy villages, washing away the dust of a century and a half ". But neither Dean Church, nor Canon Mozley, nor Thos. Mozley, nor Dr. Pusey, nor Canon Liddon could have told all this part of the story. My object is to tell some part of that story about men and places here and there, together with some account of the literature of the Tractarian Revival, the writings of the thinkers and workers. A short record of these may help to show more clearly how the movement progressed in the country generally, in the quiet towns and sleepy villages. Even a short account of the literature might form a history in itself—the tracts, theological works, sermons, commentaries, the hymns, poetry, stories, allegories, magazines and reviews, works on music, art, and architecture, books of devotion and instruction, also works of controversy to meet the endless objections of opponents—all this should make a not unattractive story to Church people generally.

One of my earliest recollections as a boy was of a conversation in my father's house in London, about 1840, between a Londoner of some cultivation and a gentleman farmer from Essex. The latter was asking of the new sect of Tractarians, then so much talked about. " Well," replied the Londoner, " the few I know who hold these opinions are among the very best people of my acquaintance in life, manners, business, and morals." " Ah," replied the farmer, " we don't want any of that sort down in Essex ; we don't want to be interfered with, but prefer to go on in the way we are used to." What that " way " was I had a chance of understanding a little later on : dining with one of those gentlemen farmers, with six or eight guests, the death of one of their neighbours was announced ; he had been a friend of the master of the house, but the only remark I heard was, " Well, every dog has his day " ; one could only conclude that the way these gentlemen preferred going was not a very elevating or refined one. Those were the times when the farmers and labourers clattered out of the fine old parish church of Ware, when the vicar (Mr. Coddington) ascended the pulpit in his surplice. Let us hope that there was more ignorance than malice about it ; of course, there were some few who stood by the vicar and his curate, the first incumbent of Ware Side (the late much lamented Dr. Butler, Dean of Lincoln), among them the names of John Sworder and Walter Tween

may still be remembered. **Mr.** Butler's *Sermons to
Working Men*, published about that time, **were dedicated to** Walter **Tween, his** churchwarden ; **these**
sermons were often used **and preached by other** clergymen.

The record of Dean Butler's **life and work** has so
recently been before us, that I cannot hope to add **anything** of moment. **He was** a most earnest preacher and
splendid parish priest, **with the** gift of organising those
sisterhoods which **have been one** of the most valued
fruits of **the** movement. **From** Wantage grew that
most **useful body of** women **who** now undertake and
superintend **the** work **of nursing,** rescue, and training,
bringing help and comfort **to the** afflicted, sick, and
fallen, and carrying on works of mercy full of untold
blessings to thousands of our fellow-creatures. Dean
Butler was one who never spared **himself,** and was ever
ready at the cost of much labour to help with his voice
and pen, with a **fixed,** determined, and fearless energy.
A wonderful **testimony to his** work is that **of the**
clergy, sisters, **school** teachers, and others who **have
worked under him ; it is** most interesting to remember
his very early labours at that small district **of Ware**
Side, Hertfordshire, **and** to see the extent and influence
of the work begun at Wantage.

Not far off, in the county of Essex, one could tell of
many unmeaning, absurd, **and** irreverent pieces of ceremony and ritual, kept **up from year to year,** the inven-

tion of some former verger, official, or parish clerk, such as the turning round to the organ of the whole congregation when that instrument began to play   A relative of mine was married at one of these churches ; on the occasion, as the altar and its covering would have disgraced the vicar's kitchen, he presented a new altar cloth ; the enlightened vicar and churchwardens carefully laid it by and put it on when the donor and his wife came to visit in the parish.   In another corner of Essex I remember a vicar who was three parts a farmer, and certainly wore in service time what one could hardly distinguish from an ordinary smock-frock as the only vestment over his usual clothes.   The whole arrangement and service were of the very worst and meanest.   It was a seaside parish, and I often went out sailing with a hearty, middle-aged fisherman, and had a quiet chat with him and his wife.   Married life was our topic one day, and to my great surprise I found that this happy-looking couple had never been married. I talked a little about it, and asked if the vicar knew of it and ever mentioned it.   The reply of the sailor was characteristic of the tone of the religion then in the county : "Oh, no, sir, our vicar's a most hexellent man, and never hinterferes with nobody's business ".

In the *Life of Louisa, Lady Waterford*, just published, her sister, Lady Canning, writes from Curraghmore, 1844 : " Lou has been reforming the clergyman. She gets him and his curate to examine (catechise) the children, and gives him plenty of work about her clothing club; and in church she has by perseverance got the whole congregation to stand when the Gospel is read and when the Psalms are sung, which was never done before."

But the Church Movement rapidly spread around and about, and quickly altered that state of things: it brought out a race of honest, earnest parish priests, who gave themselves up to the life set forth in the Tractarian works then being circulated.

It is called the Movement of 1833; but, as a fact, there were many pioneers, who, several years before that date, were teaching and working on the same lines.

Some mention, too, may be made of still earlier religious revivals — the Wesleyan, the Evangelical Movement, the work of such lovers of souls as Toplady, Simeon, Venn, Cornelius Neale and John Mason Good (the father and godfather of John Mason Neale, our great theologian, historian, liturgiologist, and hymn-writer), Wm. Wilberforce, Bickersteth, Leigh Richmond, Elliott, Pym, Villiers, Marshall, and many others. These were the men to whom Dr. Pusey refers in that preface to a volume of his sermons, where he hints that a better knowledge of such men, and more familiar intercourse with them, might show that our differences were not so great or so inevitable. We do thankfully acknowledge all that was good and true in those earlier revivals; it was something to have one side of the great truths of our holy religion so earnestly and vividly set before us. No one doubts that solid good was the result of that early evangelical revival, and that many were so led to embrace the whole of the Faith as it is presented to us in our Creeds and Prayer Book Offices. We see many of these early evangelical names in the ranks of the Tractarian Movement. The names of Simeon, Wilberforce, Dale, Villiers, and Bickersteth, occur to us at once. Here and there, no doubt, there was much bitterness and angry denunciation which has long since passed away, except in the records of some so-called Protestant associations. How inappropriate to general feeling now would be Mr. Doyle's caricature in *Punch* of "A Christian Gentleman denouncing the Pope" in Exeter Hall; or the address of a noble chairman in that same hall, who concluded a violent speech by exhorting his hearers to do all in their power to uproot and destroy the Catholic Faith—"Which except a man believe faithfully he cannot be saved"—was shouted from the body of the hall. Then the speaker explained that that was not what he meant; no doubt, in those days, men did say more than they meant in the heat and fervour of polemical debate. It may safely be affirmed that the attacks for the most part were made by our opponents; High Church folk were not often given to seek notoriety, or to attack on their part.

The story of one famous exception is worth telling, and perhaps it was one of the most severe that occurred. A certain popular dissenting preacher and D.D. in the East of London had written a book called " Lectures on Puseyism," and, either with or without permission, had dedicated it to H.R.H. Prince Albert. The author was also the proprietor and editor of two religious newspapers, in both of which, for some time after publication, appeared a great many laudatory notices of this book. A week or so after these flattering reviews, there appeared in one of these papers a letter, in large type and good position, addressed to the editor, suggesting how exceedingly useful these " Lectures on Puseyism " were, and venturing to inquire if the royal person to whom the book was dedicated had taken any notice of the work, and how valuable his opinion would be ; how it would render the work more popular, and recommend it to the youth of the country. The letter ended with a desire that some steps should be taken to obtain His Royal Highness's opinion. The letter was signed by a clergyman's name, and dated from a vicarage in Brighton. Next week a second letter appeared, urging still more the great importance of obtaining Prince Albert's opinion on the lectures, and advising a humble address to the Queen, that Her Majesty would be pleased to lay her royal command, as it were, on the Prince Consort that he should give his opinion of this valuable book. This second letter was signed by the same clergyman from the same **vicarage. Next** week a third letter appeared **in** continuation of the subject, giving **a** form **of** petition to be addressed to Her Majesty, with the object that she should request Prince **Albert to give his written** opinion of this important **work, and proposing that** some chief members of **the** nobility, etc., **should be asked to** start **the petition with** their signatures. Here **followed the names of** ten **or** twelve lords, ladies, baronets, etc. This letter **was** signed by the same clergyman from the same vicarage. **A few** days afterwards an article appeared **in a well-known** weekly review showing that the whole thing was **a joke.** The letters were readily taken and printed **by** the reverend editor, who was thought to have been praising **his own** book in his own newspapers. No such clergyman **as the one who** signed **the letters** existed, there **was no such** vicarage as that whence **the letters were dated, and of all the** noble names suggested **not one was then living.**

With many controversialists **in those days it was** the custom **to date all** religion from the Reformation, oblivious **of the fact** that they were thereby playing into the hands of Rome **more** surely than all the ritual and ceremony that was ever practised. Even in a recent Privy Council trial the counsel **for** the Church Association actually suggested that the present Church **of England had no** connection as **to canons,** councils, documents, **ritual or** rubrics, with the **Church before**

the Reformation. **Such a statement** might well, as it did, astonish even the Lord Chancellor; and next **day, as a sort of** apology, a " legal continuity " **was acknow-** ledged. **It was a** curious anachronism that such an **opinion** should **have** been uttered before a court that **was** discussing the judgment of **the 95th** *Archbishop of Canterbury !*

But to return to the earlier days. **Many years be-** fore 1833 **there were** men **of piety, learning, and renown, teaching** and preaching on the same **lines** as the Tractarian Movement, who were in **some** true sense pioneers. **I** can only mention **a few of these, such as Bishop** Jebb **(who was buried in the tomb of the Thorntons** at Clapham)**; Alex. Knox ;** Bishops **Van** Mildert and Jolly **;** Patrick **Cheyne ; Mr.** Slade **(who wrote a** commentary **on** the **Psalms) ;** Arch-**deacon R. W.** Evans, of Heversham, author **of the** *Rectory of Valehead,* **and many other works, two** espe-**cially, the** *Bishopric of Souls,* and the *Ministry of the Body,* most **useful to the** clergy, **and** like in value to **Prebendary** Sadler's *Church Doctrine,* etc. ; C. E. Kennaway, author of *Consolatio ;* H. H. Norris, **rector** of South Hackney, **who had an** important controversy with the British **and** Foreign Bible **Society ; Dr.** Mill, first Principal of Bishop's **College, Calcutta,** Regius Professor of Hebrew **at** Cambridge, author of many learned lectures, sermons, etc., a name to be remem-bered in the very foremost rank of Anglican divines ;

he afterwards took the living of Brasted, near Sevenoaks, in Kent, leading the life of an active parish
priest to the last. His *Catechetical Lectures* were
published after his death by his son-in-law, **the Rev.**
Benjamin Webb, one of the well-known Cambridge
men of the movement, a coadjutor with John Mason
Neale, especially in **art** and ecclesiology, **for many**
years vicar **of St. Andrew's,** Wells Street, **the church**
built for Mr. **T. M. Fallow,** curate to **Dean** Chandler,
Rector of All Souls, Langham Place, but he died soon
after it was consecrated. Mr. Fallow's son—also **T.**
M. Fallow—born after his father's death, **was in** holy
orders. Mr. Fallow, of St. Andrew's, was on the committee of the Motett Society, before its connection with
the Ecclesiological Society. **In** Mr. Norris's parish **of**
Hackney, **too,** lived many earnest laymen, working up
towards higher things, among them Joshua Watson,
Governor of the Bank of England, to whom Dr. Newman **dedicated a volume of** his *Parochial Sermons,* and
whose **life, written** by Archdeacon Churton, **is full of**
interest, especially in the account of the foundation of
the great Church Societies; and in the early part of Dr.
Pusey's life there are interesting mentions of his visiting
Mr. Joshua **Watson at** Brighton.

One of the most remarkable of these pioneers was of
earlier date still—the Rev. **John** Oxlee, rector of Scaw-
ton, and curate of Stonegrave, Yorkshire, who in 1819
and 1821 preached and published three sermons. The

first was preached in Thirsk Church, at the visitation of the Right Worshipful Charles Baillie, from St. John xx. 23, " in which," as the title-page tells us, " it is demonstrated, in the broadest and most fundamental principles of the Christian faith, that the full power of remitting or retaining sins, and of dispensing absolution, is an essential prerogative of the Christian priesthood ". The second sermon was thus entitled : " In which it is unanswerably proved to all believers in Divine revelation, that the Christian priesthood is a perfect hierarchy, emanating from God Himself, and that in this realm the only real and efficient Christian ministers are those of the Church of England ". The third sermon is on the Christian ministry; and the regular episcopal succession is deduced by a continued and uninterrupted list of Christian bishops, from the blessed Apostles Peter, Paul, and John, down to the present prelates of Canterbury, York, and London. All three sermons had extensive notes and extracts from the early Fathers of the Church and from English divines ; but the last had a valuable appendix, with tables of the first bishops of the Churches of Jerusalem, Antioch, Alexandria, Rome, Clermont, Tours, Autun, Vienne, Arles, and Lyons ; a list of the Archbishops of Canterbury, from St. Augustine to the present time ; of York, from Paulinus to the present time ; of London, from A.D. 604 to the present time ; and the series of Roman Pontiffs, from 336 to 1294.

This Yorkshire author and divine wrote several other learned works; one on the doctrine of the Holy Trinity, a **most** telling reply **to** the Unitarians, in **a** letter **to Mr.** Wellbeloved, **a** Unitarian minister **of York.** He was known to such men as Bishops Middleton, **Heber, Kaye,** Thirlwall, and others, as **one of** the **most profound and learned scholars of the day** in Latin, **Greek, Hebrew, Chaldee,** and Syriac. **It is** recorded **that the venerable and** learned President of Magdalen **(Routh), in 1852,** had **only just seen Mr.** Oxlee's sermons, and wrote to express his satisfaction. **It would** be a curious inquiry to ask what effect these sermons had on the fifty **or** sixty rough Yorkshire parsons of that day, probably somewhat after the type of old **Bronté,** the father of Charlotte Bronté : **one can imagine their** look of intense astonishment as they sat **in the** fine **old church of Thirsk and** listened **to** such a **passage as this :—**

From the foregoing **statements it** will manifestly appear that the present subsisting hierarchy **of the Church of** England derived its episcopal power and authority, originally and immediately, not from the Romish Pontiffs, but **from** the Gallican Metropolitans ; and this, by the way, is always a sufficient answer to the vulgar prejudice and ignorant clamour of the English Dissenters, who **contend** that if the Church of England will boast of her **episcopal** succession, she must be content to have it derived from the corrupt **and** contaminated fountain **of the** Romish Church, as though, **indeed, it** were a crime and a sin **to** have obtained episcopal power **from that** see, which, as all antiquity might be cited to testify, derived **it** from the Apostles themselves, etc., etc.

It is not **at** all certain that they took Mr. Oxlee

seriously; it is hardly to be wondered at if it were so, when we remember that the cruel sport of bear-baiting was carried on not very many years before; and the story is told that the parish clerk of a church in a neighbouring county, in a whisper, said to the clergy-man between the prayers, "the bear has arrived, and is a very fine one". These Yorkshire parsons dined as usual with the Chancellor; and it is said that after dinner a whisper went round the table that the next vacant cardinal's hat was to be bestowed on the preacher. The sermons were published with the names of Hatchard and Rivington for a firm at York, and some forty years after the remainder were unearthed from Messrs. Hatchard's cellar, and met with a ready sale.

Let us also pay a passing tribute to the popular preachers of 1840 and onwards, whose churches were crowded and their sermons listened to with atten-tion, such men as Montague Villiers, Sanderson Robins, Canon Dale, Daniel Moore, and Henry Melvill; to my knowledge such earnest and vigorous preaching was of the greatest benefit to the young men of London, and when the Church Movement came into their lives there was little to *unlearn*; the addition of some important truths, and the outward expression of the same, natur-ally followed. I think we took more trouble in re-ligious matters than young folks do in these days of trams, underground trains, and omnibuses for every few hundred yards. **As** youths we thought nothing of walking on Sunday evenings from our home in Soho to Camden Chapel, Camberwell, standing throughout the service and sermon, and walking home. **Those forty minutes'** sermons, delivered with all the power and energy **of Mr.** Melvill's prime, were something to remember. Mr. Melvill, afterwards Rector **of** Barnes, and Canon of St. Paul's, who was a good churchman, edited *Sherlock on Public Worship* for Mr. Burns's Englishman's Library, **one of** the many series that were brought out in the movement. I cannot say much for the ritual of Camden Chapel in those days, but there was good Church teaching in those popular sermons ; one especially, on November 5, was a warning to the over-zealous in reform, that, in removing, as they thought, some corrupt additions, great care was needed, some vital truth being always at the bottom ; and that by cutting **too** deeply the truth itself might be damaged **or lost.** Just as Dr. Pusey felt it of moment to distinguish what the Articles really condemned as Romish ; lest we involved therewith feelings and doctrines and practices which were primitive. Though most **of** the popular extempore preachers were Evangelicals, many of them were better Churchmen at heart than we should suppose. Canon Dale, **at St.** Bride's, and evening **preacher** at St. Sepulchre's, Snow Hill, afterwards at St. Pancras, and Dean of Rochester, was a most earnest, **excellent** preacher. St. Sepulchre's was always filled, and with a large proportion of young men ; and the Church principles of some of his children and grand-children testify to his orthodox and energetic life. Some may remember the rector's large square pew at the end of the north aisle, where the preacher's young family all appeared ; and bright, clever, intelligent young faces they were. Robert Montgomery, who came from St. Jude's, Glasgow, was one of the most popular of that day ; his chapel, Percy Chapel, Charlotte Street, Fitzroy Square (now taken down), was certainly most uncomfortably crowded ; but, much as Macaulay de-spised his poetry, he was well worth hearing : it is really a fact that once upon a time he wrote for the *Ecclesiastic*, a most pronounced Tractarian monthly ; and his volume of poems, called the *Christian Life*, on the plan of the *Christian Year*, contained much that was sweet and instructive. One of his volumes of poetry was called *Satan*, and from that he was at times called " Satan Montgomery ". It is said that, calling one day on a High Church publisher, he entered the office in his usual loud manner. " My name is Montgomery. You know me ? " The publisher got up from his seat rather startled, and said, "Oh, yes, Satan ". These overcrowded churches were rather try-ing to old-fashioned folks. An orthodox churchman, a friend of mine, who always thought it his duty to hear both sides, managed to get into Percy Chapel to hear Robert Montgomery. Coming out on the crowded staircase an old woman asked him if **he** did not think it was beautiful. " Very well for **once,** my good woman ; **very** well for **once."** " For once, sir ! " she exclaimed in dismay. This **same** old churchman **was** a regular communicant **at his** parish church of St. Martin-in-the-Fields, though in Sir Henry Dukinfield's time Church **privileges** were not abundant. He was a vestryman, and now and then **put in a few** words that showed his churchmanship—*e.g.*, he once proposed that a parochial dinner **given** in the middle **of** summer should be held at a much more salubrious and appropriate time, such as November **11,** the day of the patron saint of their church. I fear that very few **of** the vestrymen knew that there was such a day as **St.** Martin's Day in the Calendar.

The most popular preachers in the early days were **not all Low** Churchmen. Archdeacon Manning was very popular, and the churches crowded whenever he **preached in town. His** bright presence, refined features, and winning manner were most attractive ; and his sermons then seemed more telling than his later addresses in the Romish Church. I remember the practical results of one at St. Margaret's, Westminster, for Westminster Hospital. **A** friend was **there,** and the first thing he said to his wife on returning home was, " My **dear, we** have two or three spare beds and bedding in the **loft ;** we must send them down to Westminster Hospital—Archdeacon Manning said so ". These single sermons of the archdeacon's were frequently published, and many a time I have bought one and enjoyed reading it after having heard it.   A curious coincidence occurred with one of them preached for the Magdalen Hospital, from the text, "Now there stood by the cross of Jesus," etc.   A few weeks after it had been published, I happened to have the sermon in my pocket when I went to church, and sat, as usual, with my Sunday-school boys under the organ at the west end.   The curate, a young deacon, nephew of a bishop, was preaching for a Penitentiary, and gave out the same text ; it sounded familiar, and I drew the printed sermon out of my pocket, and read it after the preacher, who delivered it word for word, without a sound of acknowledgment ; he was very young, and so his rather conceited action may be forgiven.   Mr. Purchas, of Brighton, at times read Bishop Hall's *Contemplations*, but he always told his people what he was reading.

Dr. Hook was much appreciated as a preacher in London ; and I need not say that when Dr. Pusey preached in town, the churches were filled with devout hearers.   For some years he preached at St. Mary Magdalen's, Munster Square, on Ascension Day ; and many well-known men were in the church—Robert and Samuel Wilberforce, and Father Ignatius, then a young deacon.   On the evening of the consecration, F. D. Maurice preached, and Mark Pattison was in the church.   When Pusey preached at the consecration of

St. Barnabas, Pimlico, there were a great many more
people outside the church than in ; and on the occasion
of his preaching at St. Peter's Chapel, Pimlico (during
Thomas Norton Harper's short incumbency), it was full,
even up the pulpit steps. He preached in his academi-
cal gown ; and the story runs that on his way back **to
the** vestry, an old woman said, "Ah, sir, if we only
had more sermons like that, **there would** be no ' Puseyism ' in our churches ".

He preached several times in old Margaret Chapel,
when, of course, the little chapel was more than full.
He preached there at Evensong on **St.** Peter's **Day, the**
night before Mr. Oakeley was condemned **in** the Old
Arches Court. On one special occasion he preached
there the sermon, " Do all to the Lord Jesus " : it was
published, and **many** thousands **were sold.** On this
occasion, I think, **some of us were told by** the verger
that the lower part of the chapel was full, and that we
must go upstairs **into the** gallery. Dr. Pusey's young
daughter was there, and told the verger that **she was**
sure her **papa** would not like her to take so high or
exalted a place in the chapel.

Dr. **A.** B. Evans was for many years evening
preacher at **St.** Andrew's, Wells Street, coming in from
Enfield, where he was curate to **Mr.** Heath. The
church was always filled, and **no one** who heard his
sharp and telling sermons, with a great deal of wit and
occasional sarcasm—somewhat after **the style of South's**

famous discourses—could dispute his ability in his own special line. I have now a letter from a clergyman well able to judge, in which he says, "Dr. Evans gave us the grandest sermon on Thursday, June 13, at St. Peter's, Vauxhall, on 'Your reasonable service,' that I have ever heard preached; it was perfectly marvellous". He was thoroughly original, and some years after had the vicarage of St. Mary-le-Strand, where he earned the respect and affection of very many friends. When he was at Wells Street, a curious story is told. Some friends were anxious to publish a volume or two of his sermons, and it was proposed to raise a small sum to defray the cost of printing. Mr. Masters was to be the publisher. A rich, crotchety churchman was asked to help. "I know you'll go putting 'S.' for 'Saint' instead of 'St.,' and all that sort of thing." "Ah, well," said the friend, "if you will help I will undertake that 'St.' shall be put for 'Saint' throughout." "In that case," replied the gentleman, "I will give ten pounds; but I don't like the way he does his hair—those two little curls on each side I think in very bad taste." "Well," replied Dr. Evans's friend, smiling, "if you will give another ten pounds, I don't mind asking him to cut off those curls." Two volumes of sermons were printed and were valued. I think they have been out of print for some years. "St." for "Saint" was printed throughout, though many would have it that "St." stood for "Street".

CHAPTER II.

In looking back on those early London days, nothing seems more wonderful than the rapid way in which the Tractarian Movement changed the whole tone of things in religious matters : within ten years of the beginning a vast number of the London churches showed many signs of its influence. It was like a call that was sure to touch all that was earnest and real in people's hearts ; it, in fact, said to them : " Here is your own old Church, no new Church, the old foundations well laid, with its Prayer-book, preface, calendar, offices, creeds, sacraments, ordinal, its fasts and vigils, saints' and holy days ; this is what it is in theory : but what a different thing now in practice ! " This stirred the hearts of thousands ; it urged them to be consistent, to carry into practice the Church system ready to their hands : it was the old Church of their country, its historical and constitutional claims were worth contending for. And so it came to pass that very early in the movement busy merchants and others found time to go to early service and celebrations, especially on holy days and festivals, making a point at such times of returning in time for evensong. Of course, improve-

(27)

ments in the services were gradual, and in many cases
only the week-day and saints' day services were more
brightly and carefully rendered, leaving the Sunday
services just as they were, until in due time the men
of the place were led to ask why the beautiful services were given to their wives and daughters in the
week-day, and not to themselves on Sundays.

Thus within a few years most marked changes took
place in hundreds of churches in London and all over
the country ; in Scotland and even in Ireland, America
and the West Indies, there was much change in the
arrangement, order, and ornaments of the churches and
services ; new churches of great beauty and grandeur
were built; and even in the old-fashioned churches of
London much was done to give a more seemly and
reverent order of things. Old things, old neglects and
abuses were to be no more ; the days were fast passing
away when an old country rector, without the least
conscious profanity, at the monthly celebration would
consecrate nearly half a loaf, giving it at the end of the
service to the poorer communicants who flocked to the
altar rails, but without kneeling or outward sign of
reverence ; and again, which is even worse, when
another rector would leave the remainder of the consecrated elements to be removed or dealt with by the
female pew-opener ; happily, a new curate insisted on
undertaking that office, and threatened to leave at once
if the rector continued the old miserable way : or when

a young lad's preparation for Confirmation was one visit to the old rector in his dining-room, who shook hands, and said he knew how well and carefully his father and mother had brought him up, and so he had much pleasure in giving him his ticket; and that was all. A friend's experience in that way was singular. He was at school in Eaton Square; among his schoolfellows were sons of Mr. Bennett and Mr. Fuller (the incumbents of St. Paul's, Knightsbridge, and St. Peter's, Eaton Square). One day the headmaster asked him if he wished to be confirmed, and he said "Yes"; the master asked him to say the Apostles' Creed, and gave him his ticket. The master then turned to another boy, saying, " M——, you ought to be confirmed, you are big enough ". The boy was offended, and living just opposite, went across to St. Paul's, Knightsbridge, and stood up in the church to be catechised. Years afterwards we visited his grave at Preston, near Brighton, a soldier's sword at the foot of a cross. The Confirmation itself, in St. James's, Piccadilly, by Bishop Blomfield, was not a very impressive or solemn ceremonial. Compared with some Confirmations of a later time in many London churches, or with those by Bishop Hamilton of Salisbury, Harvey of Exeter, Bishop Forbes of Brechin, or by the Bishop of Chichester in St. Paul's, Brighton, it was cold and formal indeed.

But even in such a parish as St. Anne, Soho, with surroundings and arrangements of the very plainest fashion, the Church Movement **was** felt and bore fruit. **In those** days the parish had **not been invaded** by foreigners. The **fine** old houses in Dean Street, Carlisle Street, Gerrard **Street, and Soho** Square, with their historical and literary record, their handsome entrance **halls,** ornamented **ceilings, and carved** staircases, had **not yet been turned into** shops, restaurants and warehouses. **The church was** fairly **full** of parishioners, **and** all parochial work was well looked after. There **were two** thorough-working curates—one a Cambridge man, a friend **of Bishop Selwyn, to** whom Sir Edward Kerrison gave a living in Suffolk (his son **is now** rector **of a large** Midland parish **and rural** dean). The other **curate was an** Oxford man, **a very** excellent scholar **and** parish **priest, and** thoroughly **in** touch with the Tractarian Movement ; **and** from him, in spite of surroundings, came the knowledge of the higher life to **very many ; such books as Mr.** Gresley's and Mr. F. E. **Paget's, with** smaller tracts and manuals, came upon us as a revelation. **A** book like *Bernard Leslie,* giving the **portrait of a** country curate, and how he gradually swept **away** the dust of ages of neglect and indifference, set the sympathies **to work,** and all longed to take their part in the revival.

Litany on Wednesday and Friday was, I think, all **the week-day** service at **St.** Anne's, with one monthly late celebration ; but **the** Oxford curate and some of the younger folks were **at** the daily five o'clock evensong at Margaret Chapel, then recently taken by **Mr.** Oakeley, and at the early celebrations too ; part of the story of that very ordinary-looking chapel I will try **to tell later on.**

Still, at St. Anne's **the** higher teaching fell on some **good** ground ; **with a few of** the older people the bow **at the** *Gloria* had not **been** forgotten, and the week before Holy Communion was a real time **of** prepara-**tion ;** many **used** the old week's preparation, and the **old** *Whole Duty of Man* (not the editions with some **of** the Church teaching cut out), Bishop Wilson's *Sacra Privata* and *Lord's Supper*, and Robert Nelson's *Fasts and Festivals.* **The** large charity schools **were in** Rose Street, Soho ; the girls and boys, in the old picturesque dresses, **had a** gallery to themselves in **church** on each side of the great organ at the west end. The organ was a grand old instrument, with three rows **of keys and great** pedal pipes, most ably played for years as a labour of love by the young daughter of **a** parishioner who was devoted **to sacred** music and the care and good order of **the instrument.** The **children** were carefully trained, and sang admirably. **Many of** these boys in after life turned out well ; **the** two senior boys especially, who used **to** sing the duet and solo **parts** in the Collect Anthem, " Lord of all power and **might,"** for the seventh Sunday after Trinity ; they be-**came** national schoolmasters ; from charity boys they were Sunday-school boys, and then Sunday-school teachers; they were born of very humble parents in St. Anne's Court, Dean Street; but in spite of that, were, in many ways, really gentlemen in heart and feeling. There are but few now left who would remember "the two Lynches," as they were called. The church was a large and handsome building of its kind, with a circular chancel apse, ornamented ceiling, and many interesting monuments, one to a King of Corsica, 1756; to David Williams, founder of the Literary Fund; to William Hamilton, R.A.; and one that especially interested us in young days, to a Bishop of St. David's, with crozier and mitre. The lower part of the chancel, under a very stiff, gaudy window, was laid out in panels with circular tops, containing the Lord's Prayer, the Ten Commandments, and two full-length paintings of Moses and Aaron. But for the three-decker and the high oak pews it really would have had a grand appearance : now the old pews are lowered, the organ is moved down and turned into two huge erections on each side, making a sort of quasi-chancel. The three-decker was a peculiar one, the steps to the pulpit or upper erection forming a sort of arch under which you could walk. The service was not much to describe— the clergy proceeded from the vestry at the far end, headed by one beadle in green and gold, and as they left the vestry another beadle opened the door to the middle division, or prayer-desk, which drew out with steps attached, and you could hear the click with which

it caught when fully open; and then, when the reader
had safely gone up the steps, it was closed with a
similar catch—rather an awkward imprisonment if
the reader were taken ill, which occurred once. The
preacher in surplice, hood, etc., went into the chancel
apse, whence he was solemnly conducted down the
church in due time by the beadle to don his black
gown. The amen-clerk was an important person, but
he came last and let himself into his lower desk; in
appearance, though not in height, he was a regular
Falstaff, and evidently had an opinion of his own
dignity; by profession he was a clever and intelligent
engraver, but he was sorely puzzled at the increase of
reverence and solemnity that was then taking place.
He gave vent to his feelings at times in the week-days
on the occasion of a baptism or christening by the
Oxford curate, or by the rector's son, Charles Middleton MacLeod, when on a visit. He confessed "that he
could not make it out ; the latter person, he thought,
was actually frightened to touch the book, the font, the
communion-table, or anything in the church". It
would be difficult to detail the improvement, though it
was gradually evident in many matters of personal
reverence, kneeling, etc.; and in those days kneeling
was anything but easy. Some classes of the Sunday-
school were placed at the chancel steps and used to
face the congregation ; now they were turned the other
way, which was much more decent and orderly. The

master of the charity schools was a character: he was an elderly man of great learning and acquirements, and had clearly come down in the world ; a good Greek, Latin, and Hebrew scholar, and a mathematician too, was hardly needed for such a post ; he was ready to impart his knowledge of languages, etc., and would play two games of chess with us at once without seeing either board or men, and win them. Talking of charity schools reminds me that many of the old foundation deeds were written and expressed in most orthodox and religious terms, beginning in the name of the Holy Trinity, etc. ; the sick and poor were well visited and assisted ; nor does one easily forget the first occasion of joining in the Communion of the Sick with the Oxford curate : it was in one of the smaller houses in Gerrard Street, where, on the second floor, a young girl in the last stage of consumption lay dying. As we were let in at the street-door his clear " Peace be to this house and to all that dwell therein " was most impressive. All was nicely arranged for the service by him on a small table near the bed, and in cassock, surplice, and stole it was quietly and reverently done ; the solemn peace of it all was something to remember, and showed most of all in the calm, pale face of the poor girl. On one such occasion a gentleman of that parish, finding the people had no small suitable table, carried one from his own home a mile and a half through the streets of London. The Sunday-schools of this parish were very large and admirably managed by the rector's daughter and niece and other excellent **workers, and among the men** were **Edward Thornton—whose loss from among us we have just been** deploring—Theodore **Galton, Mr. Edison a barrister, etc.** Many **of the new hymn-books** and **catechisms just then** published **were used ; and it was a** great charm **to the** pupils **to have some small cate-chisms, such as lessons on the Prayer-book,** calendar, etc., with **their own** names **printed to the** answers: these **were, of** course, **written and published by the** Oxford curate. The best also **was done** to solve **the** problem how to attach and retain Sunday scholars to the Church. **One plan we** found of great service : two **or three of the teachers had an evening** school from **seven to nine twice in the** week, teaching **writing and arithmetic ; it was made** a sort **of reward for the best conducted Sunday** scholars, **and for** those out-**growing the school.** The curates were constantly in **this evening school ; and** always, **at a quarter to nine,** there was **short evensong or compline, and in this ser-**vice the **seasons,** saints' days, **eves and** vigils, **were** carefully commemorated, **and** the calendar **of the** Church's year made more of a reality.

Another plan for **keeping up the interest** of the Sunday scholars **was to take them about** to the service in **churches** where things were advancing. Many a pleasant **walk** and talk, **as** Mr. Paget says, were thus en-joyed. Sometimes to Westminster Abbey, or St. Mark's

College, Chelsea, when Derwent Coleridge was Principal, and Mr. Helmore was then beginning his life's work and devotion to the music of the Church ; it was a splendid choral service without accompaniment ; to Christ Church, Broadway, Westminster, Mr. Cyril Page's ; Christ Church, Albany Street, Mr. Dodsworth's ; Christ Church, Hoxton, where Mr. Scott was working well and thoroughly : though he was better known as a theological and critical writer, and editor of the *Christian Remembrancer*; Mr. Milman, Rector of St. Augustine's, City, was once curate to Mr. Scott. Smaller works and tracts were often written by him, and most useful they were. *Plain Words to Plain People* was the title of some excellent ones.

In these ways hold was kept on the scholars, and they were helped to start in life. In one class, two became national schoolmasters, two working jewellers, one a clever upholsterer, one a clergyman—now rector of a parish in Norfolk—two brothers were solicitors' and barristers' clerks. Not very long ago I much astonished a young friend by telling her I had met two Sunday scholars, and had invited them to spend the evening ; her idea of Sunday scholars was her own little tribe of mites at St. —— ; so what was her surprise to see two tall men, with long beards, walk in ! They joined in our games, and quite entered into them, and played chess, etc., with the best of us. They were the two brothers last mentioned then getting on in years; they both remain single, to give a good home to their crippled and invalid sisters. The Sunday-school teachers were part of the staff of district visitors; and as the parish contained one side of Wardour Street and Crown Street, Newport Court and Market, and part of Seven Dials, with the numerous courts in them, there was abundance of work. The sick scholars of the schools were always carefully visited in their homes and in the hospitals.

The influence of the movement in these early days was shown chiefly in the preaching, and in smaller matters of reverence; as, for instance, where the double cushions were retained on the altar, there was no lounging on them, and the assistant priest generally knelt at some distance, facing east; but there was nothing of what we call Ritual. Mr. Rodwell, evening preacher at St. Mark's, Myddelton Square, in delicate health, sat during the Psalms, but always stood up at the *Glorias*, in the great three-decker that then hid altar, railings, etc., in that church. Our immediate neighbours—St. James's, Piccadilly, and St. Giles-in-the-Fields—showed many signs of this influence. Mr. Ward, afterwards Dean of Lincoln, was Rector of St. James's, where they had early weekly celebrations: Mr. E. H. Thompson one of the first married converts to Rome, was curate; the late Dean Oakley was also curate there. Archbishop Tenison's Chapel, called after the first Rector of St. James's, was in this parish; and there for many years

Mr. Gay (afterwards Rector of St. Matthew's, Ipswich) carried on the work single-handed, would ring his own bell, and say his daily matins at nine from his three-decker, not at all depending on a congregation, though there was generally a very small one. He was a thorough working parish priest. He married a daughter of Henry Howard, R.A., the renowned figure-painter, who was a regular attendant at St. Anne's, Soho. One of Mr. Howard's sons, Edward Irving Howard, took a good degree at Lincoln College, Oxford, and went out to India as a barrister; it was very sad that early in his career he was killed in a railway accident, the train breaking apart. His name reminds us that it is not always a success to call children after the names of favourite divines, writers, or painters, at least with the hope that the child will in after years follow in the steps and views of his supposed patron or namesake. John Mason Neale was an instance of how things may take an almost opposite direction. In some cases (not imaginary ones) it seemed almost disastrous; what could be more distressing than to christen your son Martin Luther, and in after years see him received into the Church of Rome? or for a talented artist to call his son Michael Angelo, and that years hence he should become a very indifferent artist, and end his days as a photographer? It is not every Arthur or Horatio who turns out a brave man, nor every George Herbert who becomes a saintly and religious person. We are talking of exceptions; but, of course, one could fill pages with the successful instances, such as Copley Vandyke Fielding, etc.

From this time to its transformation into St. Thomas's, Regent Street (which is still a centre of Church work and teaching), sacrificing its valuable porch and entrance in that busy thoroughfare, Archbishop Tenison's Chapel had a good record of incumbents; among them Haselwood (first Vicar of St. Mark's, Hamilton Terrace), J. H. Thomas (sometime Archdeacon of Cape Town), Cowan (afterwards Vicar of St. John's, Hammersmith, where Hugh Monro was his curate); Mr. Burrows, of Christ Church, Albany Street, afterwards Canon of Rochester. W. H. Brookfield was there, and then for many years Vicar of St. Luke's, Berwick Street, a brilliant scholar and preacher, fearfully out of place in a parish that was nearly all like the Seven Dials and the New Cut. Many will remember his finely-chiselled features and graceful manner, and all know the very beautiful memoriam poem to him by Tennyson.

Many of these neighbours were often at St. Anne's. Those were the days of afternoon and evening lectureships and readerships. Among these were T. T. Haverfield, incumbent of York Chapel, St. James's; William Harness, the Shakespearian scholar; and Edward Dalton, afterwards Rector of Lambeth and Vicar of Highgate. Dean (then Mr.) Gregory was Incumbent of St. Mary-the-Less, Lambeth, a very populous and poor district, where he **worked hard for years, and** in 1859 **had** a mission-room near Vauxhall Gardens.

The other close neighbour **was** St. Giles-in-the-Fields, where things were also working up. James Endell Tyler, **a** Fellow of **Oriel,** the friend of Whately, Jelf, Newman, Coplestone, etc., had been appointed vicar by Lord Liverpool. His fine face and figure were **to be** seen constantly about **his** parish, which was thoroughly well worked with careful **and reverent** services; in **church** he wore bands **of a** different make to those usually seen then; instead **of two narrow** strips **of muslin,** they **were** large and **in one** piece, falling down flat like those we **see in** old prints of the Caroline **Divines, and of** Bossuet and **Fénélon. He** had some excellent men as curates; **among** them Mr. **Watts,** who had Bedford Chapel, and Mr. Swain, first **Vicar** of Christ Church, Endell Street (built by the well-known Church architect, **Mr.** Benjamin Ferrey), a street running from Holborn to the Covent Garden district, which was called after **Mr.** Tyler's second Christian **name.** The work **and influence of the** Church Movement among the **masses was undoubtedly set forward** by hundreds of clergymen in town and **country,** such as Mr. Swain, **of** Endell Street. There he laboured all **his life, a** life of **rare** self-denial and **work, had** daily service and **early** communions, was always to be found in his church **or** parish or in the workhouse, where he ministered; this workhouse surrounded the church, and **the** galleries were reserved for those of its inmates who could come—what ups and downs of life **he** must have seen and known, and what a parish it was and is! Scarcely **a** parishioner above the lower middle class! **It was** a testimony to the work here as well as at St. Anne's that the parents of **the lower** middle class, and down to the very poor, **though they** themselves did not often fall in with the " **new-fangled and** Puseyite ways," were **yet** bound to **say that their children who were** under the new influence, **were all the better sons and daughters for it;** were all the more obedient, attentive, loving, industrious, careful, well-spoken, **and** thoughtful for others.

Before **we** go **further** in the **way** of other London parishes, let us return **for a** while to St. Anne's, where the names of the higher **class** of parishioners, such as Carpue, Hertslet, Beardmore, **of** Carlisle Street, etc., **were** gradually giving way to **names well** known in commerce—good and worthy names, and in most cases good parishioners—among these were such well-known **names as** Warne, Routledge, D'Almaine, Kirkman, Novello, Crosse and Blackwell, Russell Smith, etc. **In** due course, after the old rector's death, the Rev. Nugent Wade, from **St.** Paul's, Bunhill Row, was appointed, and daily service and **weekly** communion were the rule, and **many** good men **were** serving as **curates.** Mr. Wade was **an** Irishman, and had several Irishmen as curates—the Rev. C. Ingham Black, An-

drew **Nugee,** Walter **Atkins, and Percy and** Hugh
Monro, brothers of Edward **Monro, and Dr. Henry**
Monro, **all four** sons **of the famous Dr. Monro,** the
physician. **The daily** service **was sung by** twelve **of
the Sunday scholars, led** by **two or three of the** teachers.
In a large Italian building like St. Anne's it took
some power of voice to sing the daily service without
any instrument. On one occasion a gentleman of the
choir had been singing lustily at **the** eight o'clock
matins on the morning of his wedding-day : coming
out one of the curates said, **with a** bit **of a brogue,**
" Faith, and you sing as if nothing at all **was going to**
happen to **ye"; it was odd to suppose** he **was going to**
lose his **voice on** the happy **occasion. At times** such
men as Dr. J. Henthorn **Todd, of Dublin,** and Mr.
Sewell, **Warden of Radley, preached there.** All the
curates were thorough churchmen ; Andrew Nugee was
one of **the most earnest and amiable of** these ; he took
the family living **of** Wymering, **in** Hampshire, **and**
married **the** daughter of **Mr.** Richards, Vicar of Farlington, **a** well-known country parson of the Keble
School, whose parish was quite a model. Mr. Richards
wrote telling of his death at Clifton : **" He** fell asleep
on Christmas Day (1858), which may truly **be said to
have risen** with healing in its wings **to him;** in his
bitter sufferings he was always striving to overcome
all impatience ; he **desired** affectionate remembrances
to all his friends, old **and new, and I** am sure he meant

you amongst others, but **was** too ill to specify ; he will be buried at Wymering." For years, his widow was well known as a bright and earnest churchwoman in a large **town on the** south coast. His brother George, **now also** called **to his** rest, author **of** *Words from the Cross*, *Holy Women of the Gospel*, etc., then held the **family** living for some years ; after **a** very distinguished **course at** Cambridge he had become curate to Mr. Bennett at **St.** Paul's, Knightsbridge, and **went** thence **to** Wymering. He **was well** known for **his mission work** in South London.

There was never more than a most **moderate ritual** at the parish church **of St.** Anne ; indeed, **I** think **the** altar remained **as it was,** never raised or enlarged **or** ornamented, **and in the** course of years the church became chiefly **known** for grand and elaborate musical **services and the** performance **of** special sacred **music ;** but **from the date of Mr.** Wade's appointment, **fol- lowing upon former** good teaching, several **excellent works, fruits of the Church** Movement, **were begun and carried on in this parish ;** and **as this is not supposed to be a strictly chronological record, it** may **be well to tell about them here : these were the** House **of** Charity, **Rose** Street, **Soho, opposite the** old **Charity** Schools **;** the Church of **St.** Mary-the-Virgin, Crown Street ; and Newport Market **Refuge.** The House of Charity was **opened** in January, **1847, and was** well supported and **set on foot by some of** those **best known** for good work

in the church—the **Vicar of St. Anne's, Dr. Monro, Dr.**
Brett, **Earl Nelson, Mr. Roundell Palmer, Dr. Ogle,**
the **Rev. F. H.** Murray, **Mrs.** Gladstone, Mr. **Haddan,**
of **Exeter** College ; **Mr.** Algernon Bathurst, of New
College, grandson **of a** Bishop **of** Norwich ; **and many**
others. It supplied **a want that no** other institution
met. Distressed **persons were** received on special
and **trusty** recommendations ; in-patients discharged
from **hospitals,** and out-patients unable to do full work ;
to **such it gave shelter,** food, quiet, and rest. **Persons**
dependent **on those who,** by accident or sudden illness,
had been taken into hospitals ; persons who, by **no fault**
of their **own, such as by** fire, **bankruptcy, or death**
of an **employer, were thrown out of work ; those**
coming to London in search **of** friends or employment ;
those, especially women, whose health required a short
respite from laborious work ; persons with no friends in
London, waiting for means and opportunity to emigrate ;
and **others whom it was** desired to help towards re-
covering a **position** which they had lost through miscon-
duct. **In many other ways** this house was and is of help.
Who **can tell the blessing of** a kind welcome, rest **and**
care **to a young girl, even for one** night **only, on her**
way to a distant **part ; what a real act of** charity **this**
was, what safety ; and **what misery it may have** pre-
vented! The council **of the** House **of** Charity had in
it the **names** of many **of the** best and noblest, **and it**
still goes on its useful **way. It** had its early struggles.

The wardenship **was an** office held by **some** clergy of repute and standing, and even of **renown.** In addition **to** the work of their own chapel **in the** house, they assisted at times in St. Anne's and St. Mary's, Crown **Street.** I will name some of them, not in any special order : **A. J. Butler, W. F.** Norris, J. Cosby White, for **years Vicar** of St. Barnabas, Pimlico, the kind and ever-helpful priest and gentleman, who, after many years of hard parish work, retired to the lovely home, the Warden's Lodge, Newlands, **amid the fine scenery of Malvern, with** which foundation **the memory of Earl Beauchamp** still **lives in our** hearts ; **H. A. Rawes,** formerly curate **of St.** Botolph, Aldgate, and **of St.** Bartholomew's, **Moor Lane,** who seceded to Rome **and** became a popular preacher **at the** Pro-Cathedral, Kensington. Two of **the** wardens deserve more than a passing notice.

At some of the services at St. Mary's, Crown Street, **about** 1852-3, you might have heard a set of short sermons **on** the Psalms ; the preacher, quite young, **tall, dark, but pleasant** and kindly looking, his sermon could not but **impress you—so clear** and quiet, yet earnest—and you **felt that many who** heard him might **share in** his own deep, **practical** love to God, and **all that** tended to His praise and glory. This young **man was W. G. Tupper,** warden of **the** House of **Charity,** Soho, a worthy son of the Church Movement. The story of his short life **is** soon told. **He** was for **a** few years curate to Mr. Harness, of All Saints, Knightsbridge, and was a younger brother of the poet, Martin F. Tupper, who in 1856 published a short memoir of him under the title of *Out and Home.* This memoir contained his journal, three sermons preached at sea, and a few poems. It was a small memorial of a life which, as we well know, and his brother tells us, combined the strictest self-denial with the sweetest cheerfulness; a short life spent in secret good doing; the tongue of gentleness, the heart of love, the mind of sympathy and wisdom—indeed, a character of surpassing beauty, wedded to no common powers of intellect. It was his own request that several packets of his manuscript should be burnt unread, and so all were thankful for the short glimpse this volume gave of a character at once beautiful and of great simplicity. A testimony to his value as one where sympathy and wisdom could be relied on to the utmost is on record: A parish priest of many years' standing, himself a wise and learned man (Dr. Irons, Vicar of Brompton), was known to declare that among all the intricate questions on moral, religious, or social difficulties which occur to a clergyman in his parish, he at any time felt entire confidence in leaving the most perplexing to the decision of Mr. Tupper, although his junior by many years in parish toil and experience.

The biography was well and fairly written, though it will not surprise us to know that the author of *Pro-*

verbial Philosophy had little intimate **knowledge of** his brother, as he freely acknowledges thus : " For myself, the solicited editor of these pages, let me confess **to a** great personal difficulty in the matter; friends are oftentimes more intimately known to one another than **those who are nearest of** kin—an expression which **I almost** involuntarily gave utterance to soon after **hearing of William's death—is but** the **simple** truth, and **as heart speaks to** heart in these **matters, I** will **even** set it here :—

> " Alas, how little **have** I known thee, brother ;
> How lightly prized the riches of thy worth ;
> How seldom **sought thee** out to cherish thee
> And sun **my spirit in** thy light of love !
> How have **I let the** world and all its ways,
> Absence and **distance, cares** and interest,
> The many **poor excuses that we make**
> For **lax communion with a brother's heart;**
> How have **I stood aside and left such** tares
> To grow **up rank, and** choke the precious seed !
> **How have I let such** fogbanks of reserve,
> Such idle clouds of undesigned neglect,
> **Hide from** my spirit thy most lovely light ! "

William George Tupper was the youngest son of **the** late Martin Tupper, of New Burlington Street; born in 1824 ; educated **at** Winchester, and scholar **of Trinity** College, Oxford ; **was** ordained deacon at St. Paul's Cathedral **in June, 1849,** and priest in the Chapel **Royal, St.** James's, in 1850, and very soon became warden **of** the House of Charity, where he devoted his **means and** remaining energies to the service of God and the poor. The sea voyage recorded in this book was urged on him by his friends and physicians. He started in August, 1853; visited the West Indies, Cape Town, the Mauritius, Ceylon, Bombay, Cairo, etc.; he died in his thirtieth year, at sea, in May, 1854, soon after leaving Malta on his way home, and was buried at sea; it was a privilege even to slightly know him: and who shall measure the influence of such a character?

The other warden who combined the incumbency of St. Mary's, Crown Street, with the wardenship, was the Rev. J. C. Chambers; it was an excellent work of Mr. Wade and his friends to purchase the old Baptist Chapel that in 1850 stood on the west side of Crown Street, with a frontage to the street and a court of densely-crowded small houses round; those who only know Charing Cross Road and Shaftesbury Avenue and the several wide thoroughfares about, cannot imagine the change since the days of which I write. Many of the courts right and left of Crown Street were not very safe, even for the clergy and district visitors; one with the distinguished name of "Falconberg Court" could scarcely be invaded without a policeman. When the Baptists were about to give up the chapel, and there was a chance that it might be made into a music-hall or dancing-room, the Rector of St. Anne's and his friends came forward and bought it, and it became a church where much good work was done. But it had a

history, and **a curious one :** it was originally an old
Greek church, founded in 1677, under a metropolitan
of Samos, who had been driven out by the Turks ; the
Greek service continued till 1683, and was then given
up for want of funds. In 1684 it was leased to French
Protestants, and used by them till 1822, when the
Baptists had it till 1849. Under **Mr.** Philip C. Hardwick, **the architect, himself an** active churchman, the
inside was remodelled, and made fit **for** the service of
the Church of England ; he himself **carried the** large
iron cross up the body of the church on the **way to the**
scaffold to fix it on the roof. **With a** handsome altar,
choir stalls, pulpit, lectern, etc., it made quite **an im-**
pressive building, and **its** old friends certainly would
not have known **it,** though **one of** the old Baptist
women did sometimes find her way into the church,
explaining that she could hear the Lessons, and they
were sure to be **all right.** The church was consecrated
as **a** chapel of ease to St. Anne's, on St. Peter's **Day,**
1850, **with** bright stirring services, **and** a ritual **that**
was much more **advanced than that of the parish**
church ; **and no doubt it** was felt that in an old church,
one of the largest churches **of** London, ranking with
St. Martin, **St. Giles, St.** James, **St.** George, Hanover
Square, etc., with their proper old-fashioned congrega-
tions, an advanced ritual might not be then advisable.
The choir (now in cassocks and surplices) worked well,
and attained **a** fair proficiency. They were kindly

assisted in their training by Mr. Helmore and Mr. Redhead; the latter, when practising the hymn-tunes, which they sang with much vigour, especially " Innocents," which was then new to them, advised them to beware of merely pretty tunes. An octave of services was kept, and many of the great Church preachers of the day came. On one of the days, at evensong, as the choir were robing, there came an alarm of fire: an old woman's bed curtains had caught fire in the court just opposite the vestry door; four or five of the choir soon had their surplices off, and tore down the curtains and put out the fire; the old woman had a talking starling for whose safety she seemed much more anxious than her own. The first incumbent was the Rev. Walter Blunt, a genial, bright, and most courteous man, the author of several works on the new Church lines, on ecclesiastical restoration and reform, Church rates, parish officers, education, Church bells, etc. He did not remain long, and afterwards married a Kentish lady, and held the vicarage of Bicknor. He was succeeded by the Rev. Archer Gurney, who was slightly lame; a man of unusual power and talent as a divine and a poet, though not, perhaps, quite at home in such a district and among such parishioners. He preached well, and with great energy, and it used to be said that his reading of the Lessons was quite dramatic. During his four years, 1851 to 1854, both he and his mother were devoted to the work; it was in his time that Mr.

Tupper preached, **and** at times Frederick Denison
Maurice, then **in** London, and full of his plans **of**
Christian Socialism to get a hold on **the** working men;
his refined ascetic face **and** his sharp telling sermons
were familiar to us. **Mr.** Gurney held several posts **of**
work, the most important being the chaplaincy to **the**
Court Chapel, Paris, from 1858 to **1871**: his last place
of residence was Oxford, **and he died at Bath in 1887.**
He was a very voluminous author, and many of his
works were popular: *Songs of Faith and Cheer, Songs*
of the Present, Songs of Early Summer, Sermons in
French preached **in Paris,** *Parables and Meditations for*
Sundays and Holydays, several hymns **in Mr.** Shipley's
Lyra Eucharistica, **and the** well-known carol *Come* **ye**
lofty, come ye lowly. **He** wrote special **hymns for** the
Dedication **Feast at** St. Mary's. He also took part in
the controversies **of** the day, and wrote for many of **the**
best reviews.

The next vicar was a curate of St. Anne's, the Rev.
Walter B. Atkins, **M.A., of** Trinity College, Dublin,
one in **every way** worthy **to be** named with his contemporary **and** friend, the great Irish professor **and**
theologian, Archer Butler. At St. Anne's **and at St.**
Mary's he **endeared** himself to all, and **worked on,**
spending himself **in his Master's service, in this,** one of
the **most** densely **crowded and** unhealthy districts **of**
all **London.** There, with daily prayers, frequent **Com-**
munion and constant preaching, **he** continued till **1856,**

when failing health compelled him to exchange with Mr. Chambers to the quiet country vicarage of St. Mary Magdalen, Harlow, Essex, now much enlarged and beautified under the present vicar, Mr. Elwell. Though Mr. Atkins was a scholar and theologian, all the details of his office at St. Mary's were duly attended to, and he was much valued by all who knew him. In all matters his advice and sound judgment were to be thoroughly relied on, and clear and orthodox views of Church principles were set before the inquirer with an ever cheerful and unruffled temper. He wrote several theological essays ; and a small volume on the *Eternal Sonship of Christ ; the Resurrection, and the Kingdom of Heaven,* was published in 1859, forming a memorial of this quiet Christian priest, and with some the recollection of his earnest and holy life will be more than a memory. He died at Brighton, and was buried there ; during his short stay he preached at St. Paul's Church, West Street.

Then came a bright and stirring time under the Rev. J. C. Chambers, who brought with him all the energy and strength gathered in his labour of founding and working St. Ninian's Cathedral, Perth. He worked hard for this parish of St. Mary's, and the House of Charity, of which he was warden, both grew and prospered under his powers of organisation. The House of Charity attained the new premises in Soho Square, and made great progress in its most useful work. At

the anniversary in 1859 Mr. Chambers' address was a
perfect model of what such an appeal should be,—
thoroughly to the point and eminently practical.
Under him St. Mary's became a vicarage with a
decent income; new schools, taking nearly 1000 children, clergy house, ragged schools, Church guilds,
dinners for the sick and invalids, etc. A handsome
chancel, 34 ft. long, and 60 ft. high, was built on to
the old nave, the foundation-stone being laid by Canon
Liddon in 1870. For eighteen years this most energetic parish priest laboured in every way, dealing with
men and women and caring for their souls. He was
one who spoke out, did not say smooth things, or deal
otherwise than skilfully and firmly. He published a
large volume of fifty-two sermons, and a small volume
of sermons edited by Mr. Elkington, his curate and successor in the House of Charity. Mr. Chambers died in
1874. A thoroughly loyal English Churchman, he
printed several valuable pamphlets on our position as
to the Church of Rome, one especially on St. Gregory
the Great.

One interesting incident of the work at St. Mary's
may be named; it was in 1850, its first year, when
many friends there took a last farewell of William
Fredk. Taylor, who was ordained deacon and priest in
three months, and started for the Island of Tristan
d'Acunha, in the South Atlantic Ocean, 1500 miles
from the Cape and the same from St. Helena. There

he worked bravely on for his little flock for six years, being priest and choirmaster and schoolmaster, training children for the service who had never heard a note of music in their lives, their only Hymnal the New Version bound in the Prayer-book, and a card of Hymns printed for them in Crown Street, by Mr. Blunt. Mr. Taylor's first Church teaching was from Mr. Dodsworth at Christ Church, Albany Street. A visit to the Rev. H. Moody, at Gilston Rectory, near Harlow, had resulted in his becoming a student for mission work. When they outgrew the resources of the island, the bishop sent a vessel to bring nearly all to the Cape, where Mr. Taylor is working still, being Rector of Mossel Bay, a parish of 200 square miles, where he has a record of thirty-six years' work in Africa, two churches, and three out stations, where the communicants have steadily increased in number, and the Church's work makes good way. Many clergy and laity at St. Mary's were deeply interested in him and his work, his missionary spirit having no doubt been stirred up by the devotion of such friends as Chas. Middleton MacLeod, perpetual curate of St. John Baptist, Harlow, and son of the old Rector of St. Anne's, lately mentioned. It is needful to record that Dr. Littledale was a constant and much valued visitor and preacher in the Church of St. Mary, Crown Street.

CHAPTER III.

I HAVE hinted at the enthusiasm which was aroused in many hearts by the works of Dr. Neale, Mr. Paget, Mr. Gresley, Mr. Heygate, and others; this showed itself in an interest wherever Church matters could be advanced and improved, and many valuable suggestions were made which, though but little noticed at the time, were not altogether without effect. One rather singular instance is worth recording, the result of a visit to Dover by a young Churchman in 1842, about the time when Mr. Glover was Vicar of Charlton-in-Dover, and drove out in his gig to take his daily service there; rather eccentric, and devoted to some scientific pursuits, such as the building of a sea-wall, etc. He was a staunch Churchman, and much improved the service at Charlton; he also wrote in defence of the Ancient British Church and the succession of Bishops. This was the letter that the young Churchman wrote, after his first visit to Dover; it appeared in the *Times* of November 8, 1842 :—

"THE ARMY.

"SIR,—Your important articles on the moral and religious provision for the **Army recall to my mind the** manner in which **we of this day so often neglect great** opportunities; you remind **us** that the barracks, dock-yards and fortifications **round our coast are** almost equally destitute of this most important provision. **On** a recent visit to **Dover** Castle **I** was much struck with the substantial appearance of the old Roman or Saxon Church within the walls. It **seems as** if at no very great expense a roof might be thrown **over, it** might be paved **and** fitted **up, and 500 of the garrison, their wives and** children, **might** worship **within the same consecrated** walls **where their** forefathers **did** eight **or nine** cen-**turies ago. The** interior **is still very** beautiful and most substantial. **Would it be any less** interesting to **the** antiquary **if, instead of** being **used as** a storehouse **for coals, and shown to** visitors on payment of six-pence, its doors were open **for** prayer and praise, and **the** bell of the **old** church **once** again rang over the beautiful hills of Kent, with which county our religious associations **are so** forcibly linked? **In** the earnest hope **of much** abler and worthier advocates of such **a** cause **I venture to** make this humble suggestion.

" **Your** obedient servant, **W. G.**"

I only quote this **as an** instance **of the** spirit aroused by **such works** as *Bernard* **Leslie, Warden** *of Berking-holt,* **St.** *Antholin's,* **The** *Forest of* **Arden,** *Coniston Hall, Tales of the Village,* etc., etc. The remarkable part is that ten years, twenty years, passed, and in 1860-62 that old church was restored by a grant from Parliament, under the direction of Sir Gilbert Scott ; re-dedicated, June 22, 1862. The restoration thus begun was continued during 1888-90 by Mr. Butterfield, completing the tower, nave windows, sanctuary, approach to the altar, altar piece, seats, desks, floors, pavements ; and the walls were covered with mosaics ; thus the old church was once more made a beautiful house worthy of its sacred use.

The mention of Dover would hardly be complete without naming the Vicar of St. Mary's, Mr. Puckle, and his long and earnest labours on the lines of the new movement, with regret that failing health obliged him to resign, and that he so soon passed away.

Talking of this corner of Kent, the only place where much stirring Church work was then being done, was Ramsgate, at the Parish Church of St. George, and the chapel of ease. Mr. Harvey was the vicar, and many of his curates were excellent workers and writers, and among them Shirley Woolmer, W. J. Jenkins, C. C. Snowden, S. B. Harper; I think Mr. Whitehead was then working there. Though there was but little attempt at ritual, there were frequent services, much reverence, and bright and stirring preaching. Many visitors at Margate walked or rode over to these services, and were thankful for them. In this county three Canterbury churches were forward—Folkestone,

St. Andrew's, Deal, and Walmer; also, later on, St. Peter's, Broadstairs, and Margate joined in the work.

Speaking of bright and earnest preaching reminds us how much the early part of the Church Movement was distinguished in this way, and it is hardly possible to over-rate its value and influence. One great help in this especial line was the publication in 1839 of the ten volumes of *Plain Sermons by the Contributors to the Tracts for the Times*, by Newman, Pusey, J. and T. Keble, Isaac Williams, and Copeland. Mr. Isaac Williams was the chief mover in that series, and the object was a most wise one. These sermons placed the chief truths then being put forward with such energy by the great writers, in a plain, simple, and restful way, giving a more practical turn to the movement; they were like the ballast to the brilliancy of Mr. Newman and others. What a boon these sermons must have been to hard-working parish priests who certainly could not secure the leisure to write more than one good sermon a week ! Mr. Keble mentions a saying of Justice Coleridge, before the Tracts were thought of : " If you want to propagate your opinions you should lend your sermons, the clergy would then preach them, and adopt your opinions " ; and this has really been the effect of the publication of the Plain and other Sermons. It seems a pity that the price of the volumes was so high. Dr. Irons, in his *Sermons for the People*, adopted an excellent plan ; each sermon was one penny, eight pages of print, and could be taken out of the volume and easily used in the pulpit.

This practice of lending sermons was no doubt frequently adopted, but in some cases led to rather unexpected results, as when a memoir was published and a few sermons were printed at the end, and one or two of the sermons turned out not to be by the clergyman whose memoir had been written. This rather alarmed some worthy men, and they no doubt gave special instructions as to any MSS. they might leave behind them. A rather good story came in early days from the north-west of London on this subject. Mr. Faulkner began work in an iron church in Hampstead, just off the Finchley Road, and got together a congregation on Church lines, and it is with regret we remember his early death. One Sunday morning he preached a sermon to which one of his congregation took exception, and wrote to the bishop (Blomfield) to complain. The bishop wrote a kind note to Mr. Faulkner, suggesting that it might be as well that he should see the sermon. Mr. Faulkner sent it to the bishop, at the same time telling him that it was not his own, but was lent to him by a friend, a clergyman in the north of London. In due course the bishop returned the sermon, thanking Mr. Faulkner for allowing him to see it. He had read it with pleasure, and only wished he (the bishop) could write one half as good. I may mention that Mr. Faulkner's friend not only wrote admirable sermons, but wrote them in a singularly clear and print-like handwriting.

In the north-west of London Mr. Fletcher, of St. Saviour's, Haverstock Hill, and his excellent curate Mr. J. C. Hose, were also doing good solid work, and Mr. Baines, Chaplain to the Tailors' Almshouses, Haverstock Hill, Lecturer on History in Queen's College, London, afterwards Vicar of Little Marlow, was working with much influence both as preacher and writer; for years he kept up daily prayers and weekly Communion. His *Life of Archbishop Laud, Sermons, Tales of the Empire,* and many contributions to the *Ecclesiastic,* place him in the rank of a very able scholar and writer of the Church Movement. Mr. Cutts, the vicar of a church close by, was for years a most zealous worker on the same lines, and still writes many excellent books.

One of the earliest notes of the practical results of the Church Movement was the establishment of daily service; very remarkable was the rapid increase of this revival of old custom, and happily the daily service was seldom without the other great essential, the " Weekly Communion ". So in 1849 the first edition of a small sixpenny book was issued, called *Masters's Guide to the Churches where the Daily Prayers are said in England, Wales, Scotland, and Ireland;* and in 1857 the twenty-second edition was published. Part of the preface to this little work is worth repeating.

" To travellers, this Guide may be of **use, by** enabling them so to arrange their journeys and to choose their resting-places, **as to be able** to avail themselves of **the prayers of the Church.** The parish priest manfully **standing alone in the practice of daily service in the** midst **of passive** carelessness, **or** active opposition, **will be encouraged** to find how many of his brethren persevere **in** the same holy duty, and will be more especially interested in those cases where the hours of prayer are **the same as** his **own.**

" And is it too much to hope that more may **be** stirred up to follow the many good examples here **set** before them ? **The** churches **where Holy** Communion is celebrated weekly **have here been** marked with a ┼."

In this edition over 500 churches were entered, 60 in **London and the neighbourhood, and 122** where there **was a** weekly celebration of the **Holy Communion.** The **latest edition was the** thirty-seventh, 1869, with a **map of the** London churches contained in the list. **In** this edition **the number** of country churches with daily **service was** 1004, and in 556 of these **there was weekly** Communion. In London there were 139 churches, and of these 115 had weekly Communion.

It is not difficult to imagine what the influence and teaching year by year of these 1140 churches was, and **how it** affected **the younger members of** the Church ; **how they were attracted not only** by the beauty, reverence, **and order, but by the** depth **and** reality ; the

increased **earnestness in every good work,** the care of
the sick and poor, and the instruction and catechising
of the young; the higher value set on Holy Communion, Holy Baptism, **and** Confirmation. Many **of**
these churches were models **and** working centres of the
new movement, influencing thousands besides those
immediately connected with them. Such churches as
St. Paul's, Knightsbridge; St. Barnabas, Pimlico; **All
Saints,** Margaret Street; St. Alban's, Holborn; St. Andrew's, Wells **Street; St. Matthew's, City Road;** St.
Bartholomew's, **Moor Lane;** St. Mary Magdalen's,
Munster **Square;** St. **Mary** Magdalen's, Paddington;
St. Augustine's, Kilburn; **St.** Matthias, **Stoke Newing-**
ton; St. **Peter's, Vauxhall, and** St. Philip's, Clerken-
well—**were all such special centres of work.**

It is sad **to** remember that **in** many quarters the
simple fact of daily service **and weekly** Communion
was then looked upon with dislike and suspicion. This
was really the case with some **so-called** Evangelicals **of**
this time, the second or third generation of those who
had been governed by **the** influence of teachers **like
Hervey, Romaine, Cecil, Venn,** Fletcher, Scott, **etc.
How clearly has this school been** described **by Dean
Church:** "It shrank in its fear **of** mere moralising, in
its horror of the idea **of merit or of the value of** good
works, from coming **into** contact **with the** manifold
realities of the spirit **of** man—it had nothing to say **to**
the long and varied process of building up the new life

of truth and goodness; it was nervously afraid of departing from the consecrated phrases of its school, and in the perpetual iteration of them it lost hold of the meaning they may once have had; claiming to be exclusively spiritual, fervent, unworldly, it had come, in fact, to be on very easy terms with the world". A remarkable testimony to Dean Church's judgment will occur to those who remember that through all the years of the Tractarian controversy, it was an undoubted fact that when the most secular and worldly newspapers, such as the *Weekly Dispatch*, the *Sunday Observer*, and the *Morning Advertiser*, the organ of the licensed victuallers, took note of the religious events of the day, they always and invariably took the side of the Evangelical or Low Church party; through the Liddell controversy, the St. George's Riots, this was always the case.

The chief stronghold of this phase of religion at this time was undoubtedly the parish of Islington, one of the largest parishes in London, with its 100,000 inhabitants, its many district churches (ten built up to 1856, during the incumbency of Mr. Daniel Wilson, the successor of Bishop Wilson, of Calcutta), all closely kept under the patronage of the vicar and special trustees; it seemed like an impregnable fortress of Puritanism; and although the surrounding districts of Stoke Newington, Highbury, Haggerston, and Clerkenwell, were now alive to, and stirring in the new and revived work of the Church Movement, yet there was no getting into the magic circle of that parish boundary.

The story of an attempt to do so will be instructive. In 1856 the Vicar of Islington estimated that there were 30,000 persons in his vast parish, for whose spiritual instruction no place was found either in churches or chapels, and appealed for help to build more churches. Some dwellers in Islington were also being influenced by the writings of the Tractarians, and they could not but see for themselves that in all the churches of Islington, nine-tenths of the Prayer-book was a dead letter ; that the plainest injunctions for daily service, weekly Communion, the observance of saints' days, fast days, eves, vigils, catechising, private offices, etc., were entirely ignored ; that, while those who acted up to, or seemed to go beyond, what the Islington clergy considered the order of the Church, were denounced in no measured language, they themselves entirely omitted just as much as they pleased and ignored the plainest directions. So it came to pass that in 1865 a gentleman residing in Canonbury Park, in reply to the vicar's appeal, offered to build and endow a church where daily service might be performed, such as men could join in before proceeding to their city business, to build the parsonage and endow the church, also to build schools if the district required them, upon condition that an agreement satisfactory to him could be made with regard to the patronage. He wished for no personal patronage; but he was not content to spend £8000 or £10,000 to enrich the Vicar of Islington, augment the market value of his advowson, and to increase his already enormous patronage. **This** offer was declined **by** Mr. Daniel Wilson, although the daily service **and** the patronage **were** the *only two* stipulations, on the ground that " **the proposal emanated** from one identified with the Romanising movement in our Church, associated with a congregation whose minister not long since joined **the** Church **of Rome.** I cannot doubt but that the present is an attempt to introduce into the parish such a system as is pursued at St. Barnabas, Pimlico, or St. Paul's, Brighton—on this ground **I have,** in concurrence with all the incumbents of the parish, rejected the offer; **we** feel bound to protest against the movement and boldly to maintain those Protestant and Evangelical principles which are the **glory of** our reformed Church." In his final reply the gentleman **certainly** told the Vicar of Islington some home truths. I add a few of them :—

1. That it was a want of good feeling and Christian courtesy not to have sent a copy of his circular declining the offer to the parishioner who made the offer, and the person chiefly referred to.

2. That he and **his** friends simply **wanted** a church **for themselves and their** children, through the public **services of** which **they** might enjoy the privileges and **blessings of** the reformed Church **of** England.

5

3. That the stipulation **as to patronage was made** because there were parishes where the **daily** service **and other** long-established privileges had been arbitrarily **put** down **by** new incumbents **of his school without** regard to the feelings and consciences of many parishioners.

4. **That any** generous mind, unwarped **by** party spirit, **would** give **a** voice to those who erect churches **and** liberally support them, in the disposal of that which they munificently provide.

5. That the Church of England prescribes daily service, but the vicar and incumbents of Islington proscribe it from their churches.

6. **That when** the offer was **made the** proposer was identified with an Islington incum**bent, and was one of** the committee for **St.** Paul's and St. Jude's Schools; but **that** hearing the outcry **in** Islington against St. Matt**hias,** he was led to go and **see for** himself: that he found there what he and **others** had long felt the want of in **the cold** services of the Islington churches—found how the Church of England would have her children taught to worship God in the beauty of holiness, with more of God's word and less of man's talk in the sermons, **and** no harsh judgments or uncharitable censures on either their fellow-Churchmen **or others.**

7. That the Vicar **of** Islington had no more right to charge a member of St. Matthias with Romanising than the **latter** had to **call** the vicar a Dissenter because he

was a friend of the Hon. and Rev. Baptist Noel; **or a** Socinian because he fraternised with the Swiss clergy, some of whom have denied the Divine Nature of the Son of God.

8. That the largest Dissenting Chapel in all London **was shortly to** be built **in** Islington, **and** that two Roman missions are now there.

9. **That the** *Weekly Register* in July **of** 1865 said: "**There is no** diminution of converts, but they have recently come, not so much from the rank **of** Tractarians as from the Low Church or even Presbyterian School".

10. **That** Islington is the family living **of** the Wilson family, purchased at Garraway's Coffee House; that the then vicar **had kept** under his own control the nomination to the ten churches which the inhabitants **so** liberally enabled him to build.

The vicar and the layman have long since gone to their rest, but the story is characteristic of those times. **The** effect of the **bitter** denunciation of the Oxford School by the Islington clergy was not always what **they** desired. **In Dr.** Liddon's short memoir of the saintly Bishop of Salisbury (Hamilton), we read of the result in his case, how he felt the contrast between the denunciations at Islington, and the quiet, holy, Christian **lives of** the men **who** represented the movement, and became a High Churchman.

There were not so many daily services available just then **in** and about London; a special one was a late

daily evensong at half-past eight, at All Souls, Langham Place, when Dr. Chandler, afterwards Dean of
Chichester, was rector. This was one of the earliest
attempts to improve the choral parts of the Prayer-
book Service. Mr. Ingram, a bright and talented
musician, had been brought from the country, and for
this service there was an harmonium at the west end
of the centre aisle. Mr. Ingram lived and worked as a
Church musician for some years in London, publishing
and editing, on the lines of the ancient Church music,
chants, canticles, anthems, etc. Some will remember
Dr. Chandler's never-varying kindness and care in his
pastoral duties; and the daughter churches of All Saints,
Margaret Street, and St. Andrew's, Wells Street, were
not a little indebted to his courage and care. His curates,
too, Mr. Fallow, Mr. Wollaston, afterwards Vicar of
Felpham and Canon of Chichester, Mr. Murray, and
others, should not be left out of the record. When Dr.
Chandler became Dean of Chichester, he devoted himself to the work and care of his Cathedral, and was but
little heard of out of his Deanery; the great west window was a tribute of respect to him from his parishioners
of All Souls. But for him the beautiful Sussex marble
pillars might have remained longer under their endless
coats of whitewash, the nave filled with its tall un-
sightly pews, the old monuments and pavements have
gone into more ruinous decay. He put up a beautiful
stained-glass window to the memory of his sister. His

care extended to every part of his charge : the choristers, the lay vicars, the organ, the outside of the
Cathedral, the east end, the roofs and the churchyard,
all were under his fostering care, supported by the city
and diocese, and all the Chapter ; the city, its churches
and institutions, too, were remembered by him. He
died in 1859, and his funeral was attended with every
mark of respect and affection. He left £2000 in trust
to be applied towards the decoration of the Cathedral,
or the aiding of the Theological College. Few names
were more revered among the early practical workers
in the revival of the Church principles. He was a
son of the Rev. John Chandler, of Witley, Surrey ; was
educated at Winchester, and became a Fellow of New
College, Oxford ; was Bampton Lecturer in 1825, and
was for some years tutor to the Duke of Buccleuch.
In worth and heartiness, though not in scholarship, his
name may rank with those of Dr. Mill and Dr. Pea-
cock. It was a John Chandler, of Witley, his brother,
who made the earliest translations of the old Latin
hymns under the title of *The Hymns of the Church ;*
though that work was out of print years ago, many of
the translations are familiar to us now, and are used in
all our best collections.

A little later, 1837, Bishop Mant published his
translation of hymns from the Roman Breviary. A
few words from his preface will tell us much of
how things even then were advancing, and how an

Irish bishop of that day could speak with no uncertain tongue.

"To those who are acquainted with the history of
our Book of Common Prayer it is well known that our
excellent Reformers, studious of goodness rather than
of novelty, constructed their provisions for the public
worship of the Church upon the foundation of previously
existing forms.   Accordingly our Common Prayer-
book has derived a large portion of its contents from
the Breviary or Daily Service-book of the Romish
Church, purified from corruption, reduced to the standard of Holy Scripture, as professed by the Catholic
Church of Christ.   Together with its other voluminous
provisions, the Breviary contains a considerable number of hymns used in the regular course of its daily,
weekly, or occasional services, one of which, known by
the name of 'Veni Creator Spiritus,' has been adopted
by our Church in her 'Ordering of Priests' and 'Consecration of Bishops'.

"Bishop Ken is related to have daily sung to his
lute his morning and evening hymns, which partake
much of the character of some of these hymns from
the Breviary.   As a Winchester College boy, Ken must
have been familiar with the 'Jam lucis orto sidere,'
which was sung forty or fifty years ago, when I was
one of William of Wykeham's scholars, and I presume
still continues to be sung by the College boys."

Mr. Isaac Williams' translation of hymns from the

Parisian Breviary **is** worthy of mention with these two volumes.

Westminster Abbey was then a great delight to all young Church-folk, and one special and additional daily service was often attended even from a distance: this was the 7·15 (7·45 winter) early-morning prayer, chiefly established for the young men in the National Society's Training College in Westminster. This service was attended by many whose names were familiar in the after-history of the Church Movement. **Dr.** Hook was there whenever he was in town; he was then Vicar of Leeds, the apostle of the Church to the great middle class, as Dean Church calls him; Dr. Wordsworth, Canon and afterwards Bishop of Lincoln; Dr. Williamson, headmaster of Westminster School; Canon Jennings, Rector of St. **John** the Evangelist; Sir William Henry Cope, then Minor Canon; Lord **John** Thynne; many laymen of the neighbourhood; **Mr. Maude, Mr.** and the Hon. Mrs. Talbot, father and mother **of** the Member for the University of **Ox**-ford, and **the** present Vicar of Leeds. The service, **a** plain one, of **course,** was taken by the Rev. John Aubone Cook, then curate to Dr. Milman, who held St. Margaret's, Westminster, and was afterwards Dean of St. Paul's. Few would have seen anything remarkable **about Mr.** Cook, and yet he **was** really one of those **whose** life was a perfect specimen of the country parish **priest, by** whom the principles of the Church Movement were set forth in life and conversation; and it was by the influence of such men that the revival grew and increased as it did. I give a short sketch, taken chiefly from Mr. Heygate's small biography, of him.

John Aubone Cook was of a good family, and was brought up in France, and then at a school in England, at Woolwich. In 1829, on the death of Col. Cook, his father, Mr. Cook went to India; but, not finding the opening he wished for, returned. On the voyage home the ship was dismasted, and all hope that they should be saved was taken away. In the storm he thought that if his life were preserved, it would be a right act of gratitude to dedicate it to God in His ministry. He entered Corpus Christi College, Cambridge, and came out senior optime. He was ordained as curate to Dean Milman in 1838. He devoted himself to theological study, and the bishop told him that he had done himself the greatest credit in that. He spent twelve years of unremitting toil as Curate of St. Margaret's, and those who knew him there told of his untiring industry, his tender compassion and steady devotion; " love " and " reverence " were the terms in which those who knew him at Westminster spoke. On one occasion at St. Margaret's, some Frenchmen entered the church, and walked about admiring and criticising with their hats on; Mr. Cook electrified the offenders by calling out in the very manner and accent in which such a rebuke would have been given in their own

country : " It is a church, gentlemen ! it is a church ".
The hats were promptly removed. In the autumn of
1849 Mr. Cook was overdone by attending to those who
were sick of the cholera, and at that time he buried
fifty people in one week. Those who did not know
him could form no idea of his toil. Mr. Cook did not
meet those whom he buried for the first time at the
grave, and he did not visit in a hurried or negligent
manner ; his characteristic was his earnest, thorough
treatment of every subject ; he led a man to say and do
the right thing at the last, to withdraw the slander, to
restore the unrighteous gain. During the ten years
from 1840 that he was early reader at the Abbey, he
was never once late. He resided in London with his
widowed mother, and was a head to the family.

He was appointed in 1850 to the vicarage of South
Benfleet, in Essex, then out of the way of all men ; and
so Mr. Cook passed from the society of highly-educated
men to an entire solitude. This was the one great trial
of his life. In 1852 he was made rural dean ; in this
office he had long, weary walks, and fostered much
care of the holy edifices, vestments, and sacred furni-
ture. He never yielded to any irreverent custom such
as writing his entries on the altar, but uniformly refused to do so. He never entered a church without
offering a short prayer. On one occasion, when looking over a new church, he observed that there was no
place for washing the holy vessels after a celebration of

the Sacrament. He received for reply, that such a provision was not sanctioned by the English Church. "How do you show this?" he said. "There is no order for it in the rubrics," was answered. "Is there any for washing the surplices?" was the conclusive rejoinder.

A Mormonite was once preaching on the roadside at Benfleet; the vicar passed by, and when an opportunity offered, he said, "Will you allow me to ask you one question?"

"Certainly," was the reply.

"Is it true or not that your chiefs at the Salt Lake have many wives?"

The preacher could not but allow it, and was justifying it. Mr. Cook turned round and said, "Now, my friends, you have heard that this man teaches a religion which leads to a man having many wives; do you wish this for your daughters?"

"No."

Mr. Cook went home and the people with him, and the preacher was left by himself on a heap of stones.

As rural dean Mr. Cook had to examine and report on the schools; his love for children fitted him well to instruct them. At all school-feasts he was at home, and never happier; he has been seen to take the plate of a child, and eat of its rice pudding, when it was in trouble because it had been sentenced to finish the rice or have nothing else. But some wonderful work was in store for this poor vicar. In the summer of 1854 the railway was being constructed, and a number of excavators and workmen lodged in Benfleet and **crowded** its cottages. In that summer the cholera visited England, and fell most heavily on this parish, **and** there were no well-to-do residents **to** help in **such** a calamity.

On one occasion his example was effectual. **An old man was ill in the** village, and his nurse was worn **out. Mr.** Cook went down and sat up **all night** with **the** man—offers of help came after that. In 1854 **the** terror seemed **too** great ; and while he considered the safety of others, the whole weight and labour **and danger fell on his own** shoulders. He visited the sick and dying, not from morning to night, but from week's end to week's end, and for seven whole days and nights **he** never went to his bed ; for nearly three weeks **he** had not **one** whole night's rest. From house to house he hastened, forgetting to eat, adminis**tered the** medicines, rubbed the limbs, praying when**ever one** was conscious. Physician of body and **soul,** he was spent **for his** flock, and for these godless, drunken strangers as well. One of these great navvies who, **when Mr. Cook was** urging him to come to church, replied that **he** had torment enough on week**days,** being taken with **the** cholera, sent to beg Mr. Cook to come to **him. At** his bedside Mr. Cook **passed the** whole night. It is not easy to describe the

scene ; he shrank **from no** office, **however** terrible, and
lived in the **room** occupied by several **of these** coarse
men. Doctor, nurse, **priest, without** repose and almost
without food, he comforted, assisted, supplied want,
and prayed. **He** had fresh air only when he went
about other **work in the** parish ; he himself buried
those whom he had nursed, forty in one month. **In**
such a pestilence there was little time for the thorough
spiritual treatment which was usual, but he did what
he could. One case of restitution he effected ; **a** man
who had forsaken his wife and was living with another
wrote, by Mr. Cook's hands, to his wife, asked her pardon, dismissed the **other woman, and died. A** traveller
was seized **in the** village, **every home was** closed to
him, and the people said, " There is but **one** home that
will take **you in,** and that is the vicarage ". He was
carried upstairs by Mr. Cook and a neighbour, put to
bed, nursed and attended till he recovered.

After this visitation Mr. **Cook** returned to his simple
life. **His income** was small, but the widows and sick
he always helped. His time was never his own ; **he**
was often called up, **and** would be out visiting **into the**
night ; **on one occasion** after midnight the policeman
heard a man running, **and** turned his **lantern : it was
the** vicar running to a sick man who had sent **for him.**
On **another** occasion, returning home **in the** evening,
he found that two persons had been quarrelling: he went
to their house, and spent two hours in trying to recon-

cile them, and did not leave until he had succeeded.
His sympathy was extraordinary, and no trouble was
too great if he could serve a friend by it. In 1857 he
became incumbent of Canvey Island, hoping to get an
assistant curate, but he could do so only for a time.
The hot summer of this year was followed by much
sickness. On Saturday, September 10, he left home
at midday, and was overtaken by darkness on Canvey
Island, lost his way, and reached home at ten; he felt
ill, but held the three services of Sunday, and after that
he took to his bed, from which he never rose; he lin-
gered in fever till St. Michael's Day. One who was at
his funeral tells us "there were no dry eyes; tears for
him flowed thick and fast. I never saw so many weep,
nor so worthily." Nobody knows, no one can know,
how much influence the life of this reader at the Westminster Abbey early daily service had on the neighbourhood around him.

CHAPTER IV

WHEN people spoke of the country clergy, and their not being altogether up to date in London ways, this was quite understood as applying to very few in out-of-the-way spots; indeed, I feel inclined to apologise for such speeches when I remember a very unrefined one by a London rector of some standing at that time. He was in his vestry ready to go in to the Sunday evening service, with his four curates around him. A visitor who was going to help in the service asked the rector if he was going to preach; he replied, "Oh, dear no; I do not keep dogs to bark and bark myself". I am sure no country rector, however far distant from the centre of civilisation, would have made such a speech as that.

To return to London; there were several very important centres of the Church Movement, and one of the earliest of these was Christ Church, Albany Street, built about 1836-7, when dwellers in that neighbourhood were looking on in some bewilderment at the enormous excavations being made for the cutting of the London and North Western Railway from Euston Square to Primrose Hill. We are used to such

things now ; but it really did strike young folks with
alarm to see so much of the bowels of the earth dis-
placed. Christ Church was the first church built under
Bishop Blomfield's Metropolitan Church Scheme ; it
was a semi-classical building, with nothing to attract
externally, and inside the noble proportions of the
chancel, and the altar well elevated, were the re-
deeming points, the altar-piece being a fine copy of
Raphael's Transfiguration by some well-known painter.
Plain choir stalls and lectern were added in 1850. Sir
James Pennethorne was the architect, but in 1867 the
whole was decorated and re-arranged internally under
Mr. Butterfield, the renowned church architect, to
whom the Church of England is certainly indebted for
many of her finest churches and restorations. The
first incumbent was the Rev. Wm. Dodsworth, who
had been for some years minister of Margaret Chapel,
and a popular preacher there, working his way up on
the lines of the Church Movement, but without much
attempt to improve the arrangements of that very
homely little chapel or its ritual ; he preached there
now and then in Mr. Oakeley's time, good, simple, and
thoughtful sermons ; he was originally quite an Evangelical or Low Churchman, and it was said that he had
considerable leaning to a body of men then rising into
notice, but of whom now we do not hear much, being
chiefly reminded of them by their great church of
cathedral-like proportions in Gordon Square. I refer

to the Irvingites, **or, as** they **called** themselves, the Catholic Apostolic Church. Mr. Dodsworth was not **the** only Church of England clergyman attracted by **this** remarkable body of religionists; and a **few** words about them here may not be out of place. **It was a** time of **much** progress and stirring of heart, and the claims **of the** Irvingites **to** supernatural origin **were sure** to attract. The restoration of the actual office of **the** twelve apostles, by the calling of twelve men **to** that dignity, was the main principle of **their work, and** by this **restored apostolate** the **divisions** and shortcomings of Christendom were **to be healed.** The statement **and proofs of their** spiritual **claim** had been **officially** forwarded **to every court in Europe ;** certainly the mere fact that such **a** ritual as **they then** practised **could be** accepted and approved by what was at first **a** small Presbyterian sect was in itself rather miraculous. It was, of course, easy to construct a handsome ritual and **a** devotional liturgy by using the Eastern and Western liturgies and making a good selection ; and this was done by them, though many of the **members** averred that **the** vestments and details **were specially revealed through the** revived apostolic **office.** One of **the** offices **was touching : you** might **see a** father, mother, and six **children kneeling at the** altar rails, **about to** emigrate, joining in prayer, blessed by their bishop before they **sailed.** Their church was then in Newman Street, and in the number of their priests it

was said that some Church of England clergy were to **be found** ; and it was an undoubted fact that clergy of **the** Church of England **had** submitted to what was called the laying on of the apostles' hands, and it was even currently reported that an English rector was himself **one of their** twelve apostles. **Mr.** Drummond, the banker, **was one, and** several of their priests were in business **or** official positions. One **of** the best known figures in London to be constantly met on the way from Newman Street to Euston Square was **the** noble and venerable form of Mr. Heath, the angel or bishop in Newman Street. **They** were not at all an aggressive people, or anxious to make proselytes : **a friend of** mine in a Government office had **a** very gentlemanly, quiet, well-informed **man** as his companion in work ; it was years before he found out quite accidentally that his fellow-clerk was an Irvingite priest. **Mr.** Hooper, the **then** Rector **of** Albury, a home or centre **of** the **work (where Mr. Portal, of St.** Barnabas, **was** after-**wards** rector), made no secret of his sympathy and membership; he published a *Treatise on the Revelation of St.* **John,** *Family Prayers,* etc. Mr. Armstrong, too, was one of their great preachers, and published some volumes of sermons ; Miss Leeson, a well-known **member,** wrote some exquisite poetry, such as " Hymns **and** Scenes of Childhood," and " Songs of Christian Chivalry". I cannot, of course, say how far Mr. Dods-worth **was** at one with these worthy people. He worked for ten years in Christ **Church,** Albany Street, made it a thorough centre of Church teaching, and had **a large** congregation ; all was **done with a simple** grandeur, but with very little of advanced ritual. **Among** his curates were Mr. New, Ed. Stuart, **W. H.** Milman, Mr. Gordon, **Mr.** Morton Shaw, afterwards Rector **of** Rougham, **near** Bury **St.** Edmunds, and, for a short time, **Mr.** Cavendish, a nephew of Lord Chesham's, **and afterwards Rector** of Casterton ; in younger days **he and** his brother, who **went into** the Life Guards, **were** pages to the Queen. His clerical life was a short and rather **a sad one. Mr.** Burgon, afterwards Dean of Chichester, often officiated there in those days.

Mr. Dodsworth published sermons **and** controversial tracts ; and in 1851, concluding **that** the Church of England was involved in the judgments **of** the Privy Council or responsible for them, he seceded from the Church, and was afterwards known for the attempted replies to Dr. Pusey's famous letter to the Bishop **of** London, which was one **of** the most perfect and exhaustive defences of Catholic principles in the **Church** of England—a real manual of the greatest **value for all** time. **We may** hope it will be still read : the original **cause of** that letter was one by Mr. Dodsworth to Dr. Pusey, in which he reproached him for something like lukewarmness about the Gorham judgment, and printed expressions from his adapted **works.** Copies of this were distributed in the street outside the Church of

St. Barnabas, on the night that Dr. Pusey preached
there. Christ Church still held to the Church revival,
and had a career of sound faith and practice under the
Rev. H. W. Burrows and the present Bishop Festing.
Later on, a more advanced ritual was, and still is, at
work in that neighbourhood, in the handsome Gothic
Church of St. Mary Magdalen, Munster Square, built
by the munificence of the late Rev. Edward Stuart,
from the designs of Mr. Carpenter, whose early death
was so earnestly deplored by churchmen ; Baron Alderson laid the foundation stone, and other good Church
laymen attended this church. The very earliest sisterhood in the English Church was in Osnaburgh Street,
close by. Its beginning in 1845 by three or four
ladies quietly and unostentatiously, was in a house in
Park Village West, in the parish of Christ Church,
Albany Street. The house in Osnaburgh Street, which
is in St. Mary Magdalen's parish, was built afterwards.
Now that sisterhoods are the largest and best recognised works in our Church, it is deeply interesting
to know of this first beginning, of which Miss Sellon's,
of Devonport, was really an offshoot. A full account
of the Osnaburgh Street house will no doubt be
found in the later volumes of Dr. Pusey's life. Mr.
Stuart had a most worthy successor in the incumbency
of St. Mary Magdalen's, Munster Square—the Rev. F.
J. Ponsonby, whose comparatively early death very
many churchmen have just been mourning. Mr.

Ponsonby's work and character have earned for him the respect and affection of all who were **privileged to** know him.

This, perhaps, will be **a point at** which **we can** refer to the story of Margaret Chapel under Mr. Oakeley, the successor of Mr. Dodsworth. Mr. Mozley speaks of **a** Mr. Charles Thornton, who had charge, perhaps just before Mr. Oakeley. Mr. Thornton was a cousin **of** Dr. Pusey's, a good scholar and able man. It hardly comes within my province to tell of the early history of this remarkable chapel; how **in 1776,** the Rev. **David** Williams occupied it with the object **of includ- ing in one congregation all earnest and** pious men, without reference to creed, faith, **or doctrine ;** this was **hardly a plan likely to** succeed, **and it was** a failure. **It would be curious to** know how he proposed to suit **his** chapel and services **to every one ; it** reminds one of **Mr.** Newland's story **of the** old Devonshire boatman who was rowing him across **the** breakwater at Ply- mouth, and pointed out a small chapel, the minister of which, he said, had tried several denominations **in hope** of getting **a** congregation ; if one plan did not succeed he tried another, and his last idea **was to** propitiate the Baptists, and **he even** went **so far as to** give them a **huge** tub for immersion. Mr. Newland thought " it **was** rather a hopeless **plan to** try and please every one in such matters ". " Aye, sir," **said** the boatman, " that it was : the old gentleman's course to heaven lay north-east by west southerly, and he didn't carry no small helm neither."

This Mr. Williams, of Margaret Chapel—it was said that it was named after the minister's daughter, Margaret—was the founder of the Literary Fund, and his tombstone may be **seen** in the church of St. Anne, **Soho.** After him came a congregation calling them- **selves** Bereans. **Mr.** Dodsworth held the chapel for some time up to 1837, and it was not **so** much of a centre of work during his time. **We** read **of Mr.** Philip Pusey, the squire, elder brother of Dr. Pusey, attending Margaret Chapel in Mr. Dodsworth's time. Mr. Oakeley had been elected Fellow of Balliol **in** 1827 ; **he** had also **been** made Prebendary of Lich- field, and had been Whitehall preacher, publishing his volume of sermons preached **there, in** 1839. In his earlier **years at Oxford he** has been described as an elegant and rather dilettante scholar, a musician, much **at his** piano, and avowedly sentimental rather than decisive **in** his religious views ; but the ten years **in** the thick of the Oxford Movement **had no** doubt given him very decided views on religion, and he came to London with **the** express object of carrying out those principles, of **showing that** Anglican ritual could be expressive and devotional ; and he gathered round him **a** congregation second **to** none in London, of good standing, and earnest consistent Church principles, who rallied round the old chapel, which became a wonderful London centre **for some years ; a spot** to which **people could** point **as a proof that the** Church Movement was **a** vital and real **one, not resting in** mere books, but to be seen and known of all men by its works. **If one thing** had been degraded lower **than** another in past days of neglect it was the public worship of Almighty God : so, first and foremost, it **was in** Margaret Chapel that an improvement in this was attempted. **Yet** how little of strict ritual was at first really carried out ! scarcely more than we find now in nine out of ten parish churches throughout **the** land ; yet what a power the simple, ugly building was, and what splendid work for the Church **of** England was the result ; it was a small beginning, indeed, but how it **grew** ! **About** 1839-45 as you turned, any **day,** into Margaret Street from Wells Street, just before five, the **hour of** daily evensong, you would hear a small, half-cracked bell, in **a** little cot at the top of the chapel front gable, hardly louder or more penetrating than the blow of **the** blacksmith's hammer in the forge at the **back of the** chapel, a perpetual accompaniment **to the** week-day services, to which we got quite accustomed (that blacksmith's hammer was the only remnant of old times that survived at the consecration **of** the beautiful church of All Saints). The chapel bell was ringing, and **as you** neared the doors (one on each side), from one **of** the houses **on** the opposite **side** of Margaret Street, **you** might see crossing the road a thin, short,

limping figure, with **college cap** on, dark hair closely
cropped, good features, bright eyes and square-shaped
head. This was Frederick Oakeley, minister of the
chapel. He went in at the right-hand door, and at the
far end, before going into the little vestry, knelt a few
moments, as all the clergy did, at the wooden altar-rail,
which came in a semi-circular form around the altar
itself. **This was** the *five* o'clock evensong, which **has
now** been going on for fifty years; there was then daily
matins at **eight, and** early celebrations on Sundays and
saints' days. This was an ordinary evensong; but there
was no mistake about the hearty and **unanimous re-**
sponse, **the** reverent and earnest behaviour. **Mr.**
Oakeley, in cassock and surplice, black stole and hood,
took his place, with one chorister in a surplice by his
side, at a small desk on the left side **(Mr.** Willing,
afterwards organist, **and** then at the Foundling, was
that chorister at one time); the rest **of** the choir being
with **Mr.** Redhead and the organ at the end gallery.
One verse of the Psalms was sung by the priest **and**
choir-boy, **and** the other verse by the choir upstairs
with the congregation. **The** Psalter was the *Laudes
Diurnæ,* a Gregorian **one** arranged by Mr. Redhead,
author and editor of many valuable works of Church
music, edited by Mr. Oakeley, published by Mr. Toovey;
it had a syllabic arrangement that sometimes sounded
awkwardly, but it had a dear place in the hearts of
those who used it, and it was then a step in the right

direction.   On saints' days and their eves it was a
regular thing to sing the last fourteen verses of Tate
and Brady's 118th Psalm, " Joy fills the dwelling of
the just," to a simple melody, which, to use a favourite
expression of Dr. Gauntlett's, " went like oil ".   There
was no Hymnal then, but special hymns for special times
were printed on leaflets.   Pages of special sermons,
Advent, Christmas, Lent, Easter, anniversaries, with list
of additional services and preachers, and the hymns,
were ready for circulation among the congregation.
There hardly seemed much to attract people in this ;
but the chapel was fairly full on all week-days ; many
of the highest and most learned in Church and State,
such as Lord Lyttelton, Mr. Gladstone, and Mr. Henry
Tritton, were among them, and curates of neighbouring
parishes, with a fair number of poor ; on Sundays it
was more than full.   It was ugly, not to say painfully so ; picture to yourself a square room, with flat,
whitewashed roof, two large galleries, and the whole
area covered with pews, no centre passage but only two
side ones, the east wall (it was really north) flat and
plain. ˙ In such a place the altar was the only part that
there was a hope of making decent, and this, with the
aid of dorsel and flowers at festivals, cross and candlesticks, was all that for some years was attempted ; yet
the place was loved in spite of its ugliness ; and some
were ready to say, when at last the old pews were
swept away, that they even loved the wretched old

seats, bad as they were. It was the enthusiasm, the spirit of the thing, that carried all before it. Mr. Oakeley, whose bright sermons showed the easy finish of an elegant scholar, had constantly the presence and support of his Oxford friends. I am afraid many of us now accustomed to a ritual more in accordance with the ornaments rubric, would have thought little of the ritual there, so valued by many then. They would have seen Mr. Oakeley celebrating in cassock, rather long surplice, black stole, and Oxford M.A. hood; and kneeling, one on each side below him, might be J. H. Newman and W. G. Ward, in similar dress, the latter very conspicuous from his imposing size. Many a clergyman, an Oxford man, who had left Oxford and taken a country living, attended this humble place when he was in London, and went away to carry the influence of the inspiriting service of the little chapel to his distant country parish ; so that from this chapel there was an influence, the extent of which it is not easy to measure. Outside, after service, the hearty greetings and handshakes were a sight to see; it was like a rallying point for all friends of the movement. All was thoroughly English in heart and spirit, the idea of merely imitating another branch of the Church entered into no one's head. It was as the birthright of our own Church that all contended for outward beauty, increased reverence, and every scheme for good. Very few of the books used were taken from foreign sources; the Psalter we have named. During his ministry Mr. Oakeley translated St. Bonaventura's life of Christ, a life in which the details of the daily life of our Lord in Nazareth, were reverently filled in; an edition of this had been published in 1739, evidently by an English churchman; it is not too much to say, such was the *esprit* of the place, that nearly every member of the congregation bought a copy of this book almost wet from the press. The *Devotions for Holy Communion* contained no words that an honest member of the English Church could object to: it was much valued and used, and so was the smaller edition which followed, edited by Mr. Oakeley's successor; the *Prayers for a Blessing on the Building of the New Church*, which was a plan in the hearts of all, were part of the daily devotions of the people, as was the small book of *Questions for Self-Examination*. Part of the story of this chapel can never be written, I mean its inner life, —the earnestness about the soul and spiritual things, the besetting sin broken off for ever, the penitent restored, the worldly reclaimed, the humble and persevering strengthened and built up, the business man influenced to higher things.

For more than seven years the work prospered, and though, from time to time, warnings came of trials and troubles in the Church, those in earnest felt that such trials were sure to come; those only escaped them who continued cold and indifferent; and that was the very spirit against which Margaret Chapel, and its round of prayer and praise, fast and festival, holy seasons and rejoicings, **was** a perpetual visible protest. Bishop Blomfield, in his Charge of 1842, **had** urged a more strict adherence to some of the Church's plainest rules ; **the** party in the Church represented by the Islington clergy distinctly rebelled ; to them many parts of the Prayer-book were a dead letter, and the Church was **a** Protestant community, in spite of the Catholic creeds, calendar, seasons, offices, ordinal, catechism, etc. Then, by some it began to be urged that claims to Apostolic descent and doctrine alone belonged to the Church **of** Rome ; for this view there was little proof from primitive times, history and antiquity, to which the Church of England **referred all her members** ; **it was** found impossible to reconcile the **modern system** of the **Church of** Rome with primitive times, and so **new** theories had to be invented. Between these two parties poor Bishop Blomfield was sadly troubled. The **controversy was** not gone through without a struggle, and Margaret Chapel felt it severely. As we have said, Mr. Oakeley was enthusiastic ; he was also chivalrous, and took up the cause of his friend Mr. W. **G.** Ward with vigour, and defended his book *The Ideal of a Christian Church,* published by Mr. Toovey in 1844. **He** preached two sermons on the 10th and 17th of November, 1844, **on** " Things dispensable, and things indispensable ". After that he published that remarkable letter to a friend called " **A claim** to hold all **Roman** Doctrine **without teaching it,**" still trying to **hold on to the Church in which he knew** God had placed him.   Then, too, was published the pamphlet of twenty-four pages, "Selections from **a work** entitled *The Ideal of a Christian Church,* illustrative of its ten-**dency to** promote Dutifulness to the English Church, Unity among **her** Members, and Charity towards Dis-sentients ".   **But the end was bound** to come, and then **for a few weeks Mr. Oakeley left off** officiating, and still came to **the** service, kneeling **in one of** the end pews.   **It was of this time that Dr.** Pusey speaks when telling **of the** pain that Mr. Oakeley's writings gave him, **and doubting if he had** historical knowledge for the part **he was taking.   Dean** Church **tells the** story of his **quixotic defence of Mr. Ward before the** University ; **he was, as has been said, one** who **would** follow his **friend or leader in a " Charge of the** Light Brigade ". The contrast between the thin little minister of Mar-garet Chapel, **and** the **large,** florid, and bright per-sonality of **his** friend, **both** standing up before **the University, was curious** but very impressive.   **And the contrast between their future lives was** quite as marked : **the one** spent **the rest** of his life serving a poor con-**gregation** in Islington, limping about the streets in very shabby canonicals, **eye still bright** and voice kind ; Mr. Mozley tells us that he would sometimes be induced to dine quietly at Lambeth Palace, and talk over old days with another old Fellow of Balliol, Archbishop Tait. The other had an estate, Northwood Park, Isle of **Wight, a** happy home, wife and children, and leisure for the delights of art, music, and literature. Dean Church tells us too, that during the anxious days of the condemnation of **Mr.** Ward's book, Mr. Ward was engaged to be married, and that the engagement came **to the** knowledge of his friends, to their great astonishment and amusement, very soon after the condemnation. **It** was said that the lady was a member of the congregation of Margaret Chapel, and, to add to **the** romance, that Mr. Ward's first approach to **her was on** behalf **of a** friend, **to** whom, of course, the lady **was** unfavourable. Mr. Wingfield, her brother, a Christ Church man, **and Mr.** Ward were described by Mr. **Bennett** in the *English Churchman* (**then** the only **Church** organ) as " Subtle Mr. Ward," and " Simple **Mr.** Wingfield "—Ward's subtlety **in** claiming to hold **all** Roman doctrine, Wingfield's simplicity in accepting **as the** decree **of a** pope, Sir H. Jenner Fust's judgment **against** the Cambridge round church stone altar.

It was a long and sad time before Margaret Chapel recovered from the effects of Mr. Oakeley's secession ; the loss of such men as Bellasis, Hood, Wingfield, Burns, Toovey, Baddeley, and others was a serious one, and pressure was put on many of the congregation to take the step **that** their minister and others had taken. Mr. Upton Richards was Mr. Oakeley's successor ; he had been his

curate, and for a short time held **also** an office in the
Manuscript Department of the British Museum.   He
was an Exeter College man, nephew of Dr. Richards, then
Rector of Exeter College ; and few can nowadays **imagine**
the task of keeping that congregation together, and
carrying on the work of the movement in services, etc.,
which he so bravely undertook.   Happily, there were a
goodly number who held fast to the Church of their
baptism ; but even with their help Mr. Richards' post
was one of infinite labour and anxious care. Simple,
devout, hopeful and persevering, **he held on** his way
through all the distractions and troubles **of** that time
and **for** many years after; and well he deserved the
love and confidence he won.   The building of a noble
church was kept steadily in view, but **in the** meantime
the homely little chapel was transformed ; **it** was re-
seated, and a sort of chancel choir and stalls erected,
and the services gained beauty and strength as time
went on, till it was pulled down.   The last service at
the old chapel was an early celebration on Easter
Monday, 1850, carried out with all the increased beauty
and dignity of those years under Mr. Richards.   One
who **was there described** it as most solemn and **pathetic,**
—with what beating hearts, what weeping eyes they bend
to receive there for the last time the blessing of their
priest; **how** full, how fervent did the deep Amen arise
throughout the building, uttered **by** every voice,
responded to by **every** heart ; lingering long, so loth to

die away. Some verses on this occasion by Mrs. Alexander, author of *Hymns for Little Children*, are worth **repeating.**

> How many spirits troubled with the chiding
>   Of the rough world, have hither turned for rest,
> Like storm-tossed ship awhile at anchor riding,
>   On some small haven's quiet breast?
>
> How many lips in rapturous devotion,
>   Wrought by no outward impulse, here have moved,
> How many hearts can share our hearts' emotion,
>   Here meeting with the lost and loved?

On **All Saints'** Day, 1850, the foundation stone **of** the Church of **All Saints** was laid by **Dr.** Pusey, whose name will **ever be** treasured for the deepest learning and piety, **and a** life spent in providing **good** and solid resting ground for true Catholic principles in the Church of England. On the laying of the **stone** he preached in the temporary chapel in Titchfield **Street,** and there for another nine years the work of **the old** chapel was carried forward; and on that small crowded spot more offerings for the completion of the church **were made.** And as the building opposite progressed, **so did** the building up of every spiritual and corporal work **of** mercy increase and abound. Let none think that the reverence and beauty, and minute attention to ritual stood alone—it rarely does. All Saints' **Home, with** its orphanage, hospital, dispensary, etc., began in a small **way** in 1851, governed by rules and statutes allowed by the Bishop of London, and in

1856 was more firmly established, dedicated in a special service by the Bishop of Oxford, acting for the diocesan. It was the wish of the ladies engaged in the work that it should be, as far as possible, the Church's expression of sympathy for all who are in want, or sickness, or sorrow; by Lent, 1859, there were nine sisters, ten old women, twenty-four orphans, twenty-two serving girls, and nine incurables. There was a pharmacy, a mortuary chapel, etc. I need not say that up to the present day the work is still growing. Who does not know of its grand convalescent home and chapel at Eastbourne, and many other additions? By May, 1859, the church, the clergy-house, and other houses were completed, and on the 28th it was consecrated. Mr. Helmore sang the service, and his *Manual of Plain Song* was used. The Bishop of London (Tait) preached, and in his sermon said that personally he preferred a less ornate and elaborate church and service; but if those who loved God as well, if not better, than he did, found these things aids to devotion, and a means of drawing their hearts from the love of this world, it was not for him to refuse it. Among the preachers in the octave were the Dean of Westminster (Trench), Rev. the Hon. R. Liddell, J. R. (afterwards Bishop) Woodford, R. M. Benson, T. Yard, and T. T. Carter. I need not carry this sketch beyond the death of Mr. Richards in 1873; it would be vain to attempt any adequate description of his life's work

and devotion, and how deeply it was appreciated by
many hundreds to whom he ministered. In appearance he was slight and fair, with an ever-cheerful expression, and not unlike in features to his great and
life-long friend Dr. Pusey, who was always his staunch
helper in times of trouble and anxiety. Other valued
friends were constant attendants at the church. I name
a few : The Bishop of Brechin, Lord Glasgow, Rev. R.
J. Spranger, W. J. Blew ; Mr. Walker, the well-
known engraver ; Mr. Tritton, one of the most munificent donors to the church ; Rev. G. A. Trevor, once
Rector of Rokeley, was mid-day celebrant for years;
Mr. Lyall, of Backchurch ; Rev. J. C. Crompton, who
edited the Proper Prefaces with the old music ; Lord
Forbes, Mr. G. E. Street, Mr. Butterfield, and his
churchwarden, Mr. William Holland, and many others.
Then therew ere his fellow-helpers and curates, T. W.
Perry, C. Gutch, and last, but by no means least,
the Rev. Chas. Christie (brother of Albany Christie,
formerly fellow of Oriel), a man of only one
curacy, except a short time at St. Thomas's, Oxford,
and Lewknor. All honour and praise to such men ;
there are very few of them ! Mr. Richards had a
worthy successor in Mr. Berdmore Compton. In 1880-
81 a Conference of Clergy was held at All Saints,
on the subject of ritual, which resulted in a valuable
pamphlet on the various interpretations of the rubrics
of the Prayer-book.

A short walk across Cavendish Square to Baker Street brings us to a much more pretentious looking building than that in Margaret Street, namely, Portman Chapel, the interior of which had been made more comely by the Rev. W. J. Early Bennett, M.A., of Christ Church, Oxford, who was the minister for a few years till the church of St. Paul, Knightsbridge, was finished in 1843. At the time he was but little over thirty, and full of that strength, courage, and vigour for which he was so long distinguished. At Portman Chapel he must have aroused the fashionable folks from their easy, luxurious lives, and stirred them with his pointed and scholarly sermons. There was, of course, but little that could be called ritual, but all things were done carefully and reverently ; the pulpit was not put before the altar, the prayers were not read to the people, etc., as they were then in so many proprietary chapels. Mr. Bennett was succeeded by Mr. D. A. Beaufort, who gave the font to St. Paul's, Knightsbridge ; afterwards he was chaplain to Mr. Eliot Warburton, at Arley ; at Portman Chapel in his time Mr. Palmer, of Worcester College, author of the *Origines Liturgicæ*, preached, referring in his sermon to the martyrdom of King Charles I. In 1843 Mr. Bennett began his eight years' work at the church and parish of St. Paul's, Knightsbridge, which was for a long time to be the centre of so many struggles to maintain the showing forth of Church principles before the world of London. Trials of all kinds began **very soon : even at** the consecration the bishop ordered the removal of an oak eagle supporting the bible desk; and Mr. Hodgson, rector of the mother church, St. George's, Hanover Square, read the service facing the people, ignoring the side prayer desk. **The** choir were not in surplices till Advent, 1846. It was a handsome church, built from the designs of **Mr.** Cundy, and it was not long before Mr. Bennett made his mark, and **a very** large congregation were regular attendants **at St.** Paul's. Mr. Bennett was **not only** **a** good preacher, but **he** was a writer of numerous works, putting the Tractarian Theology **into a** most popular and readable form. His two series of *Letters to my Children*, published about 1850, on religious and moral subjects, **were** admirable specimens of such works. There were also volumes of Sermons, *Essays on the Prayer-book, on the Holy Eucharist, the Church's Broken Unity*, besides the *Old Church Porch*, and **a** variety **of** short works and pamphlets as occasion arose. **He** had a wonderful gift of attracting people to himself and his cause ; one of the most remarkable was the lady **who** wrote *Tales of Kirkbeck, Tales of* **a** *London Parish, Alice Beresford, Lives of the Fathers*, **etc.,** etc., all of which were published anonymously as edited by the Rev. W. J. E. Bennett. **He** also edited *Fénélon's Counsels*. **He was a** thorough parish priest, guide, **and** friend, and had the gift of organising too. Some **of his** curates at St. Paul's were men of great

ability : Mr. Cowie, **now Dean of Exeter, Mr.** De Gex,
C. I. Smith, Archdeacon **of** Jamaica, afterwards Rector
of Erith, author **of a standard book on** Synonyms;
George Nugee, **author of** *Sermons* **on** *the* **Cross,** and
Sermons on Holy **Women;** H. Stretton (afterwards **at
Hixon,** in Staffordshire), joint author with **Sir W. H.**
Cope of the *Visitatio Infirmorum,* and author **of a**
series of sermons **on** the acts **of St.** Mary Magdalen.
In the preface to the *Visitatio,* is **a** reference to two
young friends, candidates for the holy order of deacon ;
these were Randolph Payne, **so many** years at **St.**
Paul's, Brighton, and J. **L.** Fish, **Rector of St.** Mar-
garet's Pattens, City. Mr. **Bennett's** handsome personal
presence and dignified **and courageous** bearing through
all his troubles will **be** remembered still **by** many who
knew and valued him, recalled, **too,** by the very beauti-
ful engraving, after Richmond's portrait, **a** companion
to that excellent series **of** which those of Manning,
Samuel Wilberforce, Selwyn, **F. D.** Maurice, J. H.
Newman, etc., etc., were notable examples.   At Easter
and Christmas the church was more than crowded ; and
on one well-remembered Easter Sunday **the** number
was very large, although there had been several early
celebrations.   The vicar knew that a great many (some
coming from a **distance) would** communicate, and so
the long service would be unusually trying ; on that
occasion he went up into the pulpit and gave out his
text, " Christ is risen ".   " This is my text and this is

my sermon. **Now, to God** the Father," etc., etc. But Mr. Bennett was not **one** to be satisfied with a church filled with **the** rich and well-to-do, when there was a **part** of the parish in which small streets and crowded **houses were the state of** things near the riverside. It was the plain **duty** of the well-to-do who enjoyed the privileges and services of a church like St. Paul's to provide a church **free** and open for the poor of their **own** parish; and he set to work with this object, and about 1846-9 the small but beautiful church of St. Barnabas, in Church Street, was built, and consecrated by the Bishop of London on St. Barnabas' Day, 1850. Dr. Pusey and other well-known clergy preached. **The** sermons were all published in a memorable volume: the Bishops of London and Oxford, Dr. Mill, Keble, Man-**ning,** Sewell, Gresley, Paget, Neale, Eden (afterwards Primus of the Scottish Church), Richards, Kennaway, Henry Wilberforce, Mr. Bennett and his brother Frederick. Few could compare with Mr. Bennett **as a** preacher; and one of his sermons, I think on the Day **of** Judgment, was **said by** Manning to be the finest he ever heard. **A** work for Christ and His people was begun which is still carried on and prospering. **At** St. Barnabas Mr. Bennett mostly worked and officiated; **and** feeling that in a new church a somewhat brighter **and more ornate ritual was fairly** allowable, without **reference to what** they were already accustomed to at St. Paul's, **he carried** matters out himself. All this

was not done without opposition and **dislike** on the part
of the Puritans. The popular mind was exercised, and
what were called the St. Barnabas Riots took place.
They were very mild compared **with another** notorious
riot in the East of London, part of the story of which **I**
hope to tell in another chapter, and chiefly consisted of
hisses and tokens **of** disapproval when the altar lights
were lighted, and when Mr. Bennett ascended **the**
pulpit in his surplice. It is **well** to keep in mind **how**
little then there was of what **could** be called ritual—
black stole, **surplice** and hood, with lights and eastward position, **were** sufficient to excite these angry
feelings. **Under the** excellent and well-remembered
churchwarden, Mr. Sutherland Græme, of Græmeshill,
Orkney, a goodly band of gentlemen was organised as
special constables, who attended early **and** sat or knelt
behind the seats at the west end, and so protected the
worshippers from being molested. It was a scene not
to be forgotten as **Mr.** Bennett ascended the pulpit and
stood still till the hissing somewhat abated : he looked
the very **embodiment of a** brave determined man and
priest, **one who knew** his own faithfulness, and was not
to be hissed down ; he made himself **both** heard and
felt. After **the sermon, at the** offertory sentences, Sir
Frederick Ouseley, **then a** deacon and curate of St.
Barnabas, the future church musician and founder of
St. Michael's, Tenbury, stood at the screen with the
alms-dish, quite calm and undisturbed. A touching

remembrance comes to one's mind. Those were the last few Sundays of Archdeacon Manning's life in the Church of England. He was living in town, and had for some time left off all duty, but he still attended St. Barnabas, and might be seen sitting close by the organ and looking at Mr. Bennett, as he was patiently standing in the pulpit, with an expression that one could almost interpret thus : " Well, how long are you going to **carry** on this battle, this hopeless work of defending **and** vindicating your unhappy Church ? **For** myself I despair of it, and am leaving it." Not so Mr. Bennett ; though he might be driven from his post, his work for the Church of England was *lifelong.* Though his work in the parish might be over, the result of that work lasted **on and has been** seen for years since that time. The churchwarden, Mr. Sutherland Græme, is **still** living with **his son and** his son's wife, Margaret, daughter of the late Dr. Neale, and their children ; and now **at the age of** 86, in his enforced rest from **all** bodily labour, is as enthusiastic and interested as ever in the Church and her welfare, and recalls early events with unfailing energy and pleasure.*

The laymen of the parish were many of them as earnest as the vicar, and ready **to** help in every way ; **letters to** the **Bishop of** London (Blomfield) were **numerous and** pointed. **A** series by Mr. Ramsay, a thorough churchman and scholar, were among the most

* Mr. Sutherland Græme died since this was written.

able, and the Tractarian standing-points well argued
out; but they were not all published. Mr. Bennett
was not one to give up his position and his work till all
had been tried, and every effort for peace had been
made; but the opposition current was too strong even
for this unusually strong man—strong in his sense of
truth and justice and in his allegiance to the Church.

After a time the last appeal was made, and his
famous pamphlet was published, and its modest title
was *A Plea for Toleration*—a plea that the High
Churchman and his honest interpretation of the Book
of Common Prayer, its rubrics, offices, etc., should be
at least tolerated, put up with, allowed a place, a fair
field and no favour. How different in tone and spirit
to those who opposed him, who said, as it were, Our low
standard is the only true one, and we will go to law to
force all men down to that! Their successors in our
day propose to undo the wonderful Church work, life,
influence, and literature of the last fifty years by a little
fresh law, a few more Acts of Parliament, giving less
power to bishops, and all power to the aggrieved
parishioner. Some would almost be inclined to feel
that this party, who would force all men down to their
own standard, and yet who claim the liberty to omit
and ignore nine-tenths of the Prayer-book, should be
the party pleading for toleration. Some one once
wrote some Church nursery rhymes, and concluded with
this moral :—

There once was a prince so conceited
He would have all men think as he did,
   That one si-zed shoe
   Every man should make do,
That prince he was soon superseded.

But in those days the opposing forces **were too
strong.** Mr. Bennett had been driven from his post in
1851, **as has been** said, by the prime minister, who
had temporal authority; **by the** bishop, who had
spiritual authority; **and by the** *Times* **and the mob,
who had no authority.** Probably, **Mr. Bennett** never
expected that his resignation would be accepted by **the**
bishop; **and attempts were made by friends to** dissuade
him from acting on it, **owing to** some technical irregu-
larity, but he pleaded his honour. The storm **was** the
outcome of the "Durham Letter" by Lord John Russell, and the bishop's "Histrionic" **Charge.** On the day
that it announced **the** resignation the *Times* began a
leader thus, "Protestantism has won its *spolia opima*
at the gates **of** St. Barnabas". (Can Thomas Mozley
have written that?) Scanty spoils! for now the parish
has four churches with a much more advanced ritual,
instead **of** two, to say nothing **of the** magnificent work
at Frome, and **Sir** Frederick Ouseley's work at Tenbury. **Some years** after, as a charitable answer to the
Plea for Toleration, **Mr.** Bennett's **doctrine** of the
Eucharist was attacked in Sheppard *v.* Bennett, when
it was decided that teaching an objective real and
spiritual presence was **not** contrary to the doctrine of

the Church of England ; the Church Association appealed, but their appeal **was dismissed.** Sheppard was
a Frome clothworker, "shepherd's plaid" was **said to have
been** named after him ; **his son** became one **of the**
Cowley Fathers !   During this controversy leaflets with
short extracts from the *Tracts for the Times* or the
writings of the Tractarians, were printed **and** distri-
buted to the people as they went out of church.   **An
old** churchman used to say of such folk, "Ah, they
hate Tracts which they never read, but they love
ex-Tracts which they manufacture themselves ".

Mr. Bennett's last pamphlet was a *Farewell Letter
to his Parishioners,* one of the most touching and
pathetic letters that **was ever** written ; **it not** only
affected his parishioners, who felt what **it** was to be
deprived of their priest, guide, friend, and counsellor ;
but it affected many who knew little or nothing of the
writer.   One instance of this I will quote from the
admirable life **of** Charles Lowder, whom it influenced
to begin his work in London, and who worked **for**
some **time at St. Barnabas.** He remembers well, **as**
curate of **a** country town in Gloucestershire, in 1851,
reading one evening **by the** fireside the account of the
farewell of the incumbent of St. Paul and St. Barnabas,
the touching words **which he** spoke, and the sad leave-
taking of his much-loving flock.   **The** whole history
was not to be read carelessly or reflected upon without
many burning thoughts.   Those which arose in his

mind were of deep sorrow **for the** parish which had **lost so devoted a priest ;** of prayer that his place might **be supplied by** one who would faithfully **carry** on his work ; and of ardent longing that, if it were God's will, he might be permitted to take a part, however humble, in aiding **such an** object. The last service at **St. Barnabas under Mr. Bennett was** the Holy Eucharist, on **Lady Day, 1851.** At the close the choir and clergy **all** went out by the west door singing *Super flumina*, **as they had sung** coming in at the opening, *Exsurgat Deus.* Then all went into the dining hall, and the choir sang Weldon's anthem, " In Thee, **O** Lord, have I put my trust ". That was the finish, and it was most touching. **Cosby White (not then** curate) and others **were in tears. Mr.** Skinner, **as Mr.** Liddell's **curate,** preached on the following **Sunday in** black gown, a prayer desk having been set up outside the screen. The alms, gifts, and oblations, made **at** the offertory at **St.** Paul's, are **worth** recording—from Easter, 1846, **to** Easter, 1847 **(there were** no evening collections), they were £6641 **11s. 4d. ; one day's** offering for the building **was £2153 17s. 1d.,** the largest single offering £1000 from **a penitent. Sisters of** Charity soon came to St. Barnabas, **among** them Miss Law, daughter of the Recorder of **London, and Miss Hayes, sister of the** publisher.

In 1852 Mr. **Bennett** was presented **to the** living of **Frome** Selwood, in Somersetshire, by the Marchioness **of Bath,** but his persecution did not cease ; the **presen-**

tation was brought before the House of Commons, and it was there urged that he was not a fit and proper person to hold the living. Such a proposal could hardly be carried even in those days, and it failed. Mr. Bennett spent the rest of his life, thirty-four years, in Frome; and the restoration and rebuilding of that magnificent church will ever be a memorial of him, and the services and work of the parish were in accord with the splendid church, known far and wide for costly magnificence; on it he had expended his own private fortune. He had outlived all opposition, and on his death in 1886, aged 84, his funeral was attended by 500 of his parishioners. Sir Frederick Ouseley's sisters and others followed Mr. Bennett to Frome, and worked with him there. He was not often away from his parish, but was ever ready to help others; he preached and published two sermons at the re-opening of Holy Trinity, Bordesley, Birmingham, the scene of Dr. Oldknow's and Mr. Enraght's labours; and also kindly came to preach at St. George's-in-the-East during the riots.

The record of the two churches of St. Paul and St. Barnabas after 1851 was one of many troubles; the trials and judgments have been printed, and the firm and noble stand through them all made by Mr. Liddell is well within the memory of churchmen; the inconsistencies and contradictions in some of these judgments are well set forth in that very learned series of "Privy Council Tracts" published by Mr. Pickering.

The workers at St. Barnabas now no doubt reverence the names of those, both living and departed, who steered the Church through those early troublous times —Mr. Skinner, so solemn, yet ever gentle and kind; Mr. Lowder, the saintly, fearless and self-sacrificing, both of whose biographies will, it is hoped, cheer and strengthen many a churchman for years to come. Then come the names of Cosby White, Ashley Gibson, Charles Lyford, and a host of good and true if we had space to record them. One great point is that the work in these two churches goes forward and ever forward; and we have but lately read of the enlargement of St. Paul's, a chancel and many beautiful additions, with an increase of *life* and work in the Church, the ritual, music, and devotion, under the care of Mr. Montague Villiers, Mr. Baden Powell, and others. Church folks may take heart and thank the great Head of the Church for the example of such men as Mr. Bennett and Mr. Liddell.

CHAPTER V.

THE City of London in the early days of the Church Movement was almost the last spot where we should expect its influence to be felt, at least in any practical way. The number of large churches all along the chief streets were impregnable fortresses of old-fashioned ways and customs, and in many of them the customs were perfectly unauthorised, merely a following of those who had gone before, keeping up traditions as to ritual and ceremonies some of which were anything but edifying. Walking from west to east, who can say aught against the eminent respectability of the churches of St. George, Hanover Square ; St. James, Piccadilly ; St. Martin-in-the-Fields ; St. Clement Danes ; St. Dunstan, St. Bride, St. Mary-le-bow, St. Michael and St. Peter, Cornhill ; St. Andrew, Undershaft ; St. Botolph, Aldgate ? For many years after 1833 the Tractarian Movement had not much effect on this solid array of imposing buildings. Money was certainly spent in adornment, as in the case of St. Michael's, Cornhill, where profusion of alabaster, marbles, carving, and stained glass made it a place to visit and admire ; but, in spite of such beauty, the place was dead and

cold ; there **was** little stirring of life **and** power. A
visit to that church just after the completion and orna-
mentation was rather depressing : one especial point
showed at once a want of something—the chiefest ordi-
nance **of our Church was not** honoured, the old **altar**
table was not raised or enlarged, **and had** its old dingy
velvet covering—the one thing unimproved amidst all the
surrounding beauties. The architect **was** the late **Sir
G.** Gilbert **Scott, and it** was supposed that he was
responsible. Curiously enough, he heard some remarks
on it. Travelling outside the Hampstead **omnibus one
day was Mr. G. G.** Scott, and **just** behind **him were
two** enthusiastic young churchmen, **who had** been **to**
visit the church **and** were loudly deploring the want
of dignity in the chief place of honour in St. Michael's :
they were told afterwards who their travelling companion was, and did not seem at all in a **mood** to
apologise for their strong expressions. **But,** like that
select parish of Islington, the city was surrounded with
many tokens of the new life that was then stirring. **St.
Saviour's, Southwark, was even** then, in its sad condition, dear to the hearts of all Church folk **as** the
resting-place of one of England's most saintly bishops
(Andrewes), whose *Book of Private Devotions* **was then
and** is still the manual in **very** many households. It
was, quite early in **the** movement, printed in some six
or eight sizes and editions, first by Dr. Newman as one
of the *Tracts for the Times,* and then in several forms

published by Mr. Parker, one by the S.P.C.K., one by
Mr. Masters, and lastly one in a small portable form by
Mr. Rivington, edited by Canon Liddon, for special
use by the revered Bishop of Salisbury (Hamilton)
through his long last illness. How many would then
have rejoiced if they could have known that in the
present day St. Saviour's was likely to become a real
cathedral, restored to something of its early form and
beauty? The City's own cathedral of St. Paul was
not eventually to be behind in the work of the revival;
and though for the most part preaching and teaching
were the ways in which the beginnings were set forth,
they led on and forwards to more outward and visible
beauty in worship and service. Not very far from St.
Saviour's is the parish church of St. Mary's, Newington, or Newington Butts as it was called. Very soon
after the Church Movement began there were two
curates who both did good work there : one was the Rev.
W. J. Irons, afterwards Vicar of Brompton, and Prebendary of St. Paul's, a theologian and writer of some emin-
ence. At Newington he was quite a young man, and
as a preacher was soon well known ; his was a striking
personal appearance, long fair hair, high forehead, and
large but fine features and bright blue eyes ; and judg-
ing from his after work in preaching and writing, it is
not a matter of surprise to know that Newington
Church was full. He was the son of the Rev. Joseph
Irons, also a great preacher, but among the Dissenters

of pronounced Calvinistic tenets, who thundered forth the terrors of his creed at Grove Chapel, Camberwell, from 1818 to 1852, not very far from Newington Church: the story went that the carriages of those who came to hear the father and the son reached a long way, and at times got awkwardly mixed. Dr. W. J. Irons became a foremost theologian and writer on the controversies of the day ; he was also much valued as a parish priest and a careful and wise adviser. Some of his works were of more than common interest: an elaborate review of the Court of Arches and Privy Council Judgments, with notes and comments, and a reply to the Rev. W. Goode, on *The Whole Doctrine of Final Causes*, on *The Holy Catholic Church, Ecclesiastical Jurisdiction*, on *The Royal Supremacy*, in reply to Mr. Maskell, with some useful smaller works, such as *The Christian Servant's Book*, and lastly his beautiful translation of the *Dies Iræ*, in *Hymns Ancient and Modern*, which will live as long as hymns are sung. His fellow-curate at Newington was the Rev. J. Fuller Russell, B.C.L., afterwards perpetual curate of St. James's, Enfield Highway, and Vicar of Greenhithe, a writer and also a poet, well known in after years as the owner of a splendid liturgical library, and some very fine paintings of the schools of Albert Durer and Lucas van Leyden. Mr. Russell was not, like Dr. Irons, a great preacher, but he was ever most earnest in the movement and ready to help it forward in every way, and a

8

genial and kind friend. A most interesting letter,
1836, from Mr. Fuller Russell, when a young Cambridge
man, very earnestly wishing to restore much of the
disused ritual of the Church, and Dr. Pusey's reply,
urging above all that restored outward worship should
be genuine and real, also the account of his and Dr.
Irons' visit to Dr. Pusey, at Oxford, will be found in
Dr. Pusey's life.   Among Mr. Fuller Russell's works
were *Anglican Ordinations Valid,* in reply to Dr. Kenrick, *Lays concerning the Early Church, The Judgment
of the Anglican Church on Scripture,* and a valuable
compilation entitled *Hierurgia Anglicana,* documents
and extracts illustrative of the ritual of the Church of
England after the Reformation.   In this same neighbourhood much more work was ere long to be done.
At St. George's, Camberwell, Mr. Smith was a good,
though old-fashioned High Churchman, and in memory
of his long ministry the noble chancel just added to St.
George's was built.   Mr. Going's excellent work at St.
Paul's, Lorrimore Square, is within the memory of us
all, his earliest work on that side of the water being
the chaplaincy of Price's Candle Factory : he was the
friend of the Rev. W. B. Atkins, of St. Anne's, Soho,
about whom I spoke in a former chapter.   Mr. Goulden's work in the very worst slums of South London
must be named here.   Bishop Thorold and Bishop
Davidson have vividly pictured to us the needs of
South London.   It is not much further on to St. Peter's,

Vauxhall, where Mr. Herbert has given his life work, and laboured with great and untiring zeal among the lower and lower middle classes.

On the other side, outside the circle of the city, we **come** to one of the earliest centres of the movement **in** St. Matthew's, City **Road,** begun by Mr. Howard, and carried on by Mr. **Lawrell, Mr.** Baird, and their successors. This church was well placed on the route so thronged from the City **to** Islington and Highbury. With **a** simple ritual and very hearty choral services, St. Matthew's was always full; and one special point most worthy of notice **was** that in the regular congregation a very large proportion of young men would **always be found.** St. Philip's, Clerkenwell, was a thorough working centre of the revival; and those who were privileged to **know the Rev. Warwick R.** Wroth, **the** incumbent, will understand **the** beauty and influence of such a life as his. St. Philip's, Clerkenwell, was not a good specimen of a sacred building, but **the** very best was made of it that could be made, and the sanctuary, **altar, aud** quasi-chancel were lovingly cared for and adorned. Under the untiring energy **of Mr.** Wroth and his **curates and** an earnest body **of** lay helpers, the work of building up people **in faith** and practice went forward; and in such an unpromising building and neighbourhood the amount of good work was most encouraging. Mr. Wroth **was** tall and very thin, and delicate-looking, with hair iron-grey early in life; but he worked on while **strength** lasted, living close to his church, **in** Baker Street, Granville Square, **and** died at his **post,** leaving a most loving memory in the hearts of all **his** people : he published five sermons on the **Old** Testament types of Holy Baptism, 1859. His brother was sometime Vice-Consul at Constantinople, and died in **the** midst of his work there in November, 1861.   **I** give an **extract** from **Mr.** Wroth's letter to a friend, in reply **to** his condolence :—

" Very many thanks to you **for your** kind sympathy, and the beautiful **book you sent** [*Manual for Mourners,* Masters, 1848].   It **was a real comfort, and** my father, **to whom I lent it, said** he found it **a** great help in **enabling him to bear** this **heavy** blow ; we were **so** reckoning **on** my **dear** brother's return that the blow **came** all the heavier.   A letter from the Chaplain of **the** Embassy, however, gives us great hope that his end there was **a** blessed one.   **It** comforts us greatly that he died at his post doing his duty.   The kindness and sympathy of the people at Constantinople has been most touching ; you will be interested to read the **account** of his death and funeral in the *Levant Herald ;* the *Times* also **had a kind notice of him,** and speaks of the regret **felt by the** entire **community for** his loss. Before the establishment of the new Court justice had seldom been done at Constantinople, **and** at first it was not palatable ; but it is cheering to find how if right is done, in the long run it will win the respect of all.

" P.S.—Let me get out of your debt for my sub-
scription to the Anti-Pew Society which you paid for
me."

This postscript reminds me that Mr. Wroth **had**
determined to make his church free from pew-rents, **a**
course requiring no little courage and sacrifice in those
days. **In this and** all other parts of his work he had
the strong and staunch support and friendship of Mr.
Brett, **the well-remembered** surgeon of Stoke Newing-
ton, of whom we have much to say further **on.**
Mr. Brett's known opposition to pews and pew-rents
called forth **one of** Dr. Littledale's witty nursery
rhymes :—

> A surgeon there was at Stoke Newington,
> Who never would have any pewing done ;
>   If the church wasn't free,
>   He exclaimed, " Oh ! dear me,
> Those boxes I **soon** must be hewing down ".

We pass by Christ Church, New North Road, Hox-
ton, where the Rev. Wm. Scott was for some years
working ; **he** was a clever writer and editor in **the**
Tractarian cause. One of his curates was a Mr. Rose,
a fair man, with hair parted down the middle, who
sang the Litany in lavender kid gloves ! **He** gave up
his orders, and became the famous comic author and
reciter, Arthur Sketchley ; many of us have laughed
heartily at " Mrs. Brown " and her various droll adven-
tures. They seldom referred to Church matters, except
on one occasion when she expressed her surprise at the

display of metal work, stained glass, embroidery, etc.,
at the Great Exhibition, exclaiming, "Is it church? I
don't mind, only let me know; is it church?" Not
far off at St. Barnabas, Homerton, built by Mr. Joshua
Watson, the Rev. C. J. Black and C. J. Daniel did
excellent work.

Let us enter the sacred boundary of the City of London by Charterhouse Square, then a really quiet sheltered
spot, all three gates closed at night, with watchmen,
and the curfew regularly rung from the old turret in
the school. The Square garden was carefully kept, but
the turf there could not compare with that in the master's garden inside the school walls, which was quite
an oasis in the City desert. Archdeacon Hale was
then master, and also Rector of St. Giles's, Cripplegate.
When some friends of mine went to reside in that old
City Square he very kindly offered them seats in the
Charterhouse Chapel on Sundays; but two or three visits
were all that they could manage: the very building
and pews were anything but conducive to reverence of
body or mind; and the old pensioners, scholars, and Dr.
Saunders, the headmaster (afterwards Dean of Peter-
borough, whose children have just erected a reredos
to his memory there), did not do much in that way, or
to raise the whole tone of the service. John Hullah,
then organist, had not much chance of brightening the
service, as there was as little as possible for him to do.
The service might be almost as dreary as Beresford

Hope describes that at the chapel of Harrow School in his day. Mrs. Stone, the matron, was always kind and much beloved. The master was always very courteous, and spoke **often to** my friends; he heard afterwards that they **were regular** attendants at St. Bartholomew's, **Moor Lane; and next time** he met them, he said, " Well, I always considered myself a High Churchman, **but I don't** know what to call myself now ; I hear that **you have most** wonderful ceremonies **there ".** Compared with some of our churches now, it was not much **after all. St.** Botolph's, Aldersgate; Christ Church, Newgate Street ; St. Anne and St. Agnes ; **St. Bartholo-** mew the Great, **Smithfield,** and St. Sepulchre, all had one type of service, with huge pews in which you **were** buried ; but certainly the splendid organ playing of Mr. Cooper at the latter church, and the singing of his **trained** charity children, were admirable, **and** it was also a treat to hear his out-voluntary **on** Sunday even- **ing, to** which many would hasten after **leaving their own** service ; the " Dead March " in " Saul " was **a wonder** to hear, and his Evening Hymn accompaniment **something quite** thrilling ; it would have thrown out singers less carefully **trained. As to** St. Thomas's, Charterhouse, though **it was somewhat more** bright and modern, Mr. **Rogers, now** Rector **of** Bishopsgate, **was** much too busy with **the** great Golden Lane Ragged and other Schools **to give** much attention to ritual and Church services ; **we** are bound to say that his schools

were a great success for many **years.** The Square was
a favourite residence, and several of the City clergy
lived there. One rather famous man may be mentioned
here **at No. 33, the** Rev. **Wm. Goode,** then Rector
of St. Antholin's, one of the fiercest **opponents of
the** Church Movement. **He** came of a Puritan stock,
his father before him having been curate to W. Romaine at the church **of St. Andrew by the** Wardrobe,
Blackfriars, **to** which rectory **he** succeeded in after
years. **He was** a voluminous **writer, and his** life was
written by this son. Mr. Goode was the Puritan champion, and was then **the most, I** had almost said the only
really **learned man among** the ultra-Evangelical party ;
he was always ready with huge book or pamphlet to do
battle against the Tractarian leaders. **He** wrote on the
Baptismal Controversy, replied **to Tract XC.** on the
Real Presence, against Dr. Pusey, Archdeacon Denison,
Robert Wilberforce, **and others, and** maintained the
validity of the **Scotch and foreign** non-Episcopal
Churches. In those days the Puritans were patronised,
and **one good** living after another was bestowed upon
Mr. Goode. From St. Antholin's he **went to** All
Hallows **the Great,** Thames Street ; thence to St. Mar-
garet's, Lothbury ; and **thence to** the Deanery of Ripon.
Mr. Goode was a **familiar** figure in the City till 1856.
He was of middle height, thin, pale, dark hair, and
very lame ; he had always a sad, solemn face, caused
perhaps by a great domestic affliction. He seemed to

live **much** alone, and personally had no power or influence. The Charterhouse boys would sometimes say,
" **What** a pity it is that Goode isn't better,"—that was
their little joke. But Mr. Goode might write and
declaim on paper to little avail. The time was at hand
when the writings of the Tractarians, the essays, tracts,
lectures, hymns, poems, devotional works, etc., were to
enter into the daily use and life of the people, to be
carried out and put into practice. The exhortations to
holiness, to reverence, to devotion and worship and
obedience to the Church rules **were** to be made real—
to be lived. The Church, so perfect on paper, in Prayer-
book, in canons, and documents, was to become a reality
—a daily guide and rule of life : **a** Catholic revival **in**
books and on paper only would have roused very little
opposition ; but such a revival in act and deed throughout the length and breadth of the land was a much
more formidable thing in the eyes of the worldly, the
careless, and indifferent.

On the west side of this old **City** Square lived the
Rev. W. Denton, who had in 1850 taken the living of
St. Bartholomew's, in Moor Lane, **a** turning about
half-way up Fore Street. This was a copy of the old
church of St. Bartholomew by the Exchange, one **of**
Wren's churches pulled down to make room for Mr.
Tite's Royal Exchange. The materials were sold for
£483, and a church was built in this, one of the crowded
parts of Cripplegate and Moorfields, where a church

was much needed. The font, pulpit, and all the fine old oak were used, but otherwise the new building was not thought to much resemble the old one. The tomb of Miles Coverdale was transferred to the church of St. Magnus, London Bridge. The new church was completed about 1850; and Mr. Denton was the first vicar, an Oxford man, well up in the literature of the Church Movement, a scholar and divine, who in after years wrote valuable commentaries on the Epistles and Gospels, the Lord's Prayer, works on Servia and the Servian Church, etc. Stirring sermons by himself and friends, and frequent services, especially at Advent and Lent, were at once the order of the day; and though a student and a lover and collector of books, he felt deeply the responsibility of his parish charge, and set himself to bring the Church and the Church's call into the lives of his people. In 1852 he arranged for a series of twenty-three sermons, one for every day in Advent, and they were printed in a volume afterwards. Mr. Denton's few words of introduction will best tell his hopes and object: " Various reasons have led to the printing of this volume ; but chiefly the hope that this attempt to avail ourselves of holy seasons as calls to repentance, and a deeper fulfilment of the duties of practical Christianity, may lead the way to more systematic efforts to evangelise the neglected masses of this metropolis. The shopkeeper is busier as Christmas draws on ; trade and worldly business of all kinds have their seasons of greater gain and intense labours, and must the Church alone stand all day long in the market-place idle, and the houses of God be as closely shut up as heretofore?"

Then came words that to us who have seen the hope realised sound almost prophetic : " If the feeble efforts made in **one of** the poorest and least accessible churches **in London** have yielded lasting fruit, what, by God's blessing, might not be looked for from the earnest preaching of mercy and repentance in the naves of our two cathedrals ?—what more worthy use of the mother churches of the diocese ? "

Among the preachers whose sermons were printed in this volume were **many** of the most renowned men of the Church Movement : Archdeacon Thorpe, Rev. J. Keble, T. W. Perry, **W. J.** Butler (late Dean of Lincoln), **E.** Monro, W. J. Irons, **A.** B. Evans, **J. R.** Woodford (**afterwards Bishop** of Ely), Archdeacon Grant, **J. M.** Rodwell, Rev. the Hon. R. Liddell, **W.** Scott, R. **Milman** (afterwards Bishop of Calcutta), H. Newland, **H. A.** Rawes, James Skinner, etc.

From this time Mr. Denton, assisted by his curates, made the work of the Church felt throughout his densely-crowded parish, working not only in the church but in the homes and houses of the people, the closely-packed courts that lay from Milton Street to Little Moorfields, chiefly costermongers, shoemakers, canal porters, char-women, and sempstresses, mostly one room to a family ;

and the improvement, religious and physical, was wonderful.   In a few years a parish, **part of** which once
bore so ill a character that, except under necessity, persons
carefully avoided **it, was** in many points quite altered ;
so much had been done to remedy the sad state of things.
Individuals and families were won from their neglect ;
drunkenness and brawling were less frequent; habits
of cleanliness were encouraged, and the services of the
Church fostered reverence and **devotion. A** good bright
choral service, thoroughly suited to the neighbourhood ;
all was sensible and straightforward, the music superin-
tended with much time and care by the precentor and
organist ; **the** psalms and canticles to Gregorian chants
and arrangements; the Communion office to good simple
selections from the best Church music compiled and
arranged by Helmore, Redhead, and Gauntlett ; the
hymns a small selection, one of the many pioneers of
Hymns Ancient and Modern.   In **those** days many of
the clergy, **Dr.** Irons, F. H. Murray, Dr. Oldknow, etc.,
had made selections for **their** parishes ; these were
printed and **used** by many of their friends.   The hymn
tunes, too, **were from** the *Church Hymn and Tune
Book*—by Rev. W. J. Blew and Dr. Gauntlett—Mr.
Redhead's book of *Hymn Tunes*, and the *Hymnal Noted*.
The hearty, bright singing of the services and hymns
was something to remember.   **Nor** was the care and
reverence confined to Sunday.   All the saints' day and
week-day **services and** celebrations were given with

equal care in every detail, the occasional offices were all carefully rendered; **the** Church was for the people, without money and without price. Especially **was** this the case with the funerals; if only a curate and **the** precentor and **four** or six choir boys **were** available, **the** funeral service of the poorest person **was sung** and had every attention and respect paid **to it; this** was quite unusual in those days in the **City:** I forget what it would have cost to have a church opened and the service performed, but it **was a** considerable sum; this custom had a good and solemn effect, and was thoroughly appreciated. One very touching funeral took place in 1856, the funeral of a little child, the only daughter of the Vicar. All appearance **of** gloom was avoided; the altar had its white frontal on, with white **flowers in the vases;** the legend round **the pall was,** "**Of** such is the kingdom of **heaven**". The coffin **was** met at the door by the clergy and **choristers;** it was of oak with a raised cross, **a** purple **pall with** white fringe, a white cross under the legend. The sentences were to Mr. Redhead's arrangement of Marbeck. After the lesson an introit was sung, and the Holy Communion was celebrated and received by the parents, godparents, nurse, and a few mourners. At the Cemetery, Highgate, the choir and clergy were ready to lead the way to the grave, the coffin being carried on a **bier by six choristers.** "Man that is born of a woman" **was sung to a chant, and** "I heard a voice from heaven " to Mr. Redhead's arrangement. As the echo of the last Amen died away, the hymn, " Jesus lives! no longer now can thy terrors, death, appal us," made a bright conclusion to this sacred office. This choir of St. Bartholomew's was well known for many years; the members all reverent, earnest, hearty workers in the cause of God's worship and honour; they made it a work of love and religion, and gave of their best. The late Dr. Steere, afterwards Bishop Steere, then a law-student in London, and the Rev. J. T. Fowler, then studying medicine (he is Vice-President of Hatfield Hall, Durham, an excellent churchman, and author and antiquarian of repute), were for some time members of the choir. There was one work of this choir, not a common one, which they on several occasions undertook: a well-known physician in Finsbury Square was laid up, but not by an illness that required great quiet; on Sunday evening, after church, the choir would sing the canticles, psalms, and a few hymns in the large drawing-room, and the doctor heard them from his room, and much appreciated it. One incident, which occurred in 1852, reminds me that this gift of music and singing might be much more used in the rooms and houses of the poor, the sick, and the aged: a well-known hymn or psalm or canticle sung by a district-visitor or lay-helper, would brighten up the long weary day, and cheer many a lingering illness. The incident was this: the Church Movement was spreading far and wide; from the West

Indies, Jamaica, St. Kitts, St. Vincent, and other parts, one heard of much stirring and care for all things belonging to Divine worship. An aged West Indian gentleman, a Mr. McMahon, had come over to England for an operation to his eyes, and had an introduction to Mr. Masters, and other Church folk in the City; among others who called on him was the precentor of St. Bartholomew's (who was also churchwarden). In the course of their talk, Mr. McMahon, who was aged and feeble as well as blind, said how much he missed the beautiful services to which he had been accustomed. The precentor offered to sing parts of the service to him, then and there, and told me afterwards he never should forget the look **of** pleasure on the old man's face; and on that and other visits he sang without any accompaniment, psalm, Te Deum, or canticle and **hymns.** He **stood** all the **time; nothing would induce** him to sit **down** while the singing was going on, his thin face most expressive of reverence and joy. That was his last illness: he died in a few months, but the same deep reverence was shown to the last; he would drag himself out of his bed to receive the blessed Sacrament kneeling. Dr. **Bloxam** used to tell how in Magdalen College Chapel he would carry the blessed Sacrament down to old President Routh's stall in his later days, and how **he** would totter from his stall to receive **It** in like **manner.**

To come **back to Moor** Lane, the church was before

long much improved, and the chancel stalls, reredos and panelling, all of the original dark oak, were rearranged in more orthodox plan, the Cross being substituted for flaming urns, etc., under the superintendence of Mr. J. W. Hallam, a young architect, one of the congregation, then living in Charterhouse Square. Mr. Hallam published *Monumental Memorials*, thirty-three designs for churchyard crosses, coped tombstones, mural tablets, etc. : he was for thirty years unable to move about, or he would have been more known, but he worked indefatigably at his profession the whole time ; he died at Scarborough a short time ago. His only son was a scholar of Exeter College, and is now curate of Slough.

A portrait of Mr. Denton was presented to the parish after his death by Mrs. Denton, and hangs in the vestry.

Mr. Denton preached a good deal in early days, and from his store of mediæval and patristic learning, his sermons were always interesting and instructive ; he worked on till the Moorgate Street Railway swept away a very large portion of the parish, and during his later years he was much taken up with his many theological works, commentaries, histories, etc. In early days several of his curates and helpers were men of some mark ; his neighbours in the City were ever ready to help in celebrations and sermons, among them the Rev. W. H. Milman, Minor Canon of St. Paul's and Rector of St. Augustine and St. Faith ; the Rev. J. A. L. Airey, now Rector of St. Helen's ; and H. Hayman, afterwards headmaster of Rugby School, then assistant-master at the Charterhouse School, a learned classical and theological scholar, editor and author—he did write some lighter works, which are not probably remembered now. He was preaching one night at St. Bartholomew's, and seemed a little hesitating and confused at the beginning of his sermon ; on the way home the churchwarden asked what was the matter. "Matter enough," said Mr. Hayman ; "you would have felt a little nervous if, on getting up into the pulpit, you had seen your old headmaster in the seat right under you, and looking up at you, reminding you of tasks and floggings." It was Dr. Deane, of Merchant Taylors, who at times came to the service. Later on Canon Liddon was a good friend and help (he was godfather to one of the vicar's boys). On the occasion of the secession of two of the curates, Canon Liddon came and preached and reassured many ; and I think scarcely any of the regular congregation followed the curates' step. His sermon on "Our conversation is in heaven," at that time, was, I think, printed in one of his volumes.

The secessions to Rome were of course one great trial and drawback to the movement ; they were no novelty, as such happened here and there during the Great Rebellion, and from time to time after the outward

9

visible union with the See of Rome was broken : the point to remember and insist upon is this, that, compared with the extent of the fifty years' influence, teaching, literature, devotion, and new spiritual life of the Church Movement, the secessions to Rome were but as a drop in the ocean.

One of the earliest curates at St. Bartholomew's was Charles Robins, son of the Rev. Sanderson Robins, a popular evangelical preacher in a large chapel at St. John's Wood ; he was a very fluent extempore preacher, and afterwards took charge of the Mission Chapel in Clare Market.

About the middle of 1852 a young, fair, ascetic-looking man might be seen preaching one Sunday evening in the pulpit of St. Botolph's, Aldgate ; there was no mistake about his energy and enthusiasm, he preached from a written sermon on the Golden Image of Nebuchadnezzar, and applied the lesson to the worship of money as a caution to many City men ; it was afterwards published—this young preacher was the Rev. H. A. Rawes, curate to Mr. Baker, the rector; he was rather a striking figure with his new M.A. gown, Cambridge hood, crape bands, and deep crape cuffs to his cassock sleeves ; he was in mourning for the young lady to whom he had been engaged to be married, and a very different course of life was now before him, though for some years he regularly visited her grave with flowers. He became curate to Mr. Denton, and worked vigorously on **the lines** of the movement for some years, acquiring some fame as a preacher, and favour as a parish priest, and **was** somewhat of a poet as **well**, rather eccentric and excitable. **He** became Warden of the House of Charity, Soho, where I have already spoken **of him.**

One Sunday evening later on, the vicar on the way to church came across his churchwarden with two young clergymen, both **fair and** tall, one fairly stout and the other thin, and **both in** rough serge cassocks down **to** their feet. Folks were not then much accustomed **to** such visions in the streets of the City, and the new visitors attracted some attention. These were Henry and Richard Collins, brothers of **Thomas** Collins, M.P. for Knaresborough and Boston, **and sons of** the Rev. Thomas Collins, of Knaresborough. **For a** while **they** both helped **in** the parish, and very able **men they** were. Richard remained some time as curate, and afterwards became Vicar of **St.** Saviour's, Leeds, **where he died.** Henry joined **a** monastic order after working for **a** short time at **St.** George's-in-the-East. At first, on their coming from Cornwall, they were not over-careful **as to** toilet and dress, but London helped to mend that, though **a** friend told **me that** he met Henry **a few** years after, **looking much** more like a farmer than a monk, with a large cotton umbrella and a bundle over his **shoulder.** We will not forget that to him we owe those two beautiful hymns we so often sing, " Jesu

meek and lowly," and "Jesu my Lord, my God, my
all". With these two there came to St. Bartholomew's
the knowledge of the Rev. Robert Aitken, father of the
well-known missionary preacher, Vicar of Pendeen, in
Cornwall; how in addition to the doctrines of the
movement, with a considerable amount of ritual, he
taught something like the Wesleyan view of sensible
personal conversion. This Mr. Aitken, a fine, handsome man of middle age and portly presence, came to
St. Bartholomew's, and held a mission, urging on us
the fact that we were many of us unconverted. Mr.
Aitken was certainly a most gifted preacher; few could
at all compare with him for arousing a multitude. The
secession to Rome of several who had been attracted
by his earnest preaching tended, perhaps, in his later
years, to a revulsion against the revival of Catholic
truth. His views much impressed both Mr. Collins,
and also one of the curates, the Rev. W. R. Brownlow.
About this time there were open-air services in some
of the courts around Moor Lane, the choir in cassocks
and surplices, with cross; hymns and short stirring
sermons. The well-known scholar, Henry Nutcombe
Oxenham, was for some time curate; he had been, as a
deacon, helping, I think, Mr. Monro, at Harrow Weald,
and worked with Mr. Denton for some while, and
was there ordained priest by the Bishop of London. It
was said that this ordination he never would declare
invalid; and so, though nominally a Roman Catholic,

he never was very obedient or submissive, and certainly his new friends in religion never found him work to do ; but at St. Bartholomew's he was really one of the most brilliant speakers and preachers, and would surely have attained fame in that way ; his slight, elegant figure, very dark complexion **and** handsome features helped to make him attractive. He would preach excellent sermons with no longer notice than this : just when all were ready to go in, the vicar would say, " I don't feel quite well ; will you preach, Oxenham ?" He might make a few notes while the precentor was reading the lessons, and that was all. His enthusiasm for Rome was not lasting, though at first he would drive those he could not lead there ; and one he had so driven told me that on arriving at Clapham to be **received, he was as** nearly as possible running away, instead **of** ringing the bell. His friend, **Dr.** F. **G.** Lee, then a young man living in London, and much interested in all Church literature, was a helper and **preacher** at **St.** Bartholomew's, **and a** very good **extempore** preacher : he became **a** most industrious **writer and** editor in Church history and lore.

The career of one of the curates is worth more than a few short words. This was James Marshall, an Exeter College man, a very earnest and energetic curate in **every** way. **A good** musician and preacher too ; with **dark** hair and bright dark eyes, he was one of the best workers, and was much beloved throughout the parish. He was **the son of** the Rev. James Marshall, Vicar of

Christ Church, Clifton, a great **leader** among the early
Evangelicals, and his mother was **a** daughter of Leigh
Richmond, also **a** famous writer and **preacher** of the
same school.   To be brought up in an extreme school of
the kind was **not** often a success ; and, of course, **Mr.**
Marshall was **a** High Churchman when he came to **St.**
Bartholomew's.   He had but one arm, the other having
been shot off by accident when he was a lad.   **So able**
was he to do everything with one arm, that at dinner and
all meals no **notice** whatever **was** taken **or** difference
made; **but the** question of a clergyman **with one arm
was a serious one, and it must have been in very** lax
times **indeed that a Bishop of the Church** of England
would ordain a man with one arm: certainly, Archbishop
Laud, who refused ordination to, **I** think, Shirley the
poet and playwriter on account of a disfiguring mole on
his face, would **not** have done **so.   The** celebration of
the Holy Communion was **the chief** difficulty, but
he **was** seldom alone at **St.** Bartholomew's; and if **by**
chance he was so at an early Communion, the precentor,
in cassock and surplice, carried the paten by his **side**
along the chancel **rail.   We** may say that certainly **Mr.**
Marshall should **not have** been **ordained, and after** his
secession to the Church **of** Rome he **had** to give up all
idea of it ; so, after a short time **of choir** and other work
at Bayswater, he proceeded to the Bar, and during the war
with King Koffee was judge on that West Coast of Africa,
signing despatches that appeared in the *Times*.   After

some **years of service** in that very trying climate he returned home, and was knighted, doing some political and
colonial work till his death a very few years ago.   Few
people knew that Sir James Marshall was once a curate
in an obscure City church.   Mr. Lyne (Father Ignatius)
was for some time a curate there.   There are a few other
names to be recorded.

Charles Lyford, an Oxford man of Oriel College, where
Lord Blatchford, Edward Monro, and Gathorne Hardy,
were his contemporaries.   Dr. Bloxam of Upper Beeding,
Sussex, who had been Newman's curate at Littlemore,
was always glad to show and tell many things connected
with those early days ; among other things he had **a**
" round robin " with those four names to it, addressed to
Newman when Bursar of Oriel, about the dinners in Hall.
Mr. Lyford had **been** curate to **Dr.** Mountain at
Hemel Hempstead, **and** afterwards **at St.** Barnabas,
Pimlico, and was one of the most hard-working.   He
was a specimen of the ever-cheerful, kind, helpful
parson, most active and energetic, at home with
people **of his** own standing, and just as much so in
the poorest woman's room or cottage, and ready **to** help
in the most practical way.   Nothing put him **out,** and
he enjoyed a good laugh right heartily.   He took
charge for some years of the daily Litany **at** one o'clock
at St. Ethelburga's Church, Bishopsgate Street, in con-
junction with the churchwarden and precentor of St.
Bartholomew's, Mr. Spenser Nottingham, Canon Bristow

(then a layman in the City), and a few others; only once, I think, he was away, and then by direction of the vicar, the Rev. J. M. Rodwell, the precentor sang the Litany up to the Lord's Prayer. Mr. Lyford left St. Bartholomew's to help the Rev. T. Simpson Evans, rector of St. Leonard's, Shoreditch, and was first incumbent of St. Michael's in that parish, where he was succeeded by Mr. Nihill, his curate. Mr. Baird, afterwards of Homerton, and Mr. Philip Sankey were some time curates: also, the Rev. Christopher Thompson, well known for his Church music, and now Vicar of Pensax, in Worcestershire; he was ever a kind helper and friend to the Rev. R. W. Enraght, at Bordesley, during his incumbency and troublous times.

Mr. Martin, an early churchwarden of the parish, emigrated with all his family to New Zealand, and perhaps carried there many recollections of his City parish and the services they so appreciated. Among the congregation and kind helpers one should record the names of Mrs. Kingdon (mother of Bishop Kingdon), wife of Dr. Kingdon, of New Bank Buildings; Miss Rees, sister of Dr. Rees, of Finsbury Square; the Misses Tidman and their two brothers; Mr. and Mrs. Lias, and their children (among them the present Professor J. J. Lias); and Miss Townsend, of Suffolk Lane, now Sister Zilla, of East Grinstead and Newport Market Refuge Mission fame; the Misses Beale, and their brothers, the younger of whom has a history that is pathetic. E. H. Beale was educated at Merchant Taylors' School and St. John's College, **Oxford,** and was ordained deacon, December, 1869, **and** was Curate **of** Warminster. Owing **to a** partial paralysis from his earliest years, he never took priest's **orders; his** time was given up **to** the services, teaching, **parish work, and** missionary administration. **In 1877 he went to India,** and spent the rest of his life in loving and untiring devotion to the Church in Western India. His death was recorded a few months ago. And last, but by no means least, I would record Mrs. Denton's **many** years of untiring work in the parish; the kind friend, helper, and adviser **of all,** especially of those in need or trouble.

CHAPTER VI.

THE account of the work at St. Bartholomew's, Moor Lane, given in the last chapter, would hardly be complete without a word about the very wonderful amount of unfavourable notice accorded to it in the papers: all was described with the most extraordinary inaccuracy. Reporters were sent to the services to take notes, who had evidently never attended a church in their lives, and the singular things they saw and recorded were almost beyond belief. The Oxford M.A. hoods were described thus : " Some of the clergy were robed in red and black slashings," and so on, through various parts of the service. It was in the Vestry of St. Michael's, Shoreditch, that coloured stoles were first called " ribbons," a term of contempt still used by a few who seem to think there is some law, human or divine, that all such vestments should be perpetually black. Why black ? Such worthy folk, who are to be found often quoting the Bible, might find little sanction for their gloomy preference in the beautiful account of the colours ordered to be worn in Divine Service in the Book of Exodus. The presence of many clergy and laymen, hearty workers in the movement, in this part of the

(138)

City was much due to the fact that Mr. Masters' publishing and printing works were in Aldersgate Street and the far-famed Bartholomew Close. The chief editors **and** writers in the cause were constant visitors in Aldersgate Street with MSS. copy, revised proofs, etc.; **Mr.** Brett, from Stoke Newington, having studied proofs **in** his brougham as he drove along; Mr. Chamberlain, **from** Oxford; Mr. Monro, from Harrow Weald; Mr. Heygate, from Southend; Dr. Irons, from Brompton; Dr. Neale, from East Grinstead; and a host of others.

One name, the Rev. W. B. Flower, I may mention here, **as** he was close by, a junior classical master in Christ's Hospital, **when** Mr. Collinwood was senior; he was also Curate of **St.** James's, Enfield Highway, to the Rev. J. Fuller Russell, **and** some time at Crawley, in Sussex. He was a bright scholar and preacher, and **being so** near Aldersgate Street, assisted in much of the literary **work** there. He wrote **and** edited several **works:** among others, *Tales of Faith and Providence* and *Classical Tales.* He was also first editor of the *Churchman's Companion,* till 1858, when he became Chaplain at Baden-Baden; he was succeeded in the editorship by Mr. Masters' partner till 1863, when the office was taken by the author of the *Divine Master,* and other works. **Mr.** Flower, for a short time, helped Mr. Purchas when he first took St. James's, Brighton.

Mention should be made of the Parish Church of St. **Leonard's,** Shoreditch, a large classical building on the site of the old church, designed by **Dance**, about 1736. In **its** early days the church was famous for its register of renowned players and their children. **The rector at** the **time we are** speaking of, was the Rev. **T.** Simpson Evans, M.A., son of a rather famous astronomer **and** mathematician. Mr. Evans was much beloved, and **was in every way the** model of an English parish priest of the very best kind, and had some excellent men as curates; **he** encountered fierce opposition in the few ritual improvements he made; **he had a fund of infor-**mation **about the Churchmen of the preceding century;** edited the life of Bishop Frampton, the non-**juror, and** had **made** valuable historical and biographical notes **relative to a series** of orthodox Catholic divines and **laymen in the Church** of England, during the unfavour-**able** times **of the** four Georges—from Sherlock, Sparkes, Sutton, Spinckes, Nelson, **down to** Joshua Watson, Sikes **of** Guisborough, Bishop Middleton, Boodle, **Joseph** Whiteley **of** Beeston, Sawbridge of Stretton-on-Dunsmuir, Van Mildert, and H. H. Norris. The **latter, a** most active **member** of the **orthodox** Church societies, wrote to a friend : "**I want to see a** centre formed, **to which** all zealously affected Churchmen **may** resort, **and** counterplot the numerous and most **subtle** devices against our very existence, which every **day is** bringing to light". Such men were forerunners **of the** Church Movement; and Mr. Simpson Evans was a follower of those men, whose work fitted in well with the progress of the Tractarian Movement. Mr. Evans lived on Stoke Newington Common, and his wife and children were often among the worshippers at St. Matthias, Stoke Newington.

Making our way along the Kingsland Road and through the then green lanes to the west of it, we come to this church of St. Matthias, for many years a most powerful centre of work ; it is not inappropriate to mention it here, as a larger number of City merchants and men of business were attached to that church, its work and services, than to any other suburban church. Mr. Butterfield was the architect of it, and a great friend of its founder, and ever took the deepest interest in its early work and trials connected with the secession of its first vicar. At that trying time Mr. Butterfield once asked a young friend of his just in deacon's orders to come and help, which he did for six weeks. His first sermon in London was on St. James's Day, at St. Matthias, and he was rather nervous, but consoled himself with the thought that on a week-day evening in July there would not be a critical audience. Alas! in the choir were T. S. Evans and A. B. Evans, and there was a numerous congregation. The beautiful church of St. Matthias owed its origin and completion entirely to the splendid zeal and untiring energy of one famous layman, Robert Brett, a surgeon, living in a house on Stoke Newington Green, next door to the old Unitarian Chapel there. Here with his wife and children, who were also hearty in the

work, he lived in a most simple quiet way ; working at
his profession (having no carriage for some years, till a
few friends insisted on presenting him with a brougham).
He might well be called the Robert Nelson of his day;
the Church's work and needs were ever deeply in his
heart, and his influence with all the busy City men
and merchants was wonderfully shown in the many
goodly churches that arose one after another in the
neighbourhood : Haggerston, Shoreditch, Hackney,
Clapton, etc., etc.   At first a vestry was called to pre-
vent St. Matthias being built.   " You see, sir, the vestry
are unanimous against you."   His reply was, " The
work will be done ".   While the funds for St. Matthias
were being gathered and the church was building, a
very beautiful choral service was carried on for years,
in the schoolrooms, where on Sundays there never was
room for one additional chair.   The brightness and
heartiness were to be seen and felt rather than described ; and when the large noble church was finished
and ready for consecration, many a lingering look of
affection to the old schoolroom was given in passing.
The services in the new church, with the late Mr. W.
H. Monk as organist, Mr. W. Ardley as assistant, Mr.
Spenser Nottingham as precentor, and Mr. Scott the
schoolmaster, were as grand and effective as devoted
care and talent and skill could make them ; all was
exact and reverent, even to the practices, and compared
with the frequent careless and perfunctory exercises

called choir practices, those at St. Matthias were
models indeed; nothing was slurred over or hurried,
and no boy or member dared to appear for practice in
the stalls without his cassock. The music was from
the purest Gregorian sources, and the large choir gave
effect to the ancient music with a body of voice that
would compare well with **some of** the famous choirs on
the continent. Some of the congregation did not all
at once care for so severe a style of service, but the
beauty and perfection soon overcame that feeling with
most people. One visitor came who had quite a prejudice against Gregorian music, and after the service **a**
friend asked him his opinion. "Well," he replied, "you
know I never did care much for Gregorians, but they
were so exquisitely done that I have not **a** word to say
against them." **Certainly** the whole service was rendered with a care and completeness that no church in
England could then compare with; it was a privilege
to live **near such a church,** and to know and **see con-**
stantly **the** churchwarden and founder, whose noble
presence and handsome countenance as he stood at **the**
west end of the church, is to many, even now, **a** vivid
memory. In his work as a medical man he was ever
kind, sympathising, and skilful; his presence in a sick
room was **a** very bright one, and what **he was** to
invalids through long **and** trying **illnesses, is** known
perhaps only or chiefly **where** sickness and death are no
more. With **children he** was especially kind and help-

ful, and was much beloved by them; he had his own
pet names by which he always remembered some of
them; for a long time in **writing to** a friend of mine he
would remember his favourite names for the children,
and sent his love to Fair Esther, Saint Cecilia, Loza,
Pickle, Georgey, and Tom Tucker. Yet with all his
professional work he found time to write, compile, and
edit a great many devotional and practical works, most
of which **were** widely used and **valued.** There is **only**
space to **mention a few of these books:** *Devotions for
the Sick Room, Companion for the Sick Room, Doctrine
of the Cross,* illustrated **in** a memorial **of a** humble
follower of Christ (one of his Stoke Newington patients),
Instructions, Prayers, and Aspirations **for** *afflicted
Christians, Manual* **of** *Devotion for Schoolboys, Pocket
Manual of Prayers, Simple Prayers* **for** *Little Children,
Reflections, Meditations, and Prayers, with Harmony on
the Life of Our Lord, Churchman's Guide to Faith and
Piety,* etc. On all his books he put " By the Author
of *Devotions* **for** *the Sick* **Room***,* etc. "; his name **was**
never **on the title-page.** It would be difficult to tell of
half the active work for the **Church in** the way of
councils, committees, guilds, penitentiaries, orphanages,
and sisterhoods in which Mr. Brett for many years took
a real part. He **was a** staunch Church of England
man, and in the troubles about secessions he took a
firm stand. I quote from one of his letters : "It is
worse than useless to make any advances towards

unity so long as Romanists apply the most abusive and calumnious epithets to the church of which we are members. **Could** any man of right feeling court the friendship of another who on all occasions vilified his natural mother as an adulteress, **a** blasphemer, and lying deceiver ? How, then, can we endure all this against our spiritual mother if we have a single spark of catholic principle or love within us ? '' He had **no** sympathy with such converts as were evidently only too glad to get rid of the burden of their orders, and wrote witty invitations with a P.S. : " I am always at home on a Sunday, especially during the hours of Divine service ;" or with those who a few weeks after they were with us ministering as priests, were dressing for the opera, or standing up to dance at a ball for the first time in their life, to prove that they were mere lay-men ; or, worse still, would within a short time of leaving the Church pretend to forget the catholic origin and detail of the liturgy of the Church of England, which they had used for years. Nor again with those who within **two** or three years of their secession wrote as if they were authorised to speak for the whole Western Church ; " **we** maintain," "**our** contention **is,**" "we quite understand," and that on subjects never even definitely pronounced upon by that Church. With such **as** these **Mr.** Brett **could** be severe. He could also **be** severe on the other side. The following passages **are** from a letter to a well-known Evangelical

clergyman, written some years **before the** riots, pro-
secutions, and persecutions that followed some time
after.   Parts of it were almost prophetic.

"Rev. Sir,—I read with sorrow and anguish **of**
mind the misstatements and misrepresentations **of the**
doctrines, principles, practices, and designs **of those**
called ' Anglo-Catholics '.   I ask, is the fearful struggle
so near at hand, that **every soul** holding Anglo-Catholic
opinions is to be hunted like a partridge on the moun-
tains ?   There is one point in your sermon which must
arouse every layman who has a heart to love his Saviour
and his Church ; I allude to the exhortation to every
' Christian man ' to divide the Church and scatter the
seeds of disunion through the land.   What ! are the
sanctuaries of God to be desecrated by the unhallowed
intrusion of spies and reckless agitators, entering, not to
pray, but to scrutinise and contemn the clergy who are
faithfully and laboriously ministering to their flocks ?
Oh, sad and fearful struggle, parents and children
thwarted in the best and holiest plans ! Pastors wearied
and broken-hearted by opposition and disunion ! You,
reverend sir, have sounded this trumpet **of war,** and
there are hundreds who will come **to its call ;** but who
will they be ?   Not men, mild, gentlemanly, Christian,
like yourself ; but ignorant, fiery religious partisans,
whose happiness **it** would be to bring every Anglo-
Catholic to misery or exile. **Can it** be right in you to
stir up such men to go through the length and breadth

of the Church **to sit** in judgment on her clergy ? **By all** that is holy and true, by the love and compassion of the Saviour, by whatever is lovely, peaceable and sacred, **I would** respectfully entreat **you** to reconsider and re-call **what** you **have said.** If this cannot **be,** if **the** struggle must go **on, then** 'God's will be done'. **If I** have inadvertently expressed myself **in** an unchristian or uncourteous manner, I humbly **ask** pardon. **Yours,** etc."

On his death, in 1874, he was mourned **by** church-men far and wide, and his funeral on the 7th of Febru-**ary** was indeed remarkable ; after the service and cele-bration in the church, thousands followed to the grave, and testified to their **deep sense of a great** loss, and the value to the **Church of such a holy** and beautiful character. One **can** only recall the names of **a few of Mr.** Brett's friends **and** fellow-workers, and **in most** in-stances these names will include families of sons and daughters : **Beck,** Porter, Hall, Hazard, Unwin, Dickin-son, **Charrington,** Bodley, R. Forster, Butterfield, Mack-reth, Tritton, **Parnell,** Heathfield, Nottingham, Caffin, Brooks, Elliott, **Hoole,** Knight, B. E. B., and many **more ;** from **one such** centre as this, we can measure **how** the movement grew **and** spread, for **at** the present **day** many **of the sons** and daughters of Mr. Brett's friends are doing **the same work and** living the life of the higher principles learned from such men, handed on from time to time.

It was a great loss when the **Rev.** S. W. Mangin **retired** from the **post of vicar, after four** years of the **early** struggles and trials of **the new church.** Mr. **Le Geyt** then carried on the work for some years. **The** story is told that, on **the** occasion of the opening **of** Cuddesden College, one of the gushing and enthusiastic students rushed into Oxford the day before, declaring **that the** whole thing was spoiled and must be a miserable failure, **as one of the** clergymen selected for the honour of singing the Litany on the festive occasion was not **only** married but wore whiskers ! **This was** Mr. Le **Geyt** ; his wife was a Miss Monro : there was one consolation, he certainly could, and did, sing exceedingly well. The other **singer** was Mr. Huntingford, **of** Littlemore. Of **the** curates, the names **of** Smyttan, Doran, Pantin, etc., recall good work and teaching. The series of special Lent and Advent sermons were of no ordinary kind ; those by **Mr.** Skinner, Mr. Gutch, and well-esteemed preachers were attended by large congregations. Dr. Neale, too, preached there : **once** an extempore sermon of great power. One other sermon, also extempore, **was of a** kind to make **one** wonder how it was given—it was on an Old **Testament** subject, and the long names of **places and** titles abounded throughout the **whole** sermon, **and the preacher** was the Rev. Thos. Chamberlain, late of St. Thomas's, Oxford. The carol singing by **the** splendid **choir,** well and most carefully done, was simply charming. The *First Nowell* was just published, and a friend describes the effect of it when sung under his window on Christmas morn as most thrilling and effective. While in this neighbourhood the valuable pioneering work done by the Rev. John Ross, **at St.** Mary's, Haggerstone, must be especially recorded. Ere long, by Mr. Jacomb, Mr. R. Foster, and others, many churches were built in North-East London, the latter giving his own residence at Clapton for the first Suffragan Bishop of London. It is happiness to record that although for a time the Church work seemed failing at St. Matthias, it is now in all essentials revived and well carried on by the Rev. F. Caudwell, the present vicar, son-in-law of the late Rev. Robert Aitken.

But we have wandered far away from the City and **from** those churches where **a** brighter and better state of things was soon to take the place of the dreary empty City church described in some popular novels and tales. The Golden Lectures at St. Margaret, Lothbury, **when** given by Henry Melvill, Daniel Moore, and such excellent preachers, were well attended by busy City men.

At St. Augustine and St. Faith, where the Rev. W. H. Milman, minor canon, etc., was rector, there were weekly **and saint-day** celebrations.

From 1857 to 1873 the Rev. Morgan Cowie, now **Dean of** Exeter, held the Church of St. Lawrence Jewry, **the** large church by Guildhall (with the gridiron, the emblem of the saint's martyrdom, as vane on the steeple),

and proved, most surely, that City churches need not be
empty. After its rearrangement and decoration in 1867,
under Sir **A. W.** Blomfield, **no finer church of** its kind
could **be found ; and the grand** choral service, carried on
by the old choir of St. Philip, Clerkenwell, with careful
ritual, was fully in accord with the building. These, with
bright, telling sermons, brought a large attendance, and
much good work was the result in many ways.   What
a contrast to the state in which **I saw** the church many
years before, when Robert Montgomery, then **of** Glasgow,
was preaching!   The church was filled **by a** not **very**
orderly mob, who clambered over the gallery **pews, and**
broke **some of the woodwork.** Talking of vanes sym-
bolical, **reminds me of one curious case :** when the
church of St. Mildred, Poultry, was standing, in my
early days, the vane on the steeple was *half a ship*, in
accordance with the legend that the ship in which St.
Mildred came over was broken **in two** by the waves,
and she came safely to land in one-half !   On repairing
the vane more recently the enlightened churchwardens
replaced **it by a** *whole ship*.

I may name another instance where a good service
and work has for **many** years **made its way,** and in a
church in a much less prominent position than St. Lawrence,—I mean the church of St. Clement, Eastcheap,
under Minor Canon Hall (son **of the** Rev. W. J. Hall,
whose *Mitre Hymnal* is still remembered).   Here, with a
good choral service well rendered, and weekly com-

munion, there is always an excellent congregation. In the old church of this parish, Bishop Pearson delivered his famous lectures on the Creed.

This may be the place to mention another City church where trouble arose after the removal of Dr. Cowie to the Deanery of Exeter; the new rector of St. Lawrence Jewry was making fresh plans, and the choir had a fresh post of work to seek; the Rev. Thomas Pelham Dale, who had been some years Rector of St. Vedast's, Foster Lane, gladly welcomed them to his church; and, naturally, a more ornate service, with better music and ritual, was the result. Mr. Dale, a quiet scholar, and learned in science and art, gave himself heartily to the work. They had, however, to reckon with the opposing churchwardens and vestry of the double parish of St. Vedast and St. Michael le Querne, who actually assisted the Church Association to prosecute their rector, and paid over a sum from the parish fund to that association. Mr. Dale was harassed and persecuted for a long time, holding out against such powerful odds, but was at last imprisoned in Holloway Gaol. He was the son of Canon Dale, the Dean of Rochester of whom I have spoken in some early pages, and was much esteemed by many of the best clergy of the day, who gave him much kindness and support in his trouble. The story has been told in a quiet and pathetic way in his daughter's publication of his Letters. This St. Vedast's, just at the back of the Post Office, was one of the City churches where the daily service was continued in the eighteenth century—a record of these daily services was published in a small book called *Pietas Londinensis.* On the steps of this church occurred the little incident of Mr. Sikes of Guisborough and William Stevens meeting, they being almost the only attendants at week-day service ; and William Stevens jokingly said, "Never mind, if you will not tell of me I will not tell of you". Stevens was a kinsman of Bishop Horne, and one of those churchmen in whom was found a spirit of deep primitive piety throughout the eighteenth century.

It has been to some a matter of surprise that men like Mr. Cowie at St. Lawrence, and his very able neighbour, Mr. Scott at St. Olave, formerly of Hoxton, should have made no great move ; Dean Cowie's explanation was that " from the time of the Revolution, the City has been the stronghold of Puritanism ".

We must not forget to record Mr. Fish's work at St. Margaret Pattens, which he bravely carried on, though on the day that the Public Worship Regulation Act came into force his vestry passed a resolution to prosecute him under its provisions ; nor Mr. Benham's at St. Edmund the King and Martyr, where the good work had been long carried on by Mr. Hill ; he got the church restored, and with his son gathered a good congregation. Father Ignatius preached there in his time.

At All Saints, Bishopsgate, the Rev. Thomas Hugo, a man learned in antiquity and art, much raised the whole tone of the service, and brought things to a still higher standard while at West Hackney.

Somewhat further on we come to St. Peter's, Stepney, **then** under **Mr.** (late Canon) Rowsell, where for some years were frequent services and celebrations, carried out on the lines of the Church Movement; Mr. Rowsell preached from the altar steps the sermon at the opening of Mr. Lowder's Chapel in Old Gravel Lane. His predecessor was **the** Rev. Thomas Jackson, who became the head of St. Mark's College, Battersea; it is said that on his first appearance in the pulpit of St. Peter's in a surplice, the whole congregation rose *en masse* and left!

The old Parish Church of Stepney, under Mr. Lee, was then taking part in the general increase of outward reverence and order. At St. Philip's, under Mr. Heath- **cote** Brooks, there **was a good** choral service early in **the forties.** **And in one** of the divisions of this large **parish a** work was being done, and events occurring, which had much more than merely local results. The Rev. Bryan King, M.A., of Brasenose College, Oxford, incumbent of St. John's, Bethnal Green, became rector in 1842 of St. George's-in-the-East, a very large parish, through which ran the notorious Ratcliff Highway, teeming with sailors from every country, the street laid out, as it **were, for** the reception, entertainment, and amusement of sailors, filled with boarding-houses, cheap shops, and all the attendants of a seafaring population. It has been said that a full volume would not suffice to write the records of crime and misery to be found in this place. No wonder that years of work by one or two clergy in such a parish would only serve to show that some special and extraordinary work and energy, some body of men who would give up everything to raise the men and women of that parish out of the depths of wretchedness and degradation, were needed. So about 1856 Mr. King invited some clergymen into his parish to establish a mission there, to act as missionaries, and be licensed as curates. The story has been told in very touching and thrilling words in the *Life of Charles Lowder ;* how he, with Mr. Mackonochie and others, went to live in the very midst of all the sin and misery with which they were so long to contend. There it is recorded how they began to work against the recklessness of vice, the unblushing effrontery with which it was carried on when the lowest of every country combined to add their quota to the already overflowing stock, where the children even were taught early to thieve, to swear, to be bold and immoral in their manners and talk ; how they lived first in an old house in Calvert Street, now divided into two houses, one for the clergy and one for the sisters. In that house they opened a room, licensed by the bishop, for daily prayer and frequent preaching ; here they gathered a congregation (this room is now used as the sisters' oratory). Then a choir was formed ; and in 1856 the Iron Chapel of the Good Shepherd, where they had daily Communion

from the first, and a band or guild of communicants,
Confirmation and Bible classes. Then came woman's
help, schools, and visiting, bringing children to baptism.
Then in 1857 Dr. Neale's sister began a sisterhood; then
another mission, with the **old** Danish church in Well-
close Square as its **centre.** Bishop Tait took kind and
active interest in all this work. Mr. Rowley, who was
afterwards ordained, and went with Bishop Mackenzie
to Africa, took charge of the boys' school in Old Gravel
Lane; the sisters taught the girls. Then for penitents
in 1858, a home, far **from the scene of their degradation**, was taken at **Sutton in Surrey. Then an indus-**
trial school for **girls, to rescue** many from **the** perils
in their own home; for them a building at Hendon was
taken, with laundry, kitchen, nursery, chapel, chaplain's
room, sisters' room, and dormitories. **In** January, 1857,
Mr. Mackonochie joined **the** mission, stirred **by** the
sight **of the brave soldier,** Charles **Lowder.** Thus they
worked on, winning souls to Christ in **true** repentance,
in **the** faith **of** the Church, and in the duties of **the**
Christian life. Happily, neither Mr. Mackonochie nor
Mr. Lowder knew what fear was, either of mob, riots,
or violence.

So, after fifteen years of honest but almost hopeless
work, Mr. King had all this fresh strength joined **to**
his, and the mission in its course **attacked** the very
stronghold of evil; with its six clergy, fifty-four services
a week, six hundred children taught, no wonder the

vestry saw that **their easy** time of **power** was in danger ;
moreover, many of **them were owners of** notorious
evil houses. In 1859 this **vestry** had appointed a Rev.
Hugh Allen as afternoon lecturer, against the wish of
the rector. He was one of those fierce party spirits
foretold by **Mr.** Brett, and had a noisy and **irreverent
set of followers ;** after much dispute as to the time
of the afternoon **lecture, in** which **Mr.** King was, as
ever, courteous and conciliatory, the first disturbance
certainly **came** from **some** of Mr. Allen's congregation,
who stayed on afterwards to **the** rector's **service. This**
disturbance consisted in much **the** same kind of **annoy-
ance that took** place at the morning **service for** some
time, by very different people to the wretched mob and
rabble who kept up the disgraceful riots in the evening
for ten long months, but they set the example of dis-
order, and knew well what they were about ; they were
clearly **educated people, sent** or hired for the purpose.
Their plan was to *say* or *read* **in an** aggressive tone of
voice all that the choir *sang*, including the psalms.
Now **and then it** would have been ludicrous if not so
irreverent; **as,** for instance, when **the choir began** the
Gregorian **chant to** " My **song shall be of** the loving
kindness of the **Lord**," to have **those** words shouted
in your ear in a tone **of** voice that implied very little
loving kindness was rather trying. **The** rector's people
never annoyed or interfered **with the** lecturer's service.
Mr. King submitted to the bishop in every possible way

—discontinuing for a time the use of the Eucharistic vestments which had been presented two years before by members of his congregation, with a request that he would use them. Let us hope Mr. Hugh Allen came to **a better mind.** A friend tells me that years afterwards **he was seen joining** in the service of Benediction at Mr. **Nugee's** Chapel in the Old Kent Road.

But our readers will like to know what the riots at evening service at the church of **St.** George's-in-the-East were like. The moment the church was opened for service a crowd **of** men, women, boys, **and** girls, rushed in, filling it in every corner, scrambled to **the** galleries, and called to their companions where to **sit ;** the gallery of a theatre on Boxing-night was peace and quietness compared to it. This went on till the church was quite full, and very early in the riots the stalls and reading-desk were thus occupied by **the mob.**

Then the clergy and **choir** conducted the service in the chancel apse, protected from the **mob** by the chancel railings, passing **in** from **the** vestry door for **some** time through a file of policemen. What can one say **of** the service ? Imagine a mob of the very dregs of society, howling and shouting the responses **in** front **of** the chancel ; women just as they came from the streets with shawls over their heads, howling the Lord's Prayer and some of the prayers and responses : it was more like a scene from the French Revolution than service in a Christian church ; imagine this mob all through the service, lessons **and sermon,** coughing, hissing, **stamping** feet, whistling and **slamming** pew-doors. Nothing seemed to touch them, or if they stared quietly in wonder for a few minutes at the tremendous Easter Alleluias in the Easter hymn " O Filii et Filiæ," **it was only for a** moment. Many of the most renowned **preachers** in England kindly came on these Sunday evenings; and though the mob listened perhaps to Mr. Monro's pathetic account **of** Hagar and **her** son from the double text, " The water **was** spent **in** the bottle," and " Thou **art** the fountain **of** life," **their attention** was soon diverted. The splendid and touching **sermons** of Mr. Bennett, **of** Frome, and others, had little **or** no effect **on** such a congregation ; on one occasion **dogs** purposely drugged were let loose in the church crackers were let off, musical instruments used. Outside, clergymen and laymen were spat upon, pelted with stones, and had mud thrown at **them ;** in short, this mob behaved just as the dregs of society would behave anywhere if they thought they might do so with impunity ; and indeed **they** had it all their own way : they had only to threaten the altar cross, hangings, etc., and they were removed. Giving in to such people was perfectly useless. **And so it** went on for months and months, **the** rector and his curates keeping on the services, many friends coming every Sunday **to** cheer and protect through the troublous time. Nearly through **it all, the** rector's wife and family occupied their pew with friends to keep them from harm. Many will remember the imposing form of Mr. Adams (son of **Mr.** Serjeant **Adams, and** brother of William Adams, author of *The Shadow of* the *Cross,* etc.), in this post of honour.

Will it be believed that in Christian England, where law and order are the boast, such a state of things could go on—a scandal and disgrace to every one in authority? The churchwardens and local authorities did absolutely nothing. **Mr.** King **and his** curates, who violated no law, were deprived of the protection of the law. **The** magistrate, **Mr.** Selfe, Thames Police Court, **never** convicted or punished one of the rioters, though they were over and **over** again brought before him, duly charged with brawling, etc., witnesses proving the charge. This was the style of justice : a shipwright had only to ask **to be remanded for a week,** that he might get witnesses to swear he was innocent, and Mr. Selfe most politely **said, "** Certainly, certainly, adjourn it for a week ". So one-sided, too, **was** the justice ; one day, when the rector, **having** removed a man from **a** pew-door, **was** summoned by him for an assault, and this summons came on after the business was supposed to be finished, Mr. King explained that his counsel **and** witnesses had left ; but Mr. Selfe refused to remand that case, and actually convicted the rector, and fined him five shillings! **Throughout, the** rector and his curates did everything to conciliate, were such a thing possible. Of course, no **sane** person believed that there **was** any religious principle whatever in the riotous mobs thus tolerated and connived at. So long as the magistrates refused to convict and punish such offenders, so long did the mob know that they could outrage a church or anything else sacred. Only because it was a church with a very moderate and decent ritual, that has all been since declared lawful in the Church of England, the Evangelical party declined to speak out against this violation of law and order; or, if they did speak, as at Pentonville and other places, their violent language, the hasty false statements, the unchristian sentiments, but added fuel to the flame. And so it came to pass that the magistrates never punished, and seemed to entertain the monstrous notion, shared even by some of the leading newspapers, that this wretched mob, this collection of the very dregs of society, was the united voice of the Protestant people of England against the revived practices of reverence, devotion, and worship in the Church of England! One almost wishes that those who could hold such an absurd notion might have been condemned to spend two hours in the midst of the mob for forty or fifty Sundays. But if the law would not help them, churchmen did not stand by and do nothing ; early in the times of the riots a committee was formed, called "The St. George's Church Defence Association, for the maintenance of law and order in the parish church of St. George's-in-the-East". Space will only allow of my recording a few of the names : His Excellency G. R. J.

Gordon, British Minister, Hanover ; Hon. **H.** Walpole, G. F. Boyle (afterwards Earl Glasgow), Colin Lindsay, Archdeacons Denison and Churton, Revs. Canon Jenkins, R. Lee, W. J. E. Bennett, Edward Stuart, W. **R.** Wroth, Thomas Helmore, **W. R.** Scott, etc. ; of laymen, **Colonel Owen,** Colonel Moorsom, R. Brett, Sutherland Græme, J. D. Chambers, J. Burgess Knight, James Mackonochie, William Elliott, **J.** Walter Lea, T. G. **Ramsay,** Thomas Charrington, etc., etc. These did all that **was** possible in the Ecclesiastical **and** other Courts. In July, 1860, **Mr.** Hansard took charge **of the parish** that the rector might go away for the needed rest, **but he** only kept it six months, declining to break **his agreement** with Mr. King as to the services. Then the **bishop's chap-**lain took the services, and the disgraceful riots came to an end. Nothing **could exceed** the **kindness and sym-**pathy **shown** to St. George's all **through** the sad time by the incumbents **of** the surrounding parishes : **the Revs. B. C.** Sangar, of **St.** Paul's, Shadwell ; T. **T. Bazeley, of Poplar ;** T. **W.** Nowell, of Wapping ; Mr. Lee, of Stepney, and **others.** Mr. Linklater worked in **the** mission later **on.**

Through it all the work of the mission, with its varied helps, and **the noble** church of St. Peter's-in-the-East to crown them, prospered **beyond what had been** hoped, **and our** readers will remember the account of the funeral of Mr. Lowder, and his work. **No** such funeral had **been** seen in **the streets** of London in modern times

—the record of a life and work for God in our Church that will live years and years after the miserable riots have been forgotten.

Good work went on, and still goes on, at Rotherhithe, under the Rev. E. Josselyn Beck. Years before this, the Rev. Richard Rawlins, of Limehouse, who died of the cholera in 1849, had worked on thorough Church lines ; his son is now Vestry Clerk of St. Gabriel's, Fenchurch.

CHAPTER VII.

I⟨T⟩ will be a pleasant change to go from the St. George's riots and the East End of London into some few country towns and villages where the Movement worked and spread; but there are still a few other centres of work in and around London that should take a place in our story. One was the Church of St. Ethelburga, Bishopsgate, the church in which the daily Litany at midday for business men was so long kept up. Mr. Rodwell in his day was a learned writer and preacher, and published works on Oriental history and theology, and was much interested in science, the microscope, etc.; but of late years the work has been well and entirely carried on by his curate-in-charge, the late Rev. E. N. Eldred, whose care and labour in a difficult position are well known. In the North-East we find St. Paul's, Bow Common, where for many years the Rev. Arthur Cotton carried on the work in this out-of-the-way post, where could be little encouragement or help from the surrounding neighbours; and the work still goes forward. The story of St. Alban's, Holborn, has been so well told in the life of the Rev. A. H. Mackonochie, and the account there of the early struggles of priests and people, that there is little

(163)

that need be told here. The record of all these years is written in the higher lives and holy deaths of many hundreds of people of all classes; the noble founder's hopes must have been more than realised: the constant prayer and praise, the rescues from sin and misery, the raising of life and work go on and on, with surroundings that even now would tax all the courage and energy of the most industrious parish priest. In the early days of St. Matthias, Stoke Newington, a friend remembers walking home from there with Mr. Butterfield; he stopped in Gray's Inn Lane, and pointed out a place where was to be a church with everything to be desired, though it was some years before St. Alban's was consecrated. A short walk westward and we come to the church of St. John (Evangelist), Red Lion Square, where Dr. Webber, the Bishop of Brisbane, did for so many years a great work in parish and church.

St. Stephen's, Shepherd's Bush, under Mr. Collett and Mr. Cooke, was a very early suburban centre, where excellent Church work was done. On July 27, 1859, another suburban centre was formed, and the church of St. John the Evangelist, Hammersmith, was consecrated by the Bishop of London, from a design by Mr. Butterfield; it had a spacious sanctuary and good chancel (as at St. Matthias, the services for nearly three years had been conducted in a licensed room): the service was Gregorian, and Mr. W. H. Monk played the organ; a great many Stoke Newington friends were there, among them Mr. Brett, Mr. Philip Twells, a frequent attendant at St. Matthias, Henry Twells, the Master of Godolphin Schools, close to St. John's, an admirable preacher. Edward Twells, afterwards bishop, was the first vicar. A work was begun here which was followed up by Mr. Cowan and others, and the parish church and several more district churches are now all worked on excellent Church lines. Nearer town again, there is the church of St. Mary Magdalen, Paddington, where a grand work in every way has been carried on for years by the late Dr. Temple West and his coadjutors: the veteran Church organist and composer, Mr. Redhead, is still there, and as active as ever. Then, nearer town, we come to the district of St. Cyprian's, Marylebone, where the Rev. Charles Gutch has laboured, with parts of two ordinary houses for his church, for nearly thirty years, gathering around him an earnest, hearty body of churchmen and churchwomen. Mr. Gutch was well known for his zeal and solemn earnestness in his work at St. Saviour's, Leeds, and at All Saints, Margaret Street, and has earned the greatest respect and affection. For a time, the Rev. Hugh Monro (brother of Edward Monro and Dr. Monro) worked with Mr. Gutch; and also at St. Anne's, Soho; he was for a time chaplain to a minor hospital. A small, thin, pale, quiet man, without the fire and energy of Edward Monro, but ever kind, helpful, and amiable to all who had need of his assistance. We will add to these London sketches Mr. Abbott's excel-

lent work at Christ Church, Clapham, where he was for
some years assisted by the Rev. **Robert** Gwynne, now
Vicar of St. Mary the Virgin, Crown Street, **Soho**; also
the churches of St. Mary, Primrose Hill, **aud St. Augus-**
tine, Kilburn, and the wonderful works in connection
with it.

Streatham, Tooting, Balham, and many other churches
around were soon well forward in the new work, thanks
to the veteran Rector of Streatham, Mr. Nicholl, to Mr.
Tarbutt of St. Peter's, Streatham, **whose** good start and
labours are so well carried on by his successor, H. Baron
Dickinson, and others.

On our way to the country we may pass close to the
church of St. Stephen, Lewisham, where **for** more than
twenty years the Rev. Canon R. R. Bristow has most
successfully laboured.   The church **was** built in the
time of, and owes **much** to, the **Rev. S.** Russell Davies,
to whom **Mr.** Bristow **was** curate, succeeding to the
vicarage about 1868 : **Mr.** Bristow's work is well known
both as **a** preacher and as a parish priest ; he **was for a**
short time with Mr. Wroth, at St. Philip's, Clerkenwell.
Chislehurst has long **been** a highly favoured spot, both
for natural beauty and for Church privileges ; indeed, for
Church folk it was, **and is,** a most desirable place of
residence, and the old saying about Amberley, in Sussex,
" **Where** do you live ? "   " Amberley, where would you
live ? " might be repeated of Chislehurst, with its wide
commons, hilly views, its shady trees and woods ; happily

without the reverse of the Amberley proverb in winter, **when the** lanes and roads were almost impassable, and the saying *then* was, " Where do you live ? " " Amberley, God help us ! " Chislehurst old village church **was** carefully restored ánd well kept from the year 1846, when the Rev. Francis H. Murray, son of a late Bishop of Rochester, became **rector ;** from that time its daily prayers, frequent Communions, festival services, and parish work have been well known ; the church left open some hours every day, so that **the** sorrowful, the penitent, and the thankful, the poor and the world-weary might for **a few** moments kneel before God and gain comfort and **peace.** The parish and rector have **had** their troubles : **early** in the morning of March 16, 1857, the old **spire was** destroyed by fire, the whole fabric of the spire **fell** into the ancient tower ; not a beam fell outside, and so the church was saved from destruction ; by half-past ten all danger was over, and **at** twelve the rector gathered his people into the body of the church to return thanks and praise for its preservation. Mr. Murray is a thorough worker as parish priest and divine ; is the author of some devotional works, and a *catena* of authorities on the Holy Communion. **He** was always much interested in Church hymnology, a great friend of the **late Sir** Henry Baker, and other compilers of *Hymns Ancient* **and** *Modern,* and himself did some of the work of compilation of that now widely used hymnal. The beautiful churchyard is well known, and contains the monuments to Charles Lowder and some of the best churchmen of the Movement; among others, of a much loved layman, J. L. Anderdon, father-in-law to the rector, author of the *Life of Bishop* Ken, and several other works, about whom I hope to tell more when writing of the " Laymen of the Church Movement ". Many of our best living Church laymen still make their home in Chislehurst, and no doubt fully appreciate all the privileges there. Mr. Murray was once curate to Mr. Clarke, Vicar of Northfield, near Birmingham, a staunch old churchman of the Keble and Williams school. Brasted, near Sevenoaks, had for some years, in early days, the privilege of a rector who was not only a great and learned scholar, but also one who, like Dean Church, could preach simple village sermons, and enter into the villagers' wants : this was Dr. W. H. Mill, Regius Professor of Hebrew in Cambridge, and author of *University Sermons*, and many theological works. For some years, too, there has been a good churchman as rector at Sevenoaks. In this same county of Kent, at Chelsfield and Farnborough, in very early times, the Rev. Folliott Baugh was rector ; he was afterwards Vicar of Ilford, in Essex, all in the gift of All Souls' College, of which he was a fellow ; at the latter town some antiChurch riots took place. Mr. Baugh's *locum tenens* at Farnborough was the Rev. Rowland Smith, of St. John's College, Oxford, author of the *Church Catechism, illus-*

trated by the Prayer Book, and *The Law of the Anglican Church the Law of the Land*, a good scholar and **churchman.** I remember in 1852 he wrote some most **amusing** wedding verses to a friend who had married a very musical **lady,** concluding :—

> Extend your pity **to** the bard,
> With fair Cecilia for him plead ;
> That she the goodwill for the deed
> Would fain accept ; nor deem him slack
> In courtesy ; because, alack,
> Against his " Epithal " the nine
> With spiteful malice do combine.
>
> *The Hermit of Farnborough ; indited in our* **Cell.**

Not far **off, Mr.** Caffin, of Westerham, will be re-**membered as an early** worker. **At** Markbeech, near Edenbridge, **the Rev. R. S.** Hunt **was,** and is still, vicar ; from 1857 there were daily services and frequent **Communions ;** a quiet village church, well ordered and **cared for ;** Mr. Hunt was in early life curate to Sir George Prevost, at Stinchcombe, near Dursley, and no doubt was privileged to know Mr. Isaac Williams ; he was also a friend and contemporary of Dr. Neale. At Hever, close by, was the Rev. W. Wilberforce Battye **(formerly a** curate of Brighton) ; here good Church work had been carried on. At St. James', Tunbridge Wells, Mr. Pearson stood **for** some time alone, **and** it was a matter of regret when he resigned such a centre of good work ; **there is** now the district church of St. Barnabas. At Kilndown, the parish church **of** Bedgbury, the seat of A. J. B. Beresford Hope, one of the most earnest and energetic laymen of the Movement, **there** was a very beautiful church, with **frequent services**; and a rector, Mr. Harrison, heart and soul in the work. In 1844, at Milton-next-Gravesend, at the chapel of St. John, there **was** for a time one **of** the most reverent and careful services that had been seen up to that date; **in music and** ritual all that loving care could give, besides good parish work among all the **people,** daily services, constant celebrations; saints' day services with short sermons **or** addresses, and **the same on all** the black letter **days,** thus making **the Prayer Book** a thorough **reality**: some few may yet remember **the** deep regret **felt when the** Rev. **W. J.** Blew retired **from** this post; **his** heartiest services in all ritual, liturgical, and legal points have ever since been **given** to the Church of England, as well as his work on hymnology, psalmody, **etc.** Of Kentish churchmen the name of the late Rev. **W. N.** Griffin, Vicar of Ospringe, Senior Wrangler, etc., must not be left out; the memorial just arranged testifies to the **long** and earnest labours of this learned parish priest; and Northfleet, and the work there, must be mentioned.

At Richmond, in Surrey, Mr. Procter's years of faithful **work** are appreciated by many **who** reside in that lovely spot. At Roehampton, **Dr.** G. E. Biber was incumbent for some years, and published many works in defence of the Church of England, especially replying to

Mr. Sibthorp **on the** Anti-Roman line, also *The* **Seven Voices of** *the Spirit,* **and** on Convocation. He was **a** very large contributor to the chief religious magazines and periodicals, the *English Review,* successor **to** the *Christian Remembrancer,* and others. **He** was a native of Würtemberg, and **an LL.D.** of Göttingen University, **and became a** naturalised English subject before his **ordination** in 1839. Dr. Biber lived in Brighton frequently **before his** death; **his son,** who was in holy **orders, married the Hon.** Mrs. Erskine, **daughter of Lady Cardross.**

At Egham, in **Surrey,** a well-known churchman **was** rector for some years, **the** Rev. J. S. B. Monsell, author of *Sermons* **on the** *Beatitudes,* and more especially known for his hymns and poems, among them *Hymns of Love and Praise, Parish Musings, Spiritual Songs,* etc.

At Witley, the **Rev.** John Chandler was rector. **He** compiled *Horæ Sacræ,* **and** was **one of** the earliest **translators of the** old hymns; his *Hymns of the Ancient Church* has long been scarce and out of print, **but we see how** largely it **was used** by the compilers of *Hymns* **Ancient and** *Modern.* **A** copy of this **book** had **rather** a curious adventure. It was lent first to a **clergyman** who was compiling a hymnal **for** his own parish, who at the end of **five years wrote to** borrow it again for the compilers of *Hymns Ancient and Modern,* but as **it had never** been returned the owner could **only reply that he had no** objection. Search was

made and it was found, and used by the compilers of
A. and M., and then again vanished from the owner's
ken for ten or twelve years, when it was discovered by
a lady in the Library of All Saints, Margaret Street,
recognised by a special monogram.

At Dorking, Mr. Joyce spent some years of work
while his health lasted; he is perhaps still remembered
as a hearty, genial, and most kind-hearted parish priest
and gentleman.   At Reigate, the Rev. J. N. Harrison
has been for years working on the lines of the Church
Revival.

Sussex gives a wide field for Church work and progress. We will just now go through a part of Hampshire,
returning again to Sussex.

At Basingstoke, the Rev. J. E. Millard, some time
at Bradfield, Fellow of Magdalen College, once Headmaster of Magdalen College School, was rector in 1864;
and daily services, weekly communion, and good choral
services were the use.   Mr. Millard was the author of
Historical Notice of Choristers, the *Island Choir*, and
other works.   At Highclere, near Newbury, the Rev.
W. Brudenell Barter, of Oriel College, was rector;
he was a most vigorous champion of orthodoxy, and
spoke with no uncertain sound in his *Gainsaying of
Core in the Nineteenth Century*, and in his *Tracts in
Defence of the Church*, and *On the Progress of In-
fidelity;* he was, I think, brother to Warden Barter,
of Winchester.

John Keble, the author of the *Christian Year*, is always in our mind deeply connected with Oxford and the Oxford Movement, and no doubt the influence of the boyish-looking Fellow and Tutor of Oriel was a great power there ; he has been well described as a glory to his College, present in everybody's thoughts, a comfort and a stay, for the slightest word he dropped was all the more remembered, seeming to come from a different and holier sphere : every word was, as it were, a brilliant or a pearl ; yet he gave up Oxford to assist his father at Fairford, and vacated his Fellowship some years after by marriage, so was not living much in Oxford; thus the man who had stirred the hearts of so many spent his life in the sublime work of pastoral duty at the small village of Hursley, in Hampshire, with a rural population of less than a thousand people : presented to that living by his friend and favourite College pupil, Sir William Heathcote. The *Christian Year* probably had a sale that no work of the kind ever came near, and yet it was said that Mr. Parker once refused to give the sum of sixty pounds for the copyright of the book which in a few years produced enough money to rebuild Hursley church and do many other good works. My first visit was during the rebuilding of the church, and the services were all kept up in large barns fitted up carefully with altar, stalls, open seats, etc. ; the bells were rung from the old church tower for these services, and you had to find your way to the barn, on entering which

ten or twelve minutes before the time for service, you
saw that Mr. Keble and a curate were already there in
surplice, hood, and stole, kneeling towards the altar in
private prayer; and as the parish clock struck, the simple
service began. Friends came to reside in and around
Hursley to be near Mr. Keble; among these was the
Rev. R. J. Spranger, of Exeter College, a very ripe
scholar and writer, who published a set of Confirmation
lectures, somewhat quaint and patristic, but full of
material for thought; he preached at All Saints, Margaret Street, on Church colouring, and on the same
subject at Smethwick; these were published: he also
preached a set of sermons on the Apocrypha, at St.
Paul's, Brighton. Some of Mr. Keble's curates were
men of note in the Church. One, whose name is
always connected with Hursley, was the Rev. Peter
Young, author of *Daily Readings for a Year on the Life
of our Lord*, a most useful manual for clergy and
teachers. Mr. Young was for seventeen years curate
at Hursley, most of the time as a deacon, the then
Bishop of Winchester refusing him priest's orders. The
account of this is well told in Dr. Pusey's Life. My
next visit to Hursley was in 1852, when the church
was finished and open, and a very simple but beautiful
service for a country parish it was: the cross and
candlesticks were on the altar itself, and the church
full of a congregation who joined heartily in the service; it must have been a wonderful contrast to Mr.

Keble's first Sunday in the old church, when, it is said, that after the first two lines of the General Confession Mr. Keble stopped and explained to the good folks that they were to repeat the words of the Confession after him. Dr. Moberly, headmaster of Winchester (afterwards Bishop of Salisbury), was present in the church. We must not pass from Hursley without naming Otterbourne, the home for so many years of Miss Yonge authoress of the *Heir of Redcliffe*, and so many excellent works. Certainly, no one authoress has ever done the good service to Church-folk which she has done: her vivid pictures of young people, their hearty, healthy, happy, and natural home-loving lives and characters, their failures and successes, griefs and joys, must have exercised an influence that will be felt for some generations; she has earned the deep gratitude of many and many a parent and guardian; such a work as *The Pillars of the House* is simply invaluable. Miss Yonge was ever ready, too, to help forward the work of the Movement in a kind and liberal way; one instance I can name: a friend of mine was the editor of the *Churchman's Companion*, a magazine struggling into life, and Miss Yonge liberally gave *Henrietta's Wish* and the *Two Guardians* to be printed in the first instance in that magazine, giving it a good lift upward.

At Farlington the Rev. E. T. Richards spent a long life, in the simple post of a village parish priest, bright, genial, and hearty to the last. **One** of his daughters was the wife of Dr. Huntingford, and another of the Rev. Andrew Nugee, vicar **of Wymering**, near by; after Mr. A. Nugee's death the parish and church **were** well served for many years by his brother, the **Rev.** George Nugee : of these I have spoken before.

At Dogmersfield in this county, the Rev. Charles Dyson was rector : the church was rebuilt in 1843 by him and his **sister, at a cost of** £4000. He was the College **friend of** John Keble, **and preserver of the** *Christian Year* from destruction (*Keble's Life*, p. 36). **The rectory, visited by** Keble, Manning, Sir J. **D.** Coleridge, **and Bishop** Wilberforce, was built by Mr. Dyson, to whom the late Dean Butler was once curate. Miss Dyson **was most** active in the early literature of the Movement, **and** was the authoress of *Ivo and Verena, Cousin Rachel*, **and several** popular works published by Mr. Brunt.

A little farther on, at **the far end** of the county, is Westbourne, near Emsworth, **where for** some time the Rev. Henry Newland was rector and vicar ; he is perhaps better known as the Vicar of St. Mary's **Church,** Torquay ; **but at** Westbourne **most of his work for** the Church was done ; he died in the **prime of life,** and had he lived would probably have **been** one of the leading **men of** the Church Movement : it was as a brilliant preacher and speaker, bold and fearless, ready at all points, that he made his mark in the time of his health, and a very strong and vigorous mark it was ; if he had done nothing but deliver those Lectures on Tractarianism in the Town Hall, Brighton, **at** a time when party feeling ran very high, he would have done good service : it was grand to **see** and hear him, **a** fine manly **pre**-sence, and a voice that carried his words to every part of the large hall. **In many** ways the present Dean of Rochester reminds one of him. His dedication of those **lectures to** Archdeacon Denison is truly characteristic : " **My dear** Archdeacon, —What I say in these lectures I think, and what **I** think **I** mean to act up to. **I can**, therefore, find no more appropriate pattern for them than the man who, **on the** Education question, as **on all** others, meant what he said and did it." **He** also wrote *Confirmation and* **First** *Communion, Postils* **on** *the Parables*, also **a** *catena* **on the** Ephesians and Philippians, etc. ; he partly wrote and edited **the** series of *Sermons for the Christian Seasons.* In all his works **there was** a fund of instruction and information, sensibly **and** vividly conveyed and applied. His bright **presence** and conversation were long remembered by **those who had** the privilege **of** knowing him. He was **a lover of the country and** a disciple of Izaac Walton, wrote *Forest Life,* **The** *Erne,* etc.

Returning into Sussex, at Crawley, **Dr.** Neale's first **curacy, the Rev. C. A. Fowler,** of Oriel College, was **for some time rector; he was also once at** Bradfield, and later at St. Margaret's, Canterbury, a well-esteemed champion of all that was good and orthodox, author of

a most useful volume of parochial sermons, club sermons, *The Church* **the Bond of** *Brotherhood*, etc., etc.
Horsham, with its fine old parish church, and its vicar
for forty years, John F. Hodgson, a well-known worker
in the cause, comes next.   His coadjutor at the district church, John Kenrick, was the compiler of several
manuals of devotion : *The Horology, Devotions for the
Hours of Prayer*, etc. ; his signature in the dedications,
J. K., was by some taken for that of John Keble.

On a walking tour in this part many years back, two
friends started from Horsham to Cocking, calling on
the vicar, Mr. Valentine, one of the good old school.
Near by is the sweet village of Nuthurst, with its small
but beautiful church and churchyard, where, in the
very early days before 1842, the Rev. W. J. Blew,
about whom we spoke before, began the work of the
revival which some years after was to be taken up and
continued by the Rev. J. O. MacCarogher (sometime
Prebendary of Chichester) up to the end of his life a
short time ago.   These friends never forgot a few days
spent at Nuthurst about 1870, with the most kind-
hearted, genial vicar and his wife and family, including
a special Sunday, when Dr. A. B. Evans was staying
there and preached in the morning, and Mr. Blew in
the afternoon : it was a never-to-be-forgotten day, quite
refreshing to Londoners.

They walked from there to Lavington, the beautiful
seat which Bishop Samuel Wilberforce held by right

of his wife, who **was the** eldest daughter and heiress
of the late Mr. Sargent. There were four daughters
one **had married** Archdeacon Manning, then rector of
Lavington, another, Mr. George Ryder. The park,
house, and church, all close together, made a charming
place to **live in, and** the archdeacon being away the
bishop **said** the usual daily prayers in the church. The
church **itself was** quite a model **in** arrangement and
care, and as the two were walking round the churchyard **with their** knapsacks **on,** the servants from the
vicarage **came out and** inquired if they would take any
refreshment; the **same was** done **at** Graffham, which
was held with Lavington, and was **then** in charge of
Mr. Laprimaudaye. **Both** churches were **kept** open all
day. Away towards Pulborough **is** the quiet country
village of Waltham or Coldwaltham, where the Rev. J.
M. Sandham has laboured from 1846, **after the** pattern
of a real country parson, bestowing **all care** and devotion **on the church,** services, and people, and all kindness **on friends and** visitors. **The** vicar and Mrs. Sandham **were one in the** quiet life of the Church's **order**
and care, and kindness to all with them and around
them ; his recent appointment to an honorary canonry
was well deserved. Mr. Sandham's brother, General
Sandham, of Rowdells, near by, was a thorough church-
man, too. **One** special Sunday spent at Waltham
must be recorded, when the Rev. A. R. Ashwell, Principal of the Theological College and Canon of Chiches-

ter, was staying there, and preached two special sermons.   It was quite a red-letter day to remember.
Canon Ashwell's career, from his Cambridge course
ending as wrangler, as **Vice-Principal of St.** Mark's
College, Chelsea, and in many other important positions,
is well known; as a writer, preacher, and teacher, he
ranks very highly in the record of the Church Movement; his busy, active life in all three capacities—he
was for some years editor of the *Literary Churchman*—
was more than any man could keep up for very long,
and he was not a strong man; he died in 1879.   He
wrote a valuable essay, bringing into it urgent and solid
reasons, against Evening Communions.   At Arundel
efforts were being made in the right direction under
very trying surroundings.   At Bognor was the girls'
school, somewhat answering to the Woodard Middle
Class Boys' Colleges; and the lady superior and chaplain worked bravely in the cause.   Chichester, with its
record of five deans—Chandler, Hook, Burgon, Pigou,
and Randall, proved incontestably that deans might be
not only thoroughly useful but essential in all that
appertained to Divine service and worship, and the
welfare, spiritual and temporal, of all around them.   At
Bosham, Mr. Mitchell was a sound churchman, and his
church, a fine old one, carefully kept.   On a fine summer evening, few things are more delightful than to
take a boat at high tide, row out half a mile, and then
rest to enjoy the lovely view backed by the fine Downs.

At Littlehampton **the Rev. C.** Rumball has worked well for nearly thirty years, and done much in what is, perhaps, **the** most trying sort of place—a small, popular seaside **town, with** its overcrowded and shifting population. **At** Shoreham one goes back in memory **many** years, even to the solemn opening of Old Shoreham **vicarage in Mr.** Wheeler's time, and the beginning **of Mr. Woodard's** scheme **for the** religious education **of** the thousands of middle class youths growing up in **our** midst. This was started in a few small houses **in** Shoreham, and like the Church Movement, **of** which it was a sort of practical first fruits, has moved forward till one is lost in amazement **at the many handsome** buildings, **with** chapels, **cloisters, and all** the adjuncts **of** the best colleges, **at** Hurstpierpoint, Lancing, and Ardingly in Sussex only, besides those at Denstone in the Midlands and elsewhere. **To see** the very small beginnings **in** those few **old** tumble-down houses and then **the** present proportions of this scheme is indeed **a lesson of** patience and utter perseverance. Here, **too, we** will pause to speak of the inmates of that same old Shoreham vicarage from 1857 to 1876, or rather 1872, when the wife died. These were the Rev. James B. Mozley, Regius Professor of Divinity **and** Canon of Christ Church, and his wife, twin sister **of** Mrs. Johnson, **widow of** Manuel **Johnson,** the University Astronomer, in whose house Newman spent his last night in Oxford: they were daughters of Dr. Ogle. After more than twenty **years of work with** Newman, Pusey, and **the** great leaders **in** the **Church** Movement, Canon **Mozley** settled **in Old Shoreham, and lived** there as much **as** his other work **would** allow, **for he** never left **off** writing till the very last. They **loved** their old Sussex parish, **and were** indeed much beloved **there. They** lived **much for others,** and their life was **one of** cheerfulness and **happiness, and they** both retained **a** youthfulness of spirit that **was** beautiful to see. **It was at** times difficult **to** recognise **in** the sweet quiet appearance **of the** Rector **of Old** Shoreham, the man **who** in 1833 and onwards, **had** set us **all on fire** with his Essays on Laud, Strafford, etc., in the *British Critic and Christian Remembrancer; but in* reply **to** this thought **once** expressed, **Mrs.** Mozley would smile and say, **"But** surely you **don't** expect any one to go on letting **off** fireworks for **ever!"** A more delightful book than his letters, etc., **published by his sister Anne in** 1885 **it** is difficult **to conceive.** I **must not** omit to name Cuckfield, **and** with **it the Rev. T.** A. Maberley, one **of the most** hearty, genial, and kind-hearted of parish priests, who spent a **long** life devoted to his **church and parish.** Buxted, **also, was** privileged in **early** days, **and has** advanced since, **with a** church built **and** endowed by the **Rev. A. D.** Wagner, of St. Paul's, **Brighton,** who has **a** county house there; he appointed the vicar, the Rev. J. B. de la **Bere** (formerly John Edwards, of **St.** Paul's, Knightsbridge and **Prest-**

bury): but Mr Wagner really belongs to Brighton, **of which** I shall speak further on.

It is not easy to tell, in any short space, about East **Grinstead** and the very wonderful man whose name it **recalls to our** mind. **A mere** bibliography of his writings **would** require more space than this whole chapter occupies; **and** from that you would not realise **what manner of man** was John Mason Neale, **and the way of life of one of** the most learned of English churchmen, **worthy to** be ranked with **some** of the **chiefest divines, poets,** liturgiologists, historians **and** hymn writers that **ever** lived. He died certainly in what might be **called the** prime of life, but the amount **of his** work **was much more** than most men accomplish in **a very long life.** He **was** the son of the Rev. Cornelius Neale, one of the best **known of** the extreme Puritan **school; who,** after his friend, John Mason **Good, a learned and** pious physician, named his son. We **do not know** how soon Dr. Neale broke **away** from the early traditions of his home, though we **do know** that throughout his life he retained all that **was** good and true in that system,—its reverence, **earnestness,** and great regard for Holy Scripture; and we know that when **at home as a** youth in Brighton he attended with his mother Christ Church in that town, then, and for years, **under the** charge of the **Rev.** James Vaughan, one of the best and most **earnest of the** Evangelical school **of the day.** Probably **the** first stir of the Catholic revival reached Mr. Neale as **an undergraduate at Trinity College, Cambridge, with such companions as Mr. Beres**ford Hope, E. **T. Codd, M. S.** Gillis, F. A. **Paley.** It has been said **that** the revival **there touched** different points from Oxford, and worked in a different **way.** The questions which sent Oxford men to Rome certainly did not at **first** disturb University life at Cambridge. Very early in his life there, Mr. Neale **was** one of the leaders who, accepting the **great** idea of the Catholicity of the Church of England, set themselves to **work** out how the outward aspects **of** English public worship might be made most reasonably and intelligently to **cor**respond to the ideals **and best** traditions of **the ancient and historic Church; the** Cambridge Camden **Society and** the *Ecclesiologist* were founded with this express **object,** and not by any means as matters of mere archæo**logical** and antiquarian research. It was to exercise **a practical** influence on all the churches, services, and worship; and a great many of the early papers **and** pamphlets of the society were written by Mr. Neale, **the** famous *History of Pews* among the number. He was ordained very early in life, and worked **for a short** time as a curate **at** Crawley in Sussex, but **a** threatened affection of the lungs obliged him **to give up** that work; **and though** he tried Penzance and other places, Madeira **had to be** his home **for the greater part** of three years. **But before** that, on **July** 27, 1842, Mr. Neale married Sarah Norman Webster, of the talented family **of the**

Attorney-General. He never ceased writing and translating; he became master of twenty languages, and before going to Madeira taught himself Portuguese, that he might readily read the great writers and divines in that language. In Madeira was written much of the *History of the Holy Eastern Church,* and he there always had five or six works on hand, — tales, allegories, hymns, histories, etc., etc. In 1843, also, was written, jointly with the Rev. B. Webb, *Durandus on Symbolism,* a book now long out of print, and of very high value. On any point where there was a need to stand up and defend the honour of God and His Church, Mr. Neale was ready and well-armed, and the number of smaller pamphlets and essays was wonderful. His *Lectures on Church Difficulties* was quite a volume of defence. He was, as has been said, impulsive and excitable, but thorough to the backbone; chivalrous and generous, warmly affectionate in all relations of life, with a wonderful memory and great facility in acquiring languages. He did not leave Madeira till May, 1845, and was able to winter in England for the rest of his life. By this time his works began to be known and appreciated, and he never left off writing till the last year of his life, 1866. Space will not enable me to name a fiftieth part of them. Before he left Madeira he had revised the Portuguese version of the Prayer Book for the S.P.C.K., and had translated Bishop Andrewes' *Devotions* into Portuguese; he also wrote

Murray's Guide to Portugal. In 1845 Mr. Neale won the Seatonian Prize Poem, and gained it for ten successive years. The Rev. Thomas Hankinson was, I think, the only man who came near so large a number. His power of versification was wonderfully rapid ; some of these Seatonians were begun and ended in thirty-six hours. In 1858 Mr. Neale gained the one on *Egypt ;* after he had written the poem, he wrote another on the same subject in hexameters, the metre of Longfellow's *Evangeline.* The prize was given to the first, and £20 to the second one, without any idea that they were both by one hand. This latter was a grand poem, and contained those splendid lines on his first text at Crawley, sixteen years before, and is almost a picture of his own course.

> Then from the Throne of God, that Throne where the weary have
>   refuge,
> Where in the midst of distress there is calm, that mandate was
>   uttered—
> Mandate not uttered alone that day for the thousands of Judah,
> But to all ages addressed and to all generations " *Go forward,*"
> *Forward* when all seems lost, when the cause looks utterly hopeless,
> *Forward* when brave hearts fail, and to yield is the rede of the
>   coward,
> *Forward* when friends fall off, and enemies gather around thee ;
> Thou, though alone with thy God, though alone in thy courage,
>   *go forward.*
> Nothing it is with Him to redeem or by few or by many,
> Help, though deferred, shall arrive ; ere morn the night is at
>   darkest.

In 1846 Mr. Neale took the wardenship of Sackville College, East Grinstead, an ancient foundation for pensioners; **a fine old** building with chapel, dining hall, and warden's apartments value £25 a year: it was a home, and that **was all** the preferment that ever fell to **the lot of this** great divine, historian, and poet. **As I have said, Dr. Neale was** affectionate in all relations of life; **his wedding** letter to a friend, ten years after his own marriage, was characteristic.

"**Sackville** College,

"February 9th, 1852.

"My Dear ——,

"I had **not the least idea the event which I** heard of yesterday was in **contemplation,** and **so felt quite** surprised as well **as very glad.** Pray accept my best **congratulations; they must, of course, be quite** general, inasmuch **as I know not your** fair bride's **name.** To her indeed, **if she will accept them, I can offer them** more particularly because **I do know you; I know not a** better **wish to give you** than the last **verse of the** 128th psalm. **I see you just** avoided Septuagesima. **I know not where you are, but if** it should **be** anywhere so that you **could** give us **a** look in on **your** way back **I hope** you will **do so;** *you* would **like to** see the College, **and** I **shall have the pleasure of being** introduced **to your bride.**

"Yours very truly,

"J. M. Neale."

That **visit was not paid** for some time, and indeed

not till the early struggles of Sackville College and its
warden were nearly over. They were years of misunderstanding and prejudice against daily prayers, celebrations with decent ceremonial, and frequent preaching
and teaching bestowed on the place and its inmates ;
a struggle in which it took years and years of patient
waiting and working to convince Bishop Gilbert, of
Chichester, that here was a staunch loyal son of the
Church of England, and one of her noblest defenders at
the time Newman and a few of the best known Tractarians deserted her ; a man who knew more about
Church history and liturgiology, the true story of
the Eastern Churches, and the Western claims, than
half the modern doctors of the Roman Church put
together ; the last man to believe that no true Church
could exist out of visible communion with Rome.
With reference to the Privy Council judgments, his
*Few Words of **Hope** in the **Present** Crisis of the English
Church* met with deep gratitude from thousands of
anxious hearts ; and the Sisters of East Grinstead have
done a real work for all time by reprinting it in full in
the *St. Margaret's Magazine* for January, 1892 (Skeffing-
ton & Co.). Many of Dr. Neale's early works are un-
attainable now, and it is also a most happy thought of
the sisters to reprint at times portions of essays, poems,
hymns, etc., from these scarce works in their magazine.
One of my friend's visits to Sackville College was when
most of those early trials were over, and the beginning

of Dr. Neale's great practical work of the grand nursing sisterhood he founded was in progress. In person Dr. **Neale was** tall and dark, and at first might be thought stern in expression, reminding one of the portrait of another great divine of the Church, Bishop Jeremy Taylor. After going over the old building, the pensioners' rooms, the **restored** beautiful chapel, the **hall and** the warden's rooms, commanding **lovely Sussex views, my** friend was introduced to the study, literally packed and lined and hung across with **books ;** at the four corners were four desks, at **which** the warden always **stood to work.** At one desk, perhaps, **the** history of the **Eastern** Church was in progress, **at** another poems **and hymns, at another commentaries on** the Psalms, **and at** the **fourth one of the brilliant** tales **or** stories, such as *Agnes de* **Tracey, Ayton** *Priory, Shepperton Manor, Duchenier, Tales of Christian Heroism* **and** *Endurance,* etc.

Staying a day **or** two my friend realised **the** wonderfully busy life **led by** this scholar and priest. Calls and claims on all sides, duties to the sisters, the orphans, **the old people of the** College ; and duties to those, not **a few, who** asked **for** solutions on knotty **points** of theology, **canon law, history,** politics, **and** liturgiology.

On the Sunday afternoon of the visit **a** sister was nursing at some distant town, and was in some difficulty **or trouble.** Mr. Neale went off by the first train, asking my friend to take the evening service in the College chapel, and to read one of his sermons. No duty seemed to be neglected. He wrote and printed several volumes of reading for the aged, throwing himself into the feelings, hopes, and fears of the old pensioners. Children were especially cared for in sermons, tales, allegories, and hymns. It would fill a page were I to try and name all the hymns only, Dr. Neale wrote. A very large proportion of *Hymns Ancient and Modern* was from his pen. All this was done, and home duties were carefully and brightly fulfilled. It would be out of my province to describe how, in the midst of all this absorbing outside work, his home, with Mrs. Neale, and his five children growing up, was his delight and recreation, as they themselves have said (in the *St. Margaret's Magazine*, January, 1893). " Surely children never had a happier home : the nursery and all its patter, hopping, skipping, and singing never disturbed papa ; then the walks, the talks, the teaching, the reading, the writing. Shakespeare, Milton, Southey, Coleridge, Hood and others, all introduced to those children in due course." But what of Mrs. Neale ? We admire the bright scholar and divine, but we must indeed stop to think most highly of his helpmeet ; very few women can be the wife of a great genius with anything like full success, but Mrs. Neale was this and more ; one in all his hopes, plans, works, and wishes, with a courage and energy that no complications of troubles ever seemed to quell, supplying exactly what might be needed in his simple, trustful life (a grandmother, as we used to say, to the sisterhood), musical, which he was not, and indeed the very stay of such a man in all joy and sorrow. I have not space to say more, but can add from one who knew him well that he was most unworldly, unselfish, had very modest views of his own works, and was never one to drive a bargain about them. One instance I remember when his publisher spoke highly, as every one did, of that masterpiece and brilliant historical tale *Theodora Phranza, or the Siege of Constantinople*, and suggested another story of the kind. "My good friend, I couldn't write a book to order," was his reply; and that was true; all his work was spontaneous, suggested by his own great genius. As in his home so in his life and habits all was most simple and frugal. Sleeping once at a friend's house in Brighton, there was much thought what he would like to eat after a late lecture; the good man preferred the baked potatoes to anything else on the table. Dr. Neale died in August, 1866, and his funeral was attended by hundreds of clergy and laity, and the procession reached half a mile along the street of East Grinstead. Mrs. Neale outlived her husband some eight or nine years. One of her last letters to my friend was to express her thankfulness that her youngest, Margaret, was about to be married to Malcolm, the son of Mr. Sutherland Græme (of whom I have already spoken); then, in the last words, the true mother's heart spoke, " there is only one thing— one word—the Orkneys for her home ! and that is dismaying to her mother ". The saddest of her letters is concerned with the appointment of a warden as successor to Dr. Neale, at Sackville College ; imagine the patron, Earl Delaware, being induced to go back to a warden contemplated by the statutes, a single man (in that large home), a layman in that dear chapel, a man incapable and afflicted, who had been an army surgeon and had resided in the town about one year ! Such an appointment was surely an indignity to Dr. Neale's memory. The wondrous way in which the sisterhood flourished and increased after his death showed the power and attraction of the life of him who founded it.

CHAPTER VIII.

IN a former chapter I spoke of the lonely life led by Mr. Cook at South Benfleet, but it was much the sort of life led by many of the country vicars in Essex before the day of railways; and in out-of-the-way parishes the vicar, no doubt, became much of a farmer, and more and more removed from the refinement and culture which distinguished the clergy of London and the large towns. And it was just this lowering in manners, and mode of service, that the Church Movement, when some of its endless pamphlets, tracts, sermons, lectures, verses and tales penetrated so far, influenced for a better state of things.

Perhaps it was one of these old-fashioned vicars, half farmer, half parson, of whom Bishop Blomfield related the story, how he was invited to dinner at Fulham Palace, and, arriving between six and seven, found the party in the full enjoyment of afternoon tea; he enjoyed the tea and cake, etc., and concluded that dinner was over; in this idea he was strengthened when the servants brought in the silver candlesticks, and one of them showed him to his bedroom. Then he thought what early and primitive hours the bishop kept. How-

13 (193)

ever, he partly **undressed and lay down on** the bed, **and, being** tired **with his unusual journey,** was almost dozing, **when there came a knock at the** door, and "**Dinner's** on table, sir," effectually roused him; **he was rather late** at the dinner-table, **and, of** course, apologised; **such an** unpleasant *contretemps* can hardly **occur** again.

We are now thinking **of** the brighter state of things which set in **after 1840; and in this** same county of Essex there **were** many of **these** bright spots. The remembrance of **one** such place **has quite** recently occurred, and again **it is Mr. Heygate** who has recorded a little about the life of the late Vicar of Leigh, near Southend, **to** whom he was curate for some years. **Mr. King, the vicar,** was brother to the **Bishop of** Lincoln, and a **most worthy** worker in his steps. **Just before** reaching **Southend,** the fine old tower—quite a seamark—of St. Clement, Leigh, stands **out boldly,** and the church and services **were a** blessing to **many** of the visitors to Southend, **who** gladly walked **out there.** On Sunday afternoon the grand old church **(Late** Perpendicular) **was a** sight to record; it was quite **full** of blue-jackets, **who** joined **well in** the bright, **hearty** service, and listened to the splendid preaching **of Mr. Heygate, Mr. King, and** sometimes the bishop (then chaplain at **Cuddesden** College), when **he was** staying at the vicarage.

A little lower down is Corringham, where the Rev. S.

S. Greatheed was for some years vicar. He was a high authority on old Church music, a contributor to the *Ecclesiologist*, and set to music some of Dr. Neale's beautiful carols.

Higher up again, towards Mersea Island, is Southminster, a village five miles from the sea; it has a large Perpendicular Cruciform church with Norman work. Here, for many years, the Rev. G. C. Berkeley was vicar, a thorough churchman of the Keble and Williams school, and a very bright presence among his friends in London on his occasional visits there.

At Chelmsford, Colchester, and Hadleigh (especially the latter, so well restored under Chancellor Espin), things were well advancing, and also at Messing, where the Rev. T. Henderson was vicar; he was one of the preachers at St. Bartholomew's, Moor Lane, when the Church revival was begun there with that series of sermons, "Advent Warnings". Higher up still, on the borders of Suffolk, Mr. Foster, Vicar of Foxearth, had daily service and frequent Communions.

In 1850 the fine old church of Halstead was restored while Archdeacon Burney (now Vicar of St. Mark's, Surbiton) was vicar.

In another part of Essex, the good work by Archdeacon Grant, of Romford, should be told of; and not far, at Langdon Hill, is the Rev. Alfred Poole, one of the St. Barnabas clergy who suffered in the misunderstanding and outcry about Confession. His rector, Mr.

Liddell, stood by him **loyally.   At** Barking, Mr. Liddell, **afterwards   of   St.   Paul's,   Knightsbridge,** should be thought **of.**

Coggeshall, **too,** with **its old** church and many interesting remains of the Abbey, etc., should be named. Bishop **Mant was vicar** there in 1813 ; he was chaplain to Archbishop Sutton, **and in** full correspondence with Joshua Watson, Bishop Van Mildert, and others, about the publications of the S.P.C.K. ; and among them was his *Bible and Prayer* **Book Commentary, and** other valuable work **for** those times.   **Mr. W. J.** Dampier **was,** at the time **I refer to,** and **for some** years, vicar **here; and** though **not very strong,** was well known **as an** excellent churchman, and **a kind,** hard-working parish priest; **to the poor** and afflicted he was ever most gentle and helpful.   One curious case of accident occurred in his parish, in which Mr. Dampier gave great assistance **in many ways. A** fine young fellow fell from a large **fruit tree on to** the ground, and entirely **lost the use of** his hands and feet.   As he lay on his bed, week after week, it was his great trouble that all means of earning a living seemed to **be impossible.** Then **it occurred to him that** if **he could hold** a pencil in his mouth he **could copy** some drawings' **or** prints, and he **was** encouraged **by the vicar** and others, and persevered **till in** course of time he could make drawings and etchings with his mouth, while his kind friends helped him to dispose of **them;** and so he was able to earn a little.

I remember seeing some of these copies of Vandyke's Charles the First and other heads, and they were etched with wonderful **care** and accuracy. Mr. Dampier took deep interest in this poor man all his life, and **often** helped to dispose of his works.

Mr. Neave, of Epping, **was** well known as a good churchman.

We now come to Harlow, a small market town, with a large parish church and two district churches—St. John the Baptist **and** St. Mary's. In 1835, the Rev. Charles Miller, son of a former vicar, was appointed; he was fresh from Oxford, where he had been a Demy of Magdalen, **and was** entirely in accord with the early Tractarian writers **and** leaders. He was a student, and somewhat eccentric. The subject of tithes and offerings **in Old** Testament **and** Christian history he made his **study ;** and a year after his appointment the famous Tithe Commutation Act was passed, **by which** tithes **were** commuted for a rent charge, based on average **prices of wheat, barley,** oats, etc., for seven years.

From 1836 to 1847 there were various amendments to this Act, and during the whole of these years Mr. Miller waged tremendous war with the principle of the Tithe Commutation Act, denouncing it as a distinct denial of God's providence, holding that the Divine will was that the tithe should depend on the prosperity and value of the land, the blessing **and** increase in crops, **flocks, and** cattle, and so might vary from time to time.

The following is the title of one of his protests, and will give our readers some idea of **the bold,** earnest, and enthusiastic Vicar of Harlow :—

" Tithes, or Heathenism.   Reasons **for** not accepting the **Tithe** Commissioners' award, most dutifully and respectfully submitted **to the** Queen of England, the Parliament, **and** the **People, in** a Second Letter to the Right Honourable Sir George Grey, M.P., Her Majesty's Secretary of State for the Home Department, by Charles Miller, M.A., Vicar of Harlow."

It is only fair to say that however eccentric or quixotic he was thought, he had **indeed** the courage of his convictions, **as** for years and **years** he refused to receive any tithes at all.

I will not inflict **upon** my readers much more of so **dry a** subject as tithes, but their sacred origin and **history in** connection with the course of the Church's work make them a subject **of** interest to many churchmen.   Anyway, much attention was drawn to **them** during the years following the Tithe Commutation Act; and in 1846 a most valuable society was founded, called the **"Tithe** Redemption Trust," to encourage spiritual and lay owners of alienated tithes to restore them to the spiritual purposes for which they were originally ordained, to assist such owners, either by grants of money or by paying the expenses of conveyance, or by legal advice, in applying their tithes towards relieving the spiritual destitution of the parish or chapelry whence they arose, by annexing such tithes to the endowment of the parish church or chapel, or by endowing with such tithes new district churches therein. Part of the plan was to **make** applications to Parliament to facilitate the means of accomplishing these objects. Such names as Lord John Manners, Rev. W. W. Malet of Ardeley, Sir Stephen **Glynne, Sir** Roundell **Palmer,** Dr. Irons, Arthur Powell, Charles Dingwall, with **the** archbishop and several bishops, **were** among the founders and patrons. This society continues **its labours still in** Bridge Street, Westminster. The work **was** thoroughly practical ; **by** 1864 tithes **had** by their aid been restored to the Church **to** the amount of £1035 per annum, and in June, 1885, tithes amounting to £4541 had been restored.

Mr. Miller, at **Harlow, had** frequent services, weekly **Communion, and a simple but careful ritual.** About **1839, the district church of St. John the** Baptist was **built for a** distant part of the long straggling parish ; **and it is** in this church and its incumbent I would seek to interest my readers, with the record of one of the most saintly lives in connection with **the** Church Movement —not unworthy, if all could be told, to rank with that of the Curé, d'Ars—such **a life** had a good influence on **all who were** trying **to** follow in the steps **of** holy ex- **amples.** This was Charles Middleton McLeod, who was **curate of Latton, an adjoining** parish ; and when the **district** church of St. John the Baptist was built, Mr. **Miller offered** him the **incumbency ; there he** worked for more than thirty years with the stipend of a curate, and was but little known out of his own parish. There is not a great deal to tell, but what little there is should certainly be valued by good Church folk.

Charles Middleton McLeod was born at Wheeley in Essex, where his father, Dr. Roderick McLeod, was rector, about the year 1800. Some years after, Dr. McLeod became Rector of St. Anne's, Soho, then an important parish in London, holding rank with St. James's, Piccadilly, and St. George's, Hanover Square. I fear there is nothing to tell of Mr. McLeod's youth. His mother died probably when he was quite young; and there is no doubt that the quiet, devout life of active goodness which his elder sister, Wilhelmina, led at St. Anne's, had much to do with her brother Charles's course, which developed into the higher life fostered by the Church revival.

His visits to London were not frequent, and even during his father's lifetime he was never, I think, in St. Anne's Church on a Sunday; he sometimes took a Baptism or Churching in the week-day, and, as I have said, alarmed the old parish clerk by his deep reverence and devotion, as if he quite realised the sacredness of holy places and things, even though they were not so arranged as to impress it visibly upon us, as happily they often are now.

It seemed as if he never forgot that he was the servant of his Divine Master. His time, his labour, and

all the money he possessed were spent on the Church and poor of that Master; to speak of his **way of** life as simple, would but feebly express the strictness and entire self-denial of his daily course. **He** allowed himself nothing that was not absolutely necessary; the utmost recreation that he gave himself on his few visits to London was to hear some good sacred music or concert, to which **he** was taken by some old friends in his father's parish. When **in** town, he was sure to be **at the** early service or celebration at Margaret Chapel **or** Westminster Abbey. Few country churches could compare with St. John's, Harlow, for plain and simple order; though it was but an ordinary building, with choir stalls, screen, stained-glass windows, organ, organ chamber (almost the last addition he lived **to make),** frontals, hangings, vestments, and an altar triptych of **the** Crucifixion, painted **by** O'Connor, **it was** yet a beautiful home that will speak **of** its first vicar for many **a** day to come. He himself attended **to** every minute detail of his church **and** service, and with his own **hand** prepared every single thing for **that** worship up to the very last Sunday, when he could scarcely walk to the pulpit for his evening sermon; **nothing** was too small, down to the least ornament or vessel, and its belongings, for his own special care. During his incumbency, everything that could add to **the** goodness of church, churchyard, and service was by degrees procured; and for this not only would he devote

all moneys that came into his possession, and the offerings of a few who knew him and his work, but he would
also part with any personal thing that was not really
needed by him.   To obtain what was needful for his
church or poor he would give all that could be spared
by the utmost frugality.   He strictly kept all fast-days,
Lent, and fasting Communion, with a bright, cheerful
way through it all, marking saints' days and festivals
by some changes ; and on Sundays, for many years, had
some ten or twelve of his poorest parishioners to dine
with him—in summer time out on his lawn.   No one
could visit his home—plain almost to meanness with its
simple necessaries—without feeling that his life, and all
that he had, was devoted to others.   To stay a few days
in his house, as a friend once said, was a distinct privilege, and going back to town and business was like
entering another world.   The early and other celebrations and services, which he took all those years single-
handed, were so many and so frequent that few could be
found physically able to go through them.   His choir
and its work were one of his chief cares ; and as he was
a true gentleman of refined and cultured taste, he made
the very best of what was after all but a plain village
choir.   The musical parts of his late celebration were
admirably sung by eight or ten of the elder girls in his
school, who sat in the seat nearest to the chancel.   He
was the friend and adviser of every one of his choir, and
would write to those who had left his parish and care,

and keep them up to the better way of life that he had taught and shown to them.

Though naturally of a shy and retiring nature, there **was** one occasion in each year when he came, as it were, more prominently before his friends, and that was on the dedication festival of his church, when he would issue invitations to friends **in** London and elsewhere. **On each** St. John Baptist's Day as it came round, for nearly twenty years, early in the morning, some thirty or **forty** ladies and gentlemen might be seen on the platform of the Eastern Counties Railway, on their way to spend **the** day at Harlow ; many of the clergy, churchmen, and churchwomen of London, from Stoke Newington, **St.** Barnabas, St. Bartholomew's, from his old parish of St. Anne and others, all looking forward with pleasure to **do** honour to this country dedication feast, and join in good wishes for **the vicar,** who never **failed** to welcome every individual visitor with kind **words and smile.** I must record the names of a few. The well-known and beloved physician, Mr. Brett, the **founder of** St. Matthias and the promoter of other **good** schemes of church-building, was seldom absent from these gatherings, his genial presence brightening, as it were, the whole day, and with him were often his closest friends. The names of Beck, Porter, Hazard, Nottingham ; the Rev. **T.** Simpson Evans, Vicar of Shoreditch ; Rev. W. Scott, of Christ Church, Hoxton; **J. Fuller** Russell, Vicar of St. James's, Enfield ; **the**

Rev. W. J. Blew, and very many others, come to one's
mind. The twenty-five miles were soon travelled, and
the London visitors were at once in cordial intercourse
with the country vicars and friends in the neighbourhood. The influence of this one saintly man was
surely felt all around; and more reverence, order, and
frequent services were to be found in many a quiet,
out-of-the-way church in the neighbourhood. The
preachers on these occasions were some of the very
best men in London and the country. Among his
neighbours were Mr. Houghton, of Matching; Hill, of
Sheering; Moody, of Gilston (Gilston Park was the
residence for years of J. Plumer Ward, the author of
Tremaine, and a great writer and politician in the days
of Lord Melville and Lord Liverpool); Malet, Vicar of
Ardeley, near Buntingford, and many others.

A near neighbour of some renown was W. S. Copeland, Vicar of Farnham, on the other side of the railway, for some time curate to Dr. Newman at Littlemore,
and a great writer and translator in the literature and
hymnology of the Tractarian Movement, editor also
of Dr. Newman's *Parochial Sermons*. On his death in
1885, part of his fine library, through his executor,
Mr. Copeland Borlase, found a home—let us hope a
congenial one—in the Library of the National Liberal
Club.

There was an early celebration, the choral one took
place at eleven, when a sermon was preached, and about

one rich and poor dined together in a large tent. After dinner there were toasts and speeches (these latter were anything but dry, and were thoroughly enjoyed by every one); hearty interchanges of views as to the way in which the work they all cared so much for, was making way; good sound Christian politics, and no unkindness or sarcasm; and now and then the Vicar of Harlow would bring in his subject of tithes and offerings, and speak very straightly about trade and business, and what was meant by honesty and fair dealing therein.

One year there was a grand patriarchal clergyman in the company, and he preached and spoke too with all the vigour and brightness of youth, and interested and amused us all with an account of his Gloucestershire parish; this was the Rev. James Davies, Vicar of Abenhall, not far from Stroud, then in his eightieth year; this was the vicar to whom Mr. Thomas Keble in 1829 introduced Isaac Williams for his title and first curacy, the curacy of Windrush (on which Thomas Keble had been ordained fourteen years before). Isaac Williams records it in his autobiography: " I was ordained at Christmas, and lived there for two years with James Davies, my vicar, who has been my most esteemed friend ever since ".

About 150 of the poor sat down to dinner, and evensong with a sermon was at half-past three. Tea was at five, and the rest of the day was much enjoyed, and spent in various games and amusements for the school children. The reality and earnestness of this simple festival impressed all who had the happiness to join in it, and to the London folk especially it was most refreshing and encouraging.

This dedication festival was discontinued about 1861, so far as invitations to friends at a distance went, because it involved an outlay that the vicar could not spare from the church and parish ; but it was always kept for the school children, choir and poor, and he took care that they should thoroughly enjoy St. John the Baptist's Day as it came round, up to the last that he saw on earth.

And as his life was, so was his death, on Septuagesima, 1871. In his last illness, though he was in much pain, he still thought of others, and also calmly and clearly gave all directions for his own burial to every particular, and received his last communion from an old friend and neighbour. He was, by his own desire, laid in the church till the funeral, in the vestments in which he had been wont for years to celebrate the blessed Sacrament, and many went in to pray and take a farewell look at him who had been to them a pattern and a shepherd true indeed.

The funeral was one to be remembered. Such a life, though most quiet and self-renouncing, could not but attract, and very many were there to whom such a loss could not easily be supplied. The hymns "Jesus lives,"

and "Brother, now thy **toils** are over," were sung.
After the burial service lesson, holy communion **was**
celebrated by the Vicar **of** St. Mary Magdalen's Church,
Harlow, served by Mr. Miller, vicar **of** the parish
church. The church was full of earnest, sorrowing
parishioners and friends. Among **the** special mourners
were his friend and executor, **the Rev. A. B.** Goulden,
formerly Curate of St. Peter's, **Vauxhall, and now** for
twenty **years an** earnest labourer **in** his poor South
London **parish of** St. Alphege, Southwark; Mr. and
Mrs. Gauntlett, Mr. Perry Watlington, the squire of **the**
parish, the vicars of the surrounding parishes, **and** other
old friends. The service was bright, **as he** would have
had it. The grave **was at** the back **of** the chancel, **a**
spot selected by himself.

His will was written as he dictated, with **a** profession
of faith **and an** offering of his soul to God in deepest
humility and sense of unworthiness. **He** had kept but
little money, though in his life-time **money had been**
left to him; he left remembrances to the poor and his
god-children, etc., and **the** rest was to go to keep his
old servant and his wife **for their** lives. The other dis-
trict church **of St.** Mary Magdalen's, Harlow, has a good
record of real work up to the present day. The vicar is
Mr. Elwell, whose labours have been successful in raising a substantial and beautiful church in the place of
the very small original church of the district.

In making a longer record of such lives as this, and

of Mr. Cook, of South Benfleet, it may be borne in mind that they are but specimens of many hundred such lives which could be written, and that it was by such that the Movement spread and affected the daily lives of many thousands.

There are two other short sketches of country clergy. One is of the Rev. Robert Alfred Suckling, Perpetual Curate of Bussage, near Stroud, whose memoir, with correspondence, was written by Mr. Isaac Williams in 1852, to perpetuate the influence of such a character beyond his immediate circle; and from this some of these notes are taken. He was the eldest son and heir of the ancient family of that name at Woodton, in Norfolk. The name is familiar : Sir John Suckling, the poet, and his father (who was privy councillor to Kings James and Charles I.) were of the same family, as were the mother of Lord Nelson and her brother, Captain Suckling. R. A. Suckling was a sailor from 1831 to 1839. He left the sea from no feeling of disappointment, but he aspired to some higher and better life, and this feeling was strengthened by having been twice restored, when almost beyond hope, from the yellow fever on the coast of Africa. In 1839 he submitted to a large sacrifice in consenting to cut off the entail of the Woodton property. He went to Caius College, Cambridge, and was ordained on a title to Kemerton, under the vicar, Archdeacon Thorp, a model high churchman and parish priest, through whose work with his curates, many of the best men in the Church were sent forth. Of this vicar Mr. Suckling records the kindness and generosity; he gave him a very liberal stipend, and begged him to spend the income of the living as if he were rector so frequently that he had no hesitation in laying out money in his name—five, ten, and even twenty pounds at a time. Of his curate, Archdeacon Thorp tells how great was his influence in infusing life and power into the outward forms of godliness, then assuming their place in the Movement.

Mr. Suckling set to work to know every one in the parish, opened and closed the schools daily with prayers. He made acquaintance with many who had leisure while walking, both at Kemerton and at Bussage; his was a close individual concern and sympathy for others; he did not consider it enough to take a family collectively, but every member of that family was the object of his concern and care. A neighbour noticed that it was remarkable how he would watch and wait whole days and nights on one of his flock, waiting for an opportunity, if haply he might find it, to gain that one.

In 1846 he was absent from ill-health, but even in illness and absence that watchful care and tenderness for the objects of his charge characterised all his letters, of which a great many are printed in Mr. Isaac Williams' memoir.

In 1846 he was able to accept the charge of the new

church at Bussage, near Bisley. A family at that time resident in the parish of Bisley had united to build a church there, and this became known to a party of young men at Oxford, who had among themselves raised £2000 to build a church in some place where an endowment could be procured, and the Church system carried out. The church was worthy of the lovely spot and of the good purpose of the unknown founders. There Mr. Suckling set to work; it was peculiar to him to dare and venture, and to succeed : in the parish, the church and services, the choir, the dispensary, the workhouse, and afterwards the penitentiary, all went together with real work ; the quality by which his friends described him was " reality "—his singular reality.

It was said that he realised in life the unseen to a remarkable degree. His influence was wonderful, and he felt deeply how responsible he was in that way. A friend once observed that " it was more easy to be religious in conversation and action in his house than in any other. On my first visit—it was just upon twelve o'clock—he gently asked me if I would join with him in his usual prayer for that hour from *Bishop Cosin's Devotions*." It was the custom of John Keble and his curates to be in church some time before service ; and this was Mr. Suckling's plan too, interceding for those of his flock who did come to church, and for those who were hindered.

His letters show **his** great **power** of sympathy, com-**passion, and** gentleness for every kind of difficulty, pain, distress, and suffering. He would visit the dispensary at Stroud, and the workhouse, and would **remark to his curate** that he **never** left the sick ward without feeling strengthened. Many of those who had **letters from** him would **say, "I** have known no greater earthly consolation in trouble than his gentle words and affectionate sympathy".

Mr. Suckling was liberal to the utmost extent **of his power:** he subscribed to the fund for building **Perth** Cathedral, and among the offerings were several articles of plate, with two crests upon them; and a friend hinted that they probably constituted the last articles of that **kind,** or value, that he possessed. Time **and** space would fail to tell of his care for the young, the sick, and **the poor,** and the way **in** which **he** helped them by **word and by** his letters. **I** make room for one instance: **A** woman **had a** little boy killed at **a** mill: she was **asked if** she had seen Mr. Suckling. "O yes," she **replied, "I sent** for him **at once; I** felt as if **I** knew **not how to bear** it till he **came." In** 1851, a house of mercy—a refuge—was established in that part, with sisters **of mercy,** and he threw himself heartily into the **work** as chaplain.

He died on All Saints' Day, 1851, having celebrated the Holy Communion in the morning. The last few **weeks of** his life he seemed to be preparing for the end, as if he knew it was coming; he spent, we are told, hours daily in intercession for his little flock, whose every trial was his care. His heart was set upon them. And he was laid amidst that flock in the churchyard on the lovely slope of the Gloucestershire hills. A vignette of the church engraved by Willmore is on the title-page of Mr. Williams' memoir.

One more short memory is that of the Rev. Thomas H. B. Bund, M.A., of Trinity College, Cambridge, eldest son of Colonel Bund, of Upper Wick, Worcester. After his degree he was a student of the Inner Temple, and was called to the Bar, and for two years went the Oxford Circuit. He was some short time after a candidate for ordination, and was ordained deacon and priest by the Bishop of Gloucester and Bristol. He, too, was a curate in Gloucestershire, at Stroud, then under the charge of the Rev. Matthew Blagden Hale, afterwards Archdeacon of Adelaide, South Australia, and had a district church at Whiteshill assigned to him. Here he laboured, and devoted himself to the people with all his power, and they came to love and value him. Failing health came on, and he tried the air of South Devon, and then went to Malta and Egypt. After a stay at Malvern, he felt unfit to go back to the work of his parish; yet, anxious to do his Master's work among the poor, he took lodgings at Kidderminster for that purpose. He spent some weeks at Chelsea (the air of which had still some reputation for salubrity in consumption cases), and a few weeks at Ventnor, where he died **on** the 6th June, 1846, **and** was buried **at St.** John's, Worcester. His relations **all** bore witness that he never thought of himself, **but** did all he could to assist his fellow-creatures. **Just before he died he received the first copy** of his little **book** called *Aids to a Holy Life,* in form of **self-ex-** amination on the following subjects : The Right Employ- ment of Time—Humility—Brotherly Love—Government of the Tongue—Modest and becoming Behaviour—The **Love of** Money— Chastity— Mortification—Patience— Doing **all** Things for the Sake **of God—In Time** of Sickness, on Conformity to **the Will of** God. This little work of seventy pages was his only contribution to the literature of the Church **Movement, but** it was practical **and** useful, and helped others **in the** good way which during his short life **on earth he** had so carefully trod.

CHAPTER IX.

IN recording some smaller villages where Church work was done, it is feared that there may be a great deal of sameness in the narrative; and yet, if we are to give some idea of how the Movement made its way in towns and villages, it will not do to leave them out.

Of course, there is no pretence at a complete list; indeed, to attempt that would require a small library. The power and strength of the Movement are fairly shown by the large number of towns and villages of which mention can be made. Brighton has certainly been for many years a very important centre, and the seekers after health and enjoyment there have found Church privileges that scarcely belong to any other town of its size and population. We will take first a few places near. At Ditchling, on the South Downs, Mr. Hutchinson did good work for many years; and the simple, solid restoration of that church was quite an example for those who are given to the idea that a spick-and-span newness is the true principle of restoration. Mr. Campion, of Westmeston, close by, was ever the kind, genial country parson and gentleman, while the head of his family, Mr. Campion, of Danny Park, was a

true model of an English squire and churchman, and
Mrs. Campion **was** his helpmeet in all good plans
and works **of** kindness. At St. Michael and St. Anne's,
Lewes, increase **of** services and reverence were conspicuous ; and, as we go towards Newhaven, we pass
the scene of the Rev. H. M. Buck's thirty years' labours
at Seaford, **a** bright **and** pleasant seaside resort, but
not by any means an easy kind of material on which **to**
work in Church matters ; but Mr. Buck has never been
daunted, and soon after he became vicar the ancient
parish church was restored and a spacious chancel
added. Then the fine old tower was restored, with a
new clock **and bell and a** new roof to the nave, and new
framework for the eight bells. Daily service, weekly
Communion, Saints' Day Communion, have been kept
up for years : very few small seaside towns are blessed
with all the privileges that Mr. Buck **has** given to
Seaford. Pevensey, too, has for years had a vicar of the
good old Church school, Archdeacon Sutton ; and **a**
little way inland is Hurstmonceaux, **so** long the residence of the Hares, that brilliant and talented family,
the friends of F. D. Maurice, and his sister, the authoress
of *Sickness, its Trials and Blessings*, etc. The rector of
later years, Mr. **Wilde, is one** of **a** more orthodox
school. Bexhill was in very early days under a vicar,
Mr. Simpson, one of the genuine Oxford school
of divines. Within a walk of Bexhill comes St.
Leonard's-on-Sea, where **the** pioneer of the Church

Movement in that part of the county, the Rev. C. L. Vaughan, of Christ Church, has been labouring for thirty years, and claims the gratitude of very many churchmen and churchwomen who have had the privileges in Church matters that have been provided for them, both as residents and as visitors in search of health and strength. The fine and costly church which he has built, the beautiful and constant services, with all the adjuncts of ceremonial and orthodox teaching; the influence and example afforded by him and his clergy in that now populous suburb of Hastings, call indeed for the heartfelt thanks of all true churchmen. St. John the Divine is a church close to this district, where excellent work is done. In Hastings itself, though some of the churches were in early days of an old-fashioned type, the work has more recently developed in the best direction,—especially in the church of Holy Trinity, where the genial and hard-working Dr. Sanderson, formerly Headmaster of Lancing, is doing a great work as vicar of that parish; the Canonry, which is supposed to give time for rest and study, being used to enable him to be the hard-working parish priest,—with a daily celebration and most constant and carefully arranged services, and preaching of a very high order. His Parish Magazine is a model for such a town, parish, and work.

Some way inland, again, is Little Horsted, the seat of Mr. Francis Barchard, one of those laymen whose quiet, constant life has been a considerable power, and his years of work for the community of East Grinstead alone deserve deep admiration and acknowledgment.

The work at Brighton began in the early days of the fifties, with the building of St. Paul's Church in West Street, the incumbent of which was the Rev. Arthur Douglas Wagner, son of the Rev. Henry Michell Wagner, the then Vicar of Brighton; and, no doubt, very much of the work done in Brighton afterwards was due to the fact that this clever, business-like, and earnest vicar, of the old-fashioned orthodox type, of the Joshua Watson, Churton, and Sikes school, was at the head of matters. Tall, thin, and active, Mr. Wagner about the town, in his small narrow brougham, was a familiar figure for years. A few years before the time of which we speak, it seemed quite a wonder that a little old church at the top of a steep hill—restored in 1853 as a memorial to the Duke of Wellington—was the parish church of that rapidly growing town; there assembled all the parochial officials of the town, and the church was almost inconveniently crowded at every service. In those days, too, the Evangelical party was in possession of most of the popular churches and chapels in the town—Mr. Clay at St. Margaret's, Mr. Vaughan at Christ Church, Mr. E. V. Elliott at St. Mary's, Mr. Maitland at St. James's Chapel. At the Chapel Royal, Mr. Trocke was of the old-fashioned,

orthodox school, as were also the Rev. Robert Anderson
and the Rev. C. E. Kennaway.   **Mr.** Robertson at
Trinity Chapel, Ship Street, **was of no school** but his
own.   Many of these chapels were wonderfully transformed in after days, and all of them more or less
improved in outward matters as time went **on.   Mr.**
Henry Venn Elliott's large Grecian style of chapel was
to develop **into a** very fine Gothic church, very much
after the style **of one of Mr.** Pearson's best buildings ;
St. James's **was to go through** a great transformation,
and then **to settle down into its present neat and simple**
church ; **St.** Margaret's and the Chapel **Royal (once a**
perfect wilderness of pews, with the Royal Arms as the
great piece of symbolism) were hardly to be recognised ;
and Trinity Chapel, Ship Street, was to be much adorned
and beautified.   But in 1850 these buildings still had
their set form of worship : high pews, the altar behind
the three-decker, curtains, cushions, amen-clerk, choir
in gallery, etc., etc.   The Rev. Henry Venn Elliott, of
St. Mary's, was looked upon as the successor of Cecil,
Venn, **Simeon,** and the best **of** the Puritan school.
In many **ways there** seemed a less rigid **line** drawn
between these and the early High Churchmen.   **Dr.**
Pusey's son was **at** school in Sussex Square ; **the**
school attended St. Mary's Chapel, **and** he was prepared for Confirmation by **Mr. Henry** Venn Elliott, the
incumbent : Mrs. Bartlett's was a well-known and successful school, and afterwards, under her son-in-law, the

Rev. Charles Young, who was a High Churchman, well maintained its character and success. Some of those early Evangelicals, too, improved their services in many matters, especially the Rev. James Vaughan, one of the best and most deeply respected : it was said that he was most anxious for the better observance of Ascension Day, and had a celebration of Holy Communion for his people; but even with his great influence and power it was not easy to bring many of his congregation up to that level. On the vexed subject of Evening Communion it was said that Mr. Vaughan told his people from the pulpit that if any one came to the evening celebration who could by any possibility come at any other time he would discontinue it. Mr. Vaughan was large-hearted, and always spoke of Dr. Neale with affection and regard as an early member of his congregation, and appreciated the gift of some of his books from a friend.

Mr. H. M. Wagner's curates at the parish church were of the same school as himself, such as Mr. Mitchell and C. E. Douglass : the latter published two small books, the *Doctrine of Holy Baptism*, and *The One Fold of Christ*. Later on Mr. Wagner had for one of his curates Mr. Purchas, and it was from that curacy that he took the incumbency of St. James's Chapel, in St. James's Street. The building of St. Paul's in West Street was certainly the first important step of the Movement in Brighton, and the vicar was known to take the greatest interest in his son's church

and work, and for some years was a frequent preacher
in it.   Brighton Vicarage was a large Gothic mansion
in its own grounds, at the top of Montpelier Road, and
there for years lived the vicar, his sister, Miss Wagner
(of whom very many still have a loving remembrance,
and who, up to the last days of her active life, was
ever engaged in helping forward all that was good and
true), the Rev. A. D. Wagner, and frequently Mr.
Henry Wagner, a barrister and younger brother.   St.
Paul's has been for more than forty years too well
known and valued by thousands to need much description—its grand chancel, altar, altar triptych by
Rossetti, standard lights, with everything of the very
best and most costly, lovingly added to year after year
with enrichments in metal-work, paintings, decorations,
stained-glass windows, etc., throughout.   Such an immense advance on anything Brighton had known before
1850 was much talked about, and hundreds came from
far and wide to see this beautiful church and to join in
such a service of worship, praise and thanksgiving as
few then had dreamed of.   No wonder it was thronged
with devout worshippers ; and the work of the churchwardens and vergers was no sinecure ; at the time of the
late celebration the one narrow chancel-screen door, as
the only ingress to and egress from the altar, required
careful and firm attention, and on Sunday evenings the
churchwardens and four vergers failed often to find seats
for all the people who came.   Perhaps the best time to

really impress one with the great beauty of this church
was at the early communion on fine Sunday mornings.
In early days, Mr. White, the organist, who has left a
memory **of much that was** excellent both as a church-
man and **a** musician, was present, and often collected
the offertory; and at Evensong, who can forget **the**
thrill **and** outburst **of song** in those grand Parisian
tones for the *Magnificat* and *Nunc Dimittis,* kept up for
years without change or intermission, almost a type of
the simple unchanging firmness and determination of
the first **and present** incumbent, who was never one
given to **much change in** the ritual and service of his
church ? As years went on all that could enhance and
improve would be added, till a clear, definite ceremonial
was arrived at, in thorough accordance with the rubrics
and the catholic **and historical** character of the Church
of England; **and** that ritual, come what might, through
storm and sunshine, was and has been well and truly
maintained. Of course, there were storms, and they
were bravely borne, and a brilliant record might **be**
made of the early years of St. Paul's; excellent hard-
working clergy and **a** congregation thoroughly appreci-
ating all their work and teaching. Besides the Vicar of
Brighton, Mr. Arthur Wagner had the help of the Rev.
W. Gresley, Prebendary of Lichfield, for nearly seven
years, till the Church **of** All Saints, Boyne Hill, **was**
built in 1857. Mr. Gresley's share in spreading the
truest principles of the Church Movement by his works,

sermons, tales, historical and **theological,** is well known, bringing **the various** details **of improved doctrine and ritual** into **every-day** practice **in such stories as** *Bernard Leslie,* **the modern curate** facing the dust **and neglect and** abuses of ages, and doing **battle with the** opposing churchwardens and those who liked **to "let all such** things alone "; **and in** his *Portrait of an English Churchman,* showing **us the** thorough gentleman **and churchman in heart and action;** and in his stories **for** children, so fresh **and wholesome. All** recognised **the** effect of **Mr. Gresley's** Sunday evening sermons **on the young people of** that **large congregation :** this work **has been well carried** on **by others since, especially** by **the Rev. J. H.** Ashley Gibson, **once a curate** at St. Barnabas, **Pimlico. All honour to such men of one** curacy **in our Church! As in other** matters, so **in** the case **of** his curates, **Mr.** Wagner seldom changed; **and** a record of good names **could indeed be made,** though **it** would not be **easy to make it** chronologically. About 1855, Charles Beanlands was curate, afterwards well known and respected as **the** Vicar of St. Michael's, **Brighton. A** sermon of his at St. **Paul's** on St. Michael's Day **in that year,** seemed almost **to** give, as **it were, the** key-note to his **future** church and parish ; **it was an** extempore sermon of about half-an-hour, and **in it** the preacher went through every **mention** of Angels **and their** office in the Bible ; **it was so** well done, with **no hesitation** or apparent stop for a word, that in coming out, a friend asked how it was done; I think some one who knew replied that there **was** no doubt it was learnt off by heart. **To** those who remember that sermon, it was almost a coincidence **to hear** that the preacher **was chosen as the first incumbent of** the Church **of St. Michael and All** Angels, built by the munificence of the Misses Windle, who **afterwards** resided at Oxford. St. Michael's **has a** little history of its own, and curates and **friends of its own ;** so we will go back for a while to St. Paul's and its special curates. One name, **I am** sure, still stands **out** pre-eminently in the hearts and minds of those who were privileged to know him : it is that of the Rev. Randolph **Payne, one of** a family ever devoted to St. Paul's and its **work.** The father (also **Mr.** Randolph Payne, who lived at one time in Sloane Street, and went daily to St. Paul's, Knightsbridge) was one of its earliest churchwardens; and his widow and children, ever one in **their constant** attendance and work, have devoted a **life's service.** A younger son, the Rev. Alfred Payne, worked for some time in the north part of the town, at the Church of St. Bartholomew, where he was much valued and esteemed, till on his marriage he settled **in a** Yorkshire vicarage. But we are chiefly speaking of the elder brother, for nearly forty years curate of St. Paul's. **There** is not much to tell in the story of such a life, living at home with his family, taking a full share in the services of St. Paul's, seldom preaching (though when he did he reminded one of Keble and Isaac Williams, and of the *Plain Sermons by the Contributors to the Tracts for the Times*), little known to the outside world, but very much known to those who needed him as the true friend, adviser, and guide; such a gentle influence and saintly life most surely made a lasting mark on those who knew and on some who only heard of him; a lady who knew him used to say that she could not help thinking of him when she heard the words, "O ye holy and humble men of heart". The Rev. Randolph Payne died in March, 1889, and will be best known as friend and curate to Mr. Arthur Wagner; he had first the curacy of Chilton Folliott, Wilts, under Mr. Popham, one of the chaplains to Bishop Hamilton, of Salisbury, and then, for a short time, that of Wiston, under Mr. Napier, the parish in which stands Chanctonbury Ring, that famous hill with its splendid views (the Rev. Charles Goring was and is the squire): years after, it was pleasing to hear Mr. Napier often speak of Mr. Payne, remembering him with much regard. The Rev. R. Hammond, once at Bradfield and chaplain to one of Mr. Woodard's colleges, was also curate of St. Paul's for some years. The Rev. John Purchas, who had written and compiled the *Directorium Anglicanum*, when a curate at Orwell, near Cambridge, settled down in Brighton and was curate for some time at St. Paul's, where his slight and youthful appearance and quaint sermons (somewhat after the model of

Dr. A. B. Evans) interested many people. Some years after, **Mr.** Purchas became curate to Mr. Wagner, sen., **at** the parish church, and by him **was** presented **to the** incumbency of St. James's Chapel on **the death of Mr.** Maitland,—but the story of **that** chapel will **come later on in** our sketch. When **the** *Directorium* came out with its details of ceremonial and ritual, which were at first somewhat more historical and archæological than practical, it was said that visitors to Cambridge went over to Orwell expecting to see the *Directorium* in full **force and** practice, and were really **much** surprised **and** a little disappointed to find only **a** curate, with no power to change most of the old-fashioned ritual, driving **to** church in a by no means severe clerical costume.

But **though it is** not easy or **to be** expected **that** sketches such as this will follow in their due course as **to** time **and** date, we may **now go on to** tell that **a** beautiful church and constant services, **a** large congregation and much appreciation, were **a** very small part of **Mr.** Arthur Wagner's plans for the spiritual and temporal good of his native town. Very soon St. Mary's Home, carried on in several houses in Queen Square, at the top of North Street, and up the side of the steep hill (Wykeham Terrace) leading to the old church, was in **full work ; here soon came a** goodly number of sisters. **The** first superior **of** the home, Miss Gream, was sister **to** Dr. Gream, the physician (and also sister to the

" Mother **Ann** " of East Grinstead). Sister Harriet, Miss Hutton, **Miss Milner, and others** are **still** remembered with affection. The works of **St.** Mary's Home **were many and** important. In it **was a** home and refuge for **penitents ; a home** and school **for** children whose own **homes were too sad** to be worthy of **such a** sacred **name; a** hospital and dispensary ; a middle-class **school, giving a** good education **to** the daughters of **poorer** clergy and **others who had small incomes ; and other works, in** some of **which Mr. Wagner was assisted by several of the ladies of St. Paul's congregation, some of** whom lived near at hand and devoted **themselves in many ways.** One such name I will record, though **very** many others will **come to mind ; it** is that of **Miss Phillips,** daughter **of** the well-known portrait **painter and Royal** Academician of that name.

One of the earliest district churches built **by Mr.** Wagner **was** that of St. Mary Magdalene's, Bread Street, a small street running between **Church** Street and North Road, **right in the** midst of a poor fisher and working **population. This** was opened with a bright and cheerful **service, the Bishop of** Brechin preaching. This church **was served for a time** chiefly by the St. Paul's clergy; but **one of** the earliest **of** the curates **to have** special charge of it was the Rev. James H. **Cooper,** who worked here **among the** poor people for **some** years, and had the **happy** knack of being **as** genial **and** as much at home with them all as he **was** with the richer members of St.

Paul's congregation. Mr. Cooper preached well and plainly, and had many friends, among them such men as the author of *Tom Brown's School Days*; and one evening I remember the visit of Mr. Baring Gould to say "good-bye," on his leaving St. John's College, Hurstpierpoint, where he had been for a short time a master. Who would have thought that the tall, fair, bright, youthful-looking man would develop into the voluminous author, the biographer, historian, antiquary, sermon writer, and novelist, whom we seem to know so well? The choir was hearty but rough; indeed, the material was poor, and, as Mr. Cooper used to say, what voice could you expect from boys who probably had but a few herrings a week for food? Their exceeding drowsiness was a trial in some ways;—one has heard of the schoolmaster who left his class standing, telling his wife to wake him in three minutes, and then went back to his class refreshed: one of the boys in Bread Street choir certainly excelled this in rapid somnolence; he would go fast asleep during the alternate verses of the *Magnificat*, waking up each time as his own verse came round. Mr. Cooper was for some years curate to Mr. Maberly at Cuckfield, and left to take the Vicarage of Tarporley, in Cheshire, where he had a far more beautiful and reverent service than most country towns around that part were at all accustomed to. In later years, much to his own content and happiness, no doubt, Mr. Cooper has returned to the place of his early curacy as Vicar of

Cuckfield, succeeding Archdeacon Mount, himself a worthy successor to Mr. Maberly. For some years after this, St. Mary Magdalene's, Bread Street, was worked by the Rev. J. P. Kane, a well-known worker in the Movement, first at Cowley, then at St. George's-in-the-East, a most hardworking and indefatigable man: we used to say he was made of cast-iron, nothing fatigued him; one of the churchwardens of St. Paul's helped in the choir with him and read the lessons. Dr. Littledale, when in Brighton, which he often was, would frequently help and preach here: on one occasion I remarked to him that it was rather hard on us that we could not very decently laugh outright at some of the anecdotes in his sermon. "Now, that's just what I would like you to have done," he replied.

Those who know the various steep hills that run up eastward from the Old Steyne and Lewes Road will understand that the dwellers on those heights had great distances to go to any church in those early days. St. John's, Carlton Hill, the only church near, was not at all an easy place to find, though the incumbent, the Rev. Aaron Augustus Morgan, was a genial and well-known figure in Brighton: somewhat of a poet and Shakespearian scholar, he was known more in those ways than in that of the parish priest. Up one of these steep ascents, at the top of Southover Street, Mr. Wagner built another district church, to be known as the Church of the Annunciation; then at first worked by the Rev.

Charles Anderson, **now** Vicar of St. John's, Limehouse, **and** afterwards for some years by the Rev. Christopher Thompson, an excellent churchman and good musician, **once at St.** Bartholomew's, Moor Lane, and afterwards Vicar of Pensax, Worcestershire. The work here went forward, and the **late Rev.** George Chapman was appointed first **vicar of** this church. **The** story of his wonderfully holy life, and death in the midst of **his work, is still** fresh in the memory of all who knew him. **It is now many** years since **I** first saw him, a young man who had just taken **his** degree at Cambridge; **it was at Liverpool, on the** occasion of his brother's marriage, **in the days** of Mr. Bramah and Mr. Parnell at St. James-the-Less there. **He was then** the quiet, **retiring scholar, and became one of** the most saintly of **the** Church's priests, **living a** life that seemed to command the love and regard not only **of** his own people **and flock,** but of the very town itself, as **was witnessed at his** funeral. A small volume, with **a few** sketches **and** recollections, was put together and published **by** the Rev. **J. B. De la Bere,** Vicar of the district church of Buxted, **and** a still more complete life **is now** edited **by the Rev.** Alfred Gurney.

The next advance **in** Mr. Wagner's work was the building of the great Church of St. Bartholomew, in the northern part of the town, where for some time, in a temporary church, Mr. Alfred Payne and others had **been** working. This building **is** not easy to describe:

very simple, of solid brickwork, with variations of colour, and of the grandest proportions; in height it rivals Westminster Abbey, and alarmed some people, among others the Town Council, lest the light should be obstructed; but Mr. Wagner, when he built, counted the cost in more ways than one, and throughout all obstruction and opposition went on his way. Like all that he did, everything was substantial and handsome; and this church, as most of the others, has now been for some years a separate vicarage, endowed, and worked by a staff of four or five clergy, with a most correct and beautiful service and ritual, and full parochial works and scheme, bringing the Church and her system into people's hearts and lives. Mr. Collis, the late vicar, was known for years at St. Paul's, Knightsbridge. Mr. Parnell, of St. Margaret's, Liverpool, is one of the clergy.

The next church was built by Mr. Wagner and his brothers; and the story of that magnificent Church of St. Martin, Lewes Road, further north beyond St. Bartholomew's, is full of interest. As I have said, the old vicar of Brighton was an earnest worker and full of active energy in the care of his parish, soon to surpass in size and importance any town of the kind in England. On the way to the northern part of the town, between the Downs, on the Lewes Road, was a part where was little spiritual provision of Church or parish work. On the way to the Lewes Road is the large church of St. Peter's, with its imposing Gothic ornaments and tower, standing in its **own** grounds; but beyond that and on past the Level there was no church. **In** those early days, St. **Peter's was** held by Mr. **Cooke, an** old friend of the Vicar of Brighton, and of the same orthodox school; Mr. **Cooke at least was not** afraid **to** invite **Dr.** Pusey **to** preach two **sermons at St. Peter's** during the time of his suspension from preaching at the University. **(Dr. Pusey** also preached **for** Mr. Chanter, at Ilfracombe, during that period.) **In** 1842, J. Mason Neale wondered how his friend Berkeley Addison, then curate **to** the vicar, and helping sometimes **at St.** Peter's, had **no** definite idea or feeling of the necessity and design of **a** chancel, and spoke of the symbolism of what once was, **and** will again, **he** trusted, **be a** principal **part** of a church. This hope as to **St.** Peter's was **a** long time coming; but under Dr. Hannah, St. **Peter's** became the parish church, and both he and **his son and** successor planned the addition of chancel, etc., making **St.** Peter's more worthy of its position as the parish church **of** Brighton. About the Lewes and Ditchling Road part, **a** district of some six or seven thousand was growing **up; and** Mr. Arthur Wagner had placed a temporary **church, in** which worked the Rev. J. M. Fincher, now Rector of Pett, in Sussex, and others; but the old vicar had resolved to build a church in that part, choosing his friends Mr. Vaughan and **Mr.** Cooke as a sort of **Building** Committee to select site and superintend the

building; but before this was accomplished, or the
£5000 set apart, the vicar was called to his rest, and
the scheme was at an end.   Then the Rev. A. D.
Wagner and his brothers offered to carry out the in-
tention which their father had, and would have completed.   They offered to give the £5000 for it, or to
build a church in the Lewes Road; Mr. Vaughan
decided to accept the latter offer, and hence the building of the superb church of St. Martin at the cost of
many times that amount.   It was the more complete and
graceful a gift, because the brothers placed the presentation unreservedly in the hands of the Vicar of Brighton.
In the reredos were figures of saints and doctors carved
at Oberammergau; the east window was specially given
by Mr. Henry Wagner in memory of his mother and
aunt, and filled with subjects from the Annunciation to
the Day of Pentecost; the panels of the reredos were
all painted with figures from the Old and New Testament: Abraham, Moses, Elijah, Ezekiel, Joshua, Gideon,
etc., down to early Christian saints and martyrs.   The
one unusual feature was the introduction in the fifth
panel of recent colonial and English Church worthies:
Bishops Seabury of America, Inglis of Canada, Middleton
of India, Gray of Africa, Patteson of Australia, Bishop
Wilberforce, Mr. Keble, W. Gibbs, Joshua Watson, H.
Michell, and the late vicar.   Tablets recording the gift
of the church out of filial love and respect, and to Mary
Sikes Wagner, mother of the founders, who died in

1840, and to Mary Ann Wagner, their aunt, who died in 1868, were placed in the chancel.

There is one more record of another handsome church built by Mr. Arthur Wagner in Russell Street, at the back of St. Paul's, not only relieving that overcrowded church, but giving room for sisters and schools to attend with more comfort. There is to be told in connection with the building of this, the Church of the Resurrection, a singular proof of the determined perseverance of the Vicar of St. Paul's. As the church reached the level of the roof of the large brewery next to it, notice to **stop** the building from being carried higher up was given. Mr. Wagner was equal to **the** occasion ; if he **could not** go up, he could at least go down lower, and he did so, making the church of the proportions originally intended. Among the early **curates** we must not omit **the Rev. R. W.** Enraght, who afterwards took the district church of St. Andrew's, Portslade, and **from there went** to Holy **Trinity,** Bordesley, succeeding Dr. **Oldknow.** Those who knew him at Brighton and Birmingham can bear witness to his kind and helpful life as priest and friend to all his people, and those who were witnesses of his arrest and imprisonment will never forget the solemnity and pathos of that event. All honour, we repeat, to the curates of many years' standing, and among them to the Rev. J. E. Halliwell, of St. Paul's, son of the Rev. Thos. Halliwell, curate of **St.** Andrew's, Hove (to the Rev. Daniel Winham), and nephew of the renowned Shake-

spearian and bibliographical scholar, J. O. Halliwell-
Phillips. The Rev. C. H. Maunsell was for many years
working both at St. Paul's and at St. Bartholomew's
Churches; he is now Vicar of Thorpe Malsor, North-
amptonshire; among others who worked with Mr.
Wagner, the name of Alfred Gurney, now Vicar of St.
Barnabas, Pimlico, must by no means be omitted. It
was not at all likely that among all the misapprehen-
sions and misconceptions by the public of the Tractarian
clergy, so powerful and munificent a member as Mr.
Wagner would escape. The usual exciting arguments
about confession and absolution were talked over and
over again, and so one Sunday three poor working-men
felt themselves aggrieved, and as Mr. Wagner was going
up North Street in the afternoon, after calling on his
churchwarden, they assaulted him, and were taken
into custody, though they were rather punished at the
time by Sir Thomas Barrett Lennard, who was passing.
The men had, I think, some months in prison, and Mr.
Wagner kept their wives and children all the time, and
doubtless helped them when they came out. Mr. Wagner
of his own accord very seldom came before the public in
any way. Irreverence and Erastianism would certainly
arouse his indignation, and so he was present at the
great meeting in the Birmingham Town Hall, while Mr.
Enraght was in Warwick Gaol, no doubt feeling most
the dishonour done to our Blessed Lord in the sac-
rilegious act of Mr. Enraght's prosecutors. His two

pamphlets, *Christ or Cæsar*, were very earnest protests against dishonour to our Lord **as** the Divine Head of His Church. **Then for** many a long year Mr. Wagner **had** to endure the cry **of** "Romanist," "Jesuit in disguise," etc., at which latter designation a correspon-**dent of** that day, who knew what he was saying, fairly laughed outright: **"A** Jesuit by all means if they will **have it so,** but in disguise—certainly not! Mr. Wagner **is** nothing in disguise, all is open and above-board; who ever heard of his making any secret of his **views or practices?** **No** one is more outspoken and straight-forward in his sermons and teaching; he tells every one most clearly and plainly what he means, printing and publishing this too in a letter to the chief pastor of his **Church."**

How absurdly inappropriate was the cry of "eating **the bread of the** Church of England while undermining **her** in reality," when applied to a man who was spend-**ing several** large fortunes in founding and endowing churches, schools, etc., that would perpetually belong to **that Church;** to a man who had never in his life taken **one** sixpence of endowment, fee, or income from the **Church in any way** whatever! At that **time,** the **Roman papers,** after circulating a report that Mr. Wagner had seceded, kindly allowed that he might be sincere, at least if princely munificence be a sign of sincerity, and then went on to hint that his generous **disposition** and kindliness of heart had more to do with his position than any talents or learning. This was amusing, as Mr. Wagner was a good scholar, a great reader and student, and knew more about the working of the Church of Rome, both ancient and modern, than half the recent converts put together; and another thing is certain, that he was not at all given to be much influenced by others in that way. But this is all past and over; and though much of the seceding was done in a not very genuine or straightforward way, we would gladly forget it. And now years and years have passed, and the event only proves that faithful service and a definite position have been the mainstay of the English priest of whom we are telling. We have spoken chiefly of the well-known and greater works accomplished by Mr. Arthur Wagner. It is needless to add that these were but a part of his work: the private and unknown acts of charity can of course never be recorded. His care for the poor and needy, sick and afflicted, for children and helpless, might be seen; but there are other ways in which a rich man with houses and land can help folks once better off, the struggling tradesman, those whose income had been sadly reduced, and even the higher classes, the professional man with an uphill path—these were never known, of course. When St. Paul's was built, one of the first needs to be provided was a supply of the Church literature then being published by four or five firms in the form of tracts, commentaries, devotional works, sermons, allegories, tales, manuals, **etc.** Mr. Wagner **was** a good friend to the wife, afterwards the widow, of an invalid verger of St. Paul's in a small shop close to the church, helping with stock and capital for years, and it developed into a very fair business **in a** large house and shop of her own opposite the church ; many will recall with pleasure Mrs. White **and her book and** stationery shop.

The way in which **the** work and services at St. Paul's **went** on and on, always to be relied on, made it a very restful place, and indeed to many it was as a refuge in trial and trouble. **It was a** refreshment to many clergy who could get a rest at Brighton from their own town **or** country work, and some who came to rest would often help in many ways. The Rev. E. A. Illingworth will be remembered with much regard in this way. **The Rev. E.** Field, the staunch Chaplain **of** Lancing College, often preached. **The** Rev. T. Simpson Evans, Evan Rowsell, Mr. Causton, were often there, and **Edward Monro in the** last years of his life, when health **and** strength were failing. To the aged and the ailing St. Paul's was indeed a haven of rest and a comfort ; to **complete invalids** the **Blessed** Sacrament was **taken with every** mark of deep reverence. **We** can **recall** many of the earlier church folk. Sir William **and Lady Gomm, the** benefactor **to Keble** College ; Colonel Moorsom, who spent the few years of health left him by the Crimean War in much good work, and **was** churchwarden for **a year or two ;** the sister of Colonel

Short and Bishop **Short** of Adelaide; Mr. and Mrs.
Simpson and their daughters; Miss Fielding, the **only**
daughter **of** Copley Fielding, the great painter, who on
her death was laid beside him in Hove **Churchyard ;**
Mr. and Mrs. Synnot; **at his** funeral the **choir and**
clergy all attended, Mr. **Carter,** of Clewer, celebrating,
served by **the** churchwarden of St. Paul's, who **also**
carried the black ebony funeral **cross** at the church and
at the grave. Some **may** remember the tall, **thin figure**
of a lady in black, with iron-grey **hair,** and a **calm,**
dignified face: **this** was Mrs. Jennings, the **widow of**
the Rev. H. J. Jennings, chaplain at Delhi, **who, with**
his daughter, **was cut** down **by the** first band of muti-
neers, as they were nursing two officers who had just
been wounded; happily, they were killed at once, with-
out torture or outrage ; **St.** Paul's, no doubt, helped her
to bear that fearful trial. We have no space to record
many other names: **one** occurs to us as the very earliest
of the St. Paul's attendants. In the western aisle several
seats were occupied by a ladies' **school** conducted **by**
Miss Parkinson, of the Dyke Road ; **this school was**
like a home of the Church Movement, **and could tell of**
a race **of** Church women and matrons true through life
to the faith and principles they there **learnt.** As with
his curates so it was **with** Mr. **Wagner's** churchwardens.
This sketch would **be** incomplete without naming the
years of help and work by the late **Mr.** Arthur W.
Woods, of Ship Street.

St. Paul's choir was an institution, and like **Mr.
Wagner's** curates, the larger number of his choir-men
served for many years. The choir supper, too, was a
goodly feast ; and afterwards, it was pleasing to see the
vicar patiently endure the comic songs, in which "The
Monks of Old," and "**Simon** the Cellarer," usually bore
their part. Lord Elibank **was a** member of the choir
during his residence in Brighton. Their toast **was**
"Health and long life to Mr. Wagner". **Mr.** Wagner
was chancellor of Chichester Cathedral **from** 1871 to
1879.

St. Michael's, under **Mr.** Beanlands, has ever held **a**
foremost place in the practical revival of doctrine **and**
ritual : a small, but **very** well arranged church, solid
and handsome, the ritual on an elaborate and careful
plan ; the choir and music for many years conducted by
Dr. King, now organist of the parish church, **on** the
very best Gregorian models. Two of Mr. Beanlands'
curates were well worthy of mention. **The Rev. T. W.
Perry, after being at All** Saints', Margaret Street, and at
Addington, was at St. Michael's for ten years from 1862,
and was a power for good in every way, an ecclesiastical
lawyer and solid liturgical scholar, a member **of** the
Ritual Commission, 1867, author of *Lawful Church
Ornaments*, etc. As a scholar and a preacher, **Mr.**
Perry made a distinct mark in Brighton, **and was**
valued and consulted by a large circle of friends. The
Rev. Charles Walker, **though more of** a volunteer than

an actual curate, took a full share in all the services, and was a valuable help in the ritual and worship, the owner of valuable vestments and ornaments, and a liberal donor in all matters. He will be remembered with much regard and affection; and his great help and sympathy with St. Margaret's, East Grinstead, endeared him to the sisters and friends of that noble foundation. Mr. Beanlands had good friends and supporters. Among them General Tremenheere, his wife and children, the Lindsays, Mr. and Mrs. Barchard, Mrs. Tyrwhitt, Colonel Shaw Hellyer, and many others.

The early death of Mr. Purchas, and the account of the lawsuit about his ritual, have been described again and again; but the general idea to be gathered would be anything but a true representation of the man himself. He has been pictured as a sort of apostle of ritual, a man to whom ritual was everything, and by whom certain ceremonies would be carried out, in defiance of all law, order, and peace. Mr. Purchas was nothing of the kind; he was gentle, kindly, and humble-minded. When St. James's Chapel was offered to him he felt that it was an opportunity to set out in some more distinctive way the ritual sanctioned by the Ornaments Rubric, and the demolishing of part of the old Puritan chapel fixings went on merrily; but it was at best, when all was done, an incongruous mixture; and the services, which were very elaborate, and carried out by friends and helpers not always of the wisest, seemed in **that** chapel like new cloth on an old **garment.** Things were too bright and smart for the surroundings, and it was not a success ; the lawsuit was ruinous, and no doubt helped to break down Mr. Purchas's health ; **and an** amiable and lovable man was taken from **enemies and friends.** As an elegant scholar **and poet, and a kind friend and** companion, **he** will **be best known and remembered.** His **evening hymn,** " Evensong **is hushed in silence,"** with its **sweet melody,** still lingers **in the memory.** So far were Mr. **Purchas's own feelings from a wish to press extreme** ritual **on an un-**willing **people, that I have his own** handwriting **in** November, **1860, expressing** his **grief at the** angry **feelings caused, and his** readiness **to "** seek **peace** and **ensue it at any course short of** the surrender **of** truth ". His **funeral was a very** impressive **one,** and **will** rank **with others in our** recollection, **more** especially with **those of the old vicar, the Rev. H. M. Wagner, and of Miss Wagner.**

Some years before, a funeral in Brighton was very **largely attended, but,** of **course,** without the beautiful **and hopeful** ceremonial. **It was that of the Rev. F. W. Robertson.** One might call **it, by way of contrast, an exposition of very great pulpit** influence.

We will not leave our mention **of** Brighton without **naming another Mr. Wagner,** the Rev. George Wagner **(cousin to the Rev. Arthur Wagner), once** curate of **Dallington, in Sussex,—afterwards** incumbent **of St.**

Stephen's, Brighton,—who **led a** life of self-sacrificing devotion to the spiritual interests **of his** flock. His life and letters were **published, edited by the Rev. J. N.** Simpkinson, and told **of a character most** saintly and **devout.**

CHAPTER X.

MAKING our way for a while along the coast there was not a great deal to tell then of the now working centres of Portsea, Southsea, and Landport, which have all developed so much during the last twenty years; but between thirty and forty years ago the Rev. T. D. Platt at Holy Trinity, Portsea, was standing much alone in his work of Church Revival; he was for seven years curate to Archdeacon Denison. It was said that Bishop Gilbert of Chichester, the bishop who so long inhibited Dr. Neale, was much exercised by the very open and straightforward way in which Mr. Platt proceeded, even to receiving those who wished for ghostly counsel and advice in the church itself. It must have been curious and even amusing to hear that bishop express his surprise, not so much at the thing itself, as at the thorough straightforwardness. "Surely, not openly in the church itself?" and the simple reply, "Yes, my lord". Mr. Platt was assisted for some time by the Rev. W. R. Scott, a very earnest and zealous worker, once at Enfield with the Rev. J. Fuller Russell, also chaplain to Mr. Hubbard's works in Russia, for some years at Honolulu, and perpetual curate of St. Mary

Magdalen's, **Harlow. He** was the author of some valuable pamphlets, one on the apostolical **succession, and Canon LV.** The untiring **work of Mr. Scott and** his wife, **in a district of Whitechapel, for the souls and bodies of the people during the** fearful cholera of **1866, should not be forgotten.**

Crossing to the Isle **of** Wight, we can record Mr. Wix's work at St. Michael's, Swanmore, Ryde ; and on the other side of the island must visit the tomb of Mr. Adams (son of Serjeant Adams), the author of the *Shadow of the Cross*, the *Old Man's Home*, and other allegories and sermons, leaving one of the most beautiful memories of the early days of the Movement; his tomb-stone in Bonchurch churchyard is surmounted by a cross **of** iron, raised so that the "shadow of the cross" is always thrown on to the stone slab, perpetuating the name of his chief allegory : **Mr.** Adams also wrote *The Fall of Crœsus*, an attempt to point one of Herodotus's most graphic narratives with a moral directly Christian. Here also, in Ventnor, we are reminded of Miss Sewell, the authoress of many valuable books and religious manuals, as well as of the well-known tales, *Amy Herbert, Ursula, Laneton Parsonage, The Experience of Life*, and many other thoroughly bright, wholesome tales of domestic and social life, inculcating excellent Church principles ; they had **a** very large circulation, forming a literature most valuable to the rising generation of young girls. Before leaving the island we gladly tell of the Catholic **work and services,** from a very early period **of the** Movement, of Mr. Oliver of Whitwell. A name **much** connected with the Church Movement was that of Richard Waldo Sibthorp, rather a remarkable character, **who had a** church for some years in Ryde.

A little farther along the coast we come to Bourne-**mouth,** which, **like** Portsea and Southsea, has grown **and increased immensely,** with **its** several churches; **here, in** 1857, **Mr.** Bennett was working up on Church **lines, with** good choral service, weekly celebration, etc.

The Movement influenced Jersey and Guernsey early in the forties, and Dr. Godfray of Jersey was a thorough **worker in the cause, not only as** a parish priest and **preacher in a most** difficult charge, but as a writer in the *Ecclesiastic,* and other Church reviews. He trans-lated the *History of the Reformation,* by Chancellor **Massingberd, of** Lincoln, and many smaller works into **French.**

In Wiltshire, Avebury, Bishop Canning, Calne, and Chippenham were forward in the work; and in Dorset-shire, Batcombe, Dorchester, and Compton Valence under its able vicar, Perceval Ward, where Mr. Ferrey, **the architect, restored the** church and was a frequent visitor.

Ottery St. Mary was well known **for** some years as a country centre.

Exeter had many working clergy: Mr. Alleyne at St.

Edmund's, **Mr.** Ingle at St. Olave's, **Mr.** Bliss at St. James's, Mr. Armstrong at St. Paul's. These churches, and that of St. Mary Steps, advanced in the work. **The Rev. C. C.** Bartholomew, perpetual curate of St. David's **(afterwards** prebendary), also author of *Thirty-nine Sermons*, chiefly practical, was a good divine and parish priest. Another divine was the Rev. John Lincoln Galton, incumbent of St. Sidwell's, who was author of *Notes of Lectures on the Book of Canticles*, and of one hundred and forty-two lectures on the Book of Revelation; the principal excellence of **these volumes lay in** the careful and intelligent preference for ancient expositors. There lived also in Exeter Prebendary James **Ford,** who published some works of value to the clergy; **six** volumes of commentaries were published, *The Four Gospels, The Acts of the Apostles,* and *The Epistle to* **the** *Romans*, illustrated chiefly, in the doctrinal and moral sense, from ancient and modern authors. Mr. Ford also translated twelve sermons by P. Paolo Segneri from the Italian. Then Canons Woolcombe and F. C. **Cook** should be named, and last, but not least, comes **the** Bishop, Henry of Exeter, the sturdy champion of all that was orthodox, the outspoken prelate in the House of Lords, most famous for his *Letter to the Archbishop of Canterbury in the* **Gorham Case;** **that** letter, a thick 8vo., 2s. 6d. pamphlet, in paper cover, had a circulation that might astonish **the** publishers of the present day; for weeks it was sold as fast as it could be produced,

almost wet from the press. The pamphlet **was** certainly
one to **cause** a considerable amount of excitement : such
a bold and forcible attack **by a** bishop on his archbishop
was rare in the history **of** polemics, though the language
was more moderate than that used by some Reformation
bishops, as told by Mr. **S. R.** Maitland. Pamphlets are
now almost a thing of the past ; but in those days if
any one had a difference or a grievance **or** a pet theory,
a pamphlet was the natural weapon, and the war was
often carried on fierce and fast ; I need not say we have
changed all that : the day of pamplets is past and over,
and the large number **of** monthly reviews are **the re-**
ceptacles for the plans **and** proposals, the views **and**
opinions **on all** possible and impossible subjects in earth
and heaven, from the Corn Laws, Reform, and **Home
Rule, down to the most** sacred institutions of marriage
and home life. We will not complain ; under this new
plan we get, as it were, six or eight well-written pamphlets for the shilling or two ; and to the writer it **must**
be much **more** pleasant to write the article and **get a**
cheque for it, than to print a pamphlet and have a heavy
balance to pay when the printing and advertising account
is made up. Most **of** us remember the story of the
country parson who had written **a** sermon **he** thought
sure to interest **every** single clergyman, and sent it to be
printed, ordering **a** number that would come near to the
number of clergy in the Church ; and the distress of the
worthy priest **on** receiving a bill for some hundreds of

pounds; and then his relief at hearing from his good publishers that the **bill** really represented his order, which had happily **not** been executed, **and** that a few shillings were due to make up the balance on the few sold out of the 250 printed. The Bishop of Exeter's pamphlet **no** doubt produced a small fortune. **His** name was brought to the front very much in the long examination **as to the** troubles and difficulties of Miss Sellon in one of the earliest sisterhoods of the Revival at Devonport; much **wisdom and care** has since been gained in sisterhood work, through **such men** as the Vicar of Wantage, Dean Butler, the Rev. **T. T.** Carter, Mr. Chamberlain of Oxford, Bishop Armstrong, Mr. Scudamore of Ditchingham, Mr. Sharp of Horbury, Rev. **G. R.** Prynne, and Dr. Neale. The pioneers in this most difficult work were sure to suffer, but woman's **work** in the Church and the Revival is more than an established fact, **it** is now an immense power for good, acknowledged **and** approved on every side, one of the glories of our land. At Torquay and St. Mary Church, excellent work was carried on while his health lasted by Henry Newland, of whom we have spoken before; he **was** for some time the brilliant preacher and hard working Vicar of St. Mary Church. **At Newton** Abbot the **Rev. W. B.** Flower was working. **Mr. Prynne, of** St. Peter's, Plymouth, **was** undoubtedly **the** great worker and **leader in** the Church Movement in the West of England; he had a daily celebration of the Holy

Eucharist from 1849. The increase in the number of churches with daily celebrations would have rejoiced the hearts of early Tractarians. With him the work of sisterhoods revived. His *Eucharistic Manual* was in general use years before such manuals were common ; he wrote a small manual on the benefit of absolution that went through many editions. If the Church tone of the Plymouth churches is higher than almost any town in England, he was the leader, and went through severe persecution in the course of the work. He also wrote that beautiful hymn, in *Hymns Ancient and Modern*, on whose original committee he was a worker, "Jesu, Meek and Gentle". The record of his *Thirty-five Years of Mission Work in a Garrison and Seaport Town*, published in 1883, is the account of some most perfectly ordered parochial work. In Plymouth, when the late Bishop of Exeter sent Mr. Prynne, no parochial machinery existed, scarcely a place of worship or a school. He began with the stipend of £100 a year, £30 more when a room was licensed, and £20 more when a church was consecrated. The amount of false and wicked statements made before the bishop, Henry of Exeter, in 1852, was almost inconceivable ; the whole matter concluding with the bishop's solemn declaration that Mr. Prynne was entirely blameless in every way. He was in his younger days Curate of St. Andrew's, Clifton, and there published his first volume of *Plain Sermons*. He published afterwards two more series of plain parochial sermons,—short, practical, sound, and earnest, with a manly style of eloquence and full of sound doctrine, just the sermons by townspeople most needed. At Devonport, all four churches, and especially St. Stephen's, were well worked. About 1859, **a friend** spent Christmastide at what was then called **the Mission** of St. Stephen, Devonport, when he was much impressed **by the warm** and devotional worship and **the** good fellowship **at** this **great** festival **between parson and** flock, and **at the** steady progress made by the Church, bringing vital and spiritual religion among a once indifferent and even unfriendly people.   **It** was the first Christmas and Epiphany since the consecration of their **new** church on the previous St. Matthew's Day; the church was decorated by a band of young mechanics **and** needlewomen, and **the** sisters of the incumbent, **who** gave their lives **to** church and parish work; the choral services **and** celebrations were simple and hearty, led by a choir of ten, chiefly mechanics, and twelve boys of the same class.   On New Year's Eve, the Rev. James Bliss, Vicar **of** St. James's, Plymouth, preached, and there was an early celebration on New Year's Day.   A course of Advent sermons had been preached, **and after** the last an offertory was made, by which sixty of the poorest families had good Christmas fare provided.   **On** January 4th, the choir, assisted by that of St. James's and St. Mary's, Devonport, and St. Peter's, Plymouth, gave a bright musical evening and social gathering to all the members of the church—glees, carols, songs—a help to **those** who had but little brightness or recreation in their lives. This was followed by a presentation to the Rev. G. W. Proctor, the incumbent, of an address, telling how his labours had been appreciated.

Cornwall had not a few parishes where the work of **the Church** Movement had **penetrated;** among them, **Morwenstow, under** R. S. Hawker, the well-known **poet, author** of *Echoes from Old Cornwall,* and of **that** beautiful poem, ***The*** *Poor Man* **and** *his Parish Church;* Mr. Williams **of** Porthleven; also Baldhu, Falmouth (the Church of King Charles the Martyr), Kenwyn, Helston, Laneast, Marham, Penzance, Sheviock, **St.** Ives, **St. Veep, Truro, and St.** Columb Major, where **Dr.** Walker laboured for many years, **and** afterwards **was founder** of All Saints', Notting Hill, in memory of **his father and mother.** In North **Devon,** Barnstaple **and Bideford** were well forward, and at Ilfracombe, the years of earnest parish work of the late Rev. J. M. **Chanter,** the vicar, are fresh in the memory of many a churchman who visited that lovely place, as well as in the hearts of his own people; a model of the old ortho-**dox** Tractarian, friend of Dr. Pusey and many others of the School. He was **the** author of a volume of sermons published in 1858, and also of *Help to an Exposition of the Church Catechism.*

In Somersetshire, Wrington, near Chard, was for years **under a vicar who was** a theologian, scholar, poet, a thorough churchman, and a worker among his people and schools; the **Rev. Henry** Thompson was a Cambridge man of good **standing; his** parish festivals were **from year to** year very happy times indeed. Among **other** works he wrote a life of Hannah More, who was a parishioner; he also wrote *Concionalia*, outlines of sermons for the year. He was editor of a book of *Original Ballads by Living Authors*, 1850, a work well illustrated; besides **an** admirable **preface Mr.** Thompson wrote the *Martyrdom of St. Edmund*, **Cromwell** *and his Daughter*, and *The Morning Sacrifice*. Among the contributors were E. **A.** Freeman, Archdeacon Churton, Mackenzie Walcott, **Rev. W. J.** Deane, and J. M. Neale. There **was** also daily service and weekly communion at Buckland Dinham, Butleigh, Leigh-on-Mendip, Mells (where **was** Mr. Horner, a well-known and most able man), and St. Paul's, Bedminster, under Mr. Eland: daily services **at Milverton,** North Petherton, Shepton Beauchamp, and Kingston. In this county also is Frome, the scene of Mr. Bennett's life-work after leaving St. Paul's, Knightsbridge, work still well kept up by the present vicar. Neither must we omit East Brent, the parish of the ready and valiant champion, Archdeacon Denison, the preacher of the sermons on the Holy Eucharist at Wells Cathedral, all prepared most carefully beforehand, and, **I think, preached from the** printed copy; bravely were **the** sermons defended in the trial, "Ditcher v. Denison," in the proceedings against the Archdeacon of Taunton, in 1854, 1855, 1856, and **in** the printed defence and evidence. A dignitary of Wells was said to have complained that the Archdeacon kept them **all** in hot water **for so** many years; to which the Archdeacon gave the characteristic reply: " Well, hot water **is** better than **cold**". **Many** will remember the Charges of 1852, 1859, and 1860, **given** with all the Archdeacon's force and spirit, **and his sermons on** "Church and School," and " National Unthankfulness ". Such brilliant enthusiasm **and energy** had its value in the **work of** the Church Movement—without it, but little would **have been** effected.

In much **of the work of** defence and research, **Arch**deacon Denison **had a** most painstaking and learned assistant in the Rev. C. S. Grueber, incumbent of Hambridge, **in** this county; **he** was author of *Considerations on the Opinion of the Court at Bath, Two Letters to the Archbishop of Canterbury,* one to the Right Hon. Stephen **Lushington,** on Articles XXVIII. and XXIX., *Facts on the Court at Bath and Commission at Clevedon.* **Mr.** Grueber **is also the** author of manuals on Church **teaching and doctrine.** The research bestowed by Mr. Grueber on some of the Thirty-nine Articles was almost beyond conception; some who were brought up to think the Articles a sort of bulwark of Puritanism, must **have been very** much surprised **at** the result of those researches.

Many recollections **of the** early Church Movement

centre about Gloucestershire, recollections of the deepest interest; of the two Kebles especially, John, some time curate to his father at Fairford, and Thomas, so many years Vicar of Bisley; of Abbenhall, under James Davies, one of Isaac Williams' first curacies; of Stinchcombe, where Isaac Williams lived and wrote his poems and commentaries, acting as curate to his brother-in-law, Sir George Prevost, quite recently called to his rest, leaving us his valuable memoir of Isaac Williams. Bussage was the scene of Mr. Suckling's few years of labour, and where one of the earliest penitentiaries was founded. At Tidenham, Bishop Armstrong (of Grahamstown) was vicar eight years; he it was who was so deeply interested in penitentiaries, and wrote and worked for them; here, as at St. Paul's, Exeter, Mr. Armstrong lived all opposition down, and was a pattern of the hard-working parish priest. He published several volumes of sermons, a set for the festivals, and edited and wrote for the series of Sermons, and Tracts for the Christian seasons, the *Pastor in his Closet*, etc. The Rev. T. T. Carter wrote the life of Bishop Armstrong, a book still most interesting.

At St. Mark's, Lower Easton, and at Kempsford, Bishop Woodford, of Ely, was vicar for some years; his brilliant preaching and devout care for the services of the Church, were as conspicuous and telling as were his higher labours afterwards as Vicar of Leeds and Bishop of Ely. At Cheltenham, in the reign of Mr.

Close, the opponent of the Cambridge Camden and Ecclesiological Society, the Rev. Alexander Watson was at St. John's, then the only church in Cheltenham with daily service and weekly Communion. **Mr.** Watson was a busy writer in the cause, and edited five volumes of *Sermons for Sundays*, by the first preachers of the day; the *Churchman's Sunday Evenings at Home*, a set of family readings; and the *Devout Churchman*. He was also author of *The Seven sayings on the Cross*, *Sermons on the Beatitudes*, *A Catechism on the Prayer-Book*, and other works. Clifton was for some years a centre of the Evangelical school, but in 1868 the church of **All Saints** was commenced; it was finished **in 1872,** and for twenty years a record of church work under Mr. (now Dean) Randall can be made, bringing home the Church's work and worship to many thousands. St. Raphael's, Bristol, built by the munificence of Canon Miles in **1859, fell a victim to** the opposition, and was closed for some years; it has happily just **been** re-opened, let us hope to **a** brighter and even more useful future. We may not forget to name the early Bristol Church **Union** under Archdeacon Denison and Mr. Coles, **a** forerunner of our English Church Union. Many other places in Gloucestershire might be named, such as Cam, Cirencester, Dursley, Frenchay, Overbury, Sodbury, Stow-on-the-Wold, Stroud, Tetbury, and Stapleton the beautiful church built by Bishop Monk where the Rev. R. R. Chope was some time curate;

not forgetting Kemerton, near Tewkesbury, where Archdeacon Thorp was vicar; **his** influence among the younger clergy was of the very best and highest. Almost within sight of Gloucester, though in Herefordshire, is the beautiful church of Eastnor rebuilt by the late Lord Somers. Mr. Pulling, one of the compilers of *Hymns, Ancient and Modern*, was the rector.

Passing by Worcester **with** its beautiful cathedral and hard-working clergy, such **as** the Rev. the Hon. H. Douglas of St. Paul's, we **come to the** Midlands and the towns surrounding Birmingham; Wednesbury under Mr. Trigg; West Bromwich, Mr. Willett; Walsall, Mr. Allen and Mr. Hodgson; S. Michael's, Caldmore, **Mr.** J. Fenwick Laing; and at Aldridge, Willenhall, Rugeley, and Atherstone Church work was done, and great progress made. That Birmingham was the most **unlikely** town to **fall in** with **a** movement, the object of which was to revive **the** Catholic doctrine and practice of **the** Church **of** England, a glance at the religious life **of** Birmingham during the past century will convince **us**. The Unitarianism of Dr. Priestly, the Congregationalism of John Angell James, **and the** secular Christianity of George Dawson, had leavened a large proportion of the inhabitants; and the parish churches, some twenty in number, were nearly all in the hands of Evangelical **or** Low Church incumbents; there was very little of hearty life and work; Socinianism, Erastianism, and Dissent were the really active and working agencies, and so they continued till long after the Church Movement had penetrated into other towns and villages. Few of the churches added much to the architectural beauty of the town (or city which it now is). The presence of a building like Christ Church, directly opposite to the handsome erections of the Council House, Art Gallery, Free Libraries, Mason College, and Midland Institute, was a positive eyesore, and the dreary formal service seemed to vie with the building in plainness; but what could be hoped of a church the foundation stone of which was laid with the following words: " I lay this stone in the name and by command of his most gracious Majesty King George the Third ". A special work in Birmingham is worth naming, the early Sunday morning classes at half-past seven for working people, at which writing, arithmetic, geography, etc., were taught by some of the leading laymen of the city. Many hundreds attended these classes, and the fact was a complete reply to those who argued against the Archbishop of York's plea for early instead of evening Communions; the people could and did get up early, and go some distance for this secular learning, and it was said they would do the same in religion if they had been taught to set a high value on its means of grace. The earliest sign of a stirring of Church life was at St. Paul's about 1841, under Mr. Latimer and his curate, James Pollock. Aston, a suburb almost larger than Birmingham, was for a short time under a good churchman, Mr. Peake, and in this parish was the district of Holy Trinity, Bordesley, where Dr. Oldknow, a learned divine and writer and an excellent parish priest, worked till his death; he was the friend of Dr. Neale and many of the early Tractarians, and the result of his labours was shown in a hearty and beautiful service appreciated by a large congregation. The district church of All Saints, Small Heath, was started in his time. Dr. Oldknow was succeeded by Mr. Enraght, of whom we have spoken, and he brought youth and strength, and an increase of life and beauty to the work and services, together with a hearty loving kindness and helpfulness that made the vicarage and its inmates most deeply loved. The prosecution of the vicar and his separation from his people was the work of a party persecution, and, unfortunately, it prevailed. No one could say that Mr. Enraght did not do his utmost; there were no aggrieved parishioners, but a regular congregation of 400 or 500 every Sunday morning, and 700 or 800 every Sunday evening, with a large proportion of early Communicants; not one of these complained of the service or wished it altered; and, moreover, for months Mr. Enraght discontinued the things complained of at the express desire of his bishop, in the hope of peace and of stopping the prosecution; but in spite of this the persecutors determined to carry it on to the bitter end, and in due course Mr. Enraght was imprisoned in

Warwick Gaol. To describe his **leaving the** vicarage **where his people had ever** found in himself **and Mrs. **Enraght **helpers in all** times of need and trouble, **is beyond my power; most** pathetic and touching was the **going to Warwick,** his friends, and even those who had **to** carry out the sentence, were far more touched **and overcome** than was the vicar himself, who went through **it with a calm** fixed patience, with thorough **cheerfulness and** resignation. **For** nearly **two** months he **was kept in** Warwick Gaol, **and during that** time the great **meeting was held** when Birmingham **Town Hall was** filled **from end to end,** and so many came from far **and near to protest** against **the** imprisonment; **the** singing **of the "Church's one** Foundation" **at the end was something impressive and** touching. **In** the **gaol** he **received correspondence** from all parts **of** the country, **a fair specimen was the** letter: "Your imprisonment, **sir, is a disgrace** to all concerned in it, except your**self".** **He was** visited by numerous friends, all anxious **personally** to express their sympathy; he was of course visited **by his wife, and by his** children, most of whom **were then very** young; **on** one occasion when going to **dine in** the prison, **one of the** youngest, a little girl, was pathetically **anxious** to know "if they would have to dine with **the other robbers".** **At** the end of nearly **two months the question of** the original writ was raised, **and Mr. Enraght was released, not, as he** said, that he **wished to get out of prison by** a legal quibble. Lord

Justice James said that he **thought it** was quite as trivial a thing to prosecute a **clergyman for wearing a** chasuble, as it was to **get a clergyman out** of gaol **on a** bad writ. **As the** governor of the gaol, no High Church-man, **said to one** of his visitors: "The sooner that gentleman is **out,** sir, the better, for he is altogether in the wrong **place**". **So after** nearly two months **in** prison, Mr. Enraght was released, and many friends went over to Warwick, and **a** host also met him at the station **in New Street,** Birmingham; **Mr.** Jacob **Row-**lands, his solicitor; the Rev. **W.** Elwin, **his** curate (now Vicar **of** St. Andrew's, Worthing); the Rev. **J. Lupton** Taylor also assisting, who afterwards **went to Africa as a** missionary, **and there was early called to his rest (he was** brother to a well-known surgeon in **Brighton, J. E.** Taylor, some time churchwarden **to** Mr. Enraght); **Rev.** F. B. Cross, and James and T. B. Pollock, Mr. Harris, vicar's warden, and many others. They **in the** evening welcomed Mr. Enraght back **with** enthusiasm at a crowded meeting. These **imprison-**ments are **now** matters of past history, the Church Association, no doubt, feeling that the effect of such an one as I have tried to describe, would do anything but **advance** its cause. **The** persecutors did not cease until **they had driven Mr.** Enraght **from** his living, and **deprived** the congregation **of** one of the very best of **friends** and parish priests.

Some years before this **a** work in the same parish

was begun, which has, happily, not only not been crushed, but has prospered and increased in a most wonderful way. **From** his curacy at St. Paul's, the Rev. James Pollock started the mission of St. Alban's in a temporary building, and laboured on through the **most violent** opposition and rioting; living it all down **and gaining over** large numbers of people in **a** district **not very** different at first **from** that of St. George's-in-**the-East and Ratcliff Highway. In this** work, his **brother, the Rev. T. B. Pollock,** joined, **and in** the **course of years** a noble church, one **of Mr.** Pearson's grand designs, **was built,** and after a while consecrated; **a very beautiful Ritual, and a** large congregation, with **a great proportion** of men, testified **to the** success **of the** unsparing labour and devotion of these two **brothers. To** James Pollock **we** are indebted for **several** useful **and** practical manuals, and **to T. B. Pollock for some of** those **metrical** Litanies in *Hymns Ancient and Modern* **with which we are all** familiar.

Though not with success as to numbers, **the Rev.** Robert Dell **worked at St. Peter's,** Dale End, almost as **difficult to deal** with **as one of** our own City parishes; **not that the** people all lived away and came **in** only for **business** during **the** week, but it seemed as if from **Saturday night to** Monday morning all **the** shops and **houses were sealed up,** and the inhabitants not to be **found or got at. There** was **a** good choir, and the **service** was **carefully** rendered; the poor and schools were well cared for and helped by Mr. Dell, his wife, and children, who also brought as much brightness and recreation into their work as they possibly could.

In the surrounding villages and small towns, matters were here and there advancing on Church lines. Northfield for years was, of course, prominent under Mr. Clarke, a very well-known early Tractarian, and at Moseley, King's Heath, King's Norton, Smethwick, Smallheath, Sparkbrook, careful and choral services were the rule.

Coming nearer still, Edgbaston, the old parish, and the district churches of St. James and St. George were shaking off the old-fashioned ways, and making religion brighter and nearer to the Prayer-Book model; this was especially the case with old Edgbaston Parish Church, under the Rev. Creswell Strange. It is some years since I was there, and then the additions and improvements were only just beginning, but many of the old-fashioned forms and ceremonies were giving way to some brighter and more reverent ways. But then the old pews were still there, and that admirable and successful romance, *John Inglesant*, had been published; and, I must confess, it was a shock to me to see the author of that good book go into a pew and fasten the door after him; it did seem out of the order of things that the author, who had just made us all so interested in Nicholas Ferrar and his family, George Herbert and other church worthies of the seventeenth century should occupy a nineteenth-century pew! One did not expect that, like the late Mr. Pugin at Ramsgate, he should sit under a mediæval canopy at the head of his dining hall—but a pew!—George Herbert speaks about it—

> Kneeling n'er spoilt silk stockings ; quit thy state,
> All equal are within the church's gate.

—and how can that be if some are in pews ?

On my declining a seat in a pew, the verger kindly gave me one where I was close to some mural tablets, one of which attracted my attention by its wonderful inscription recording the death of the two wives of a Birmingham magistrate ; the virtues and perfections of the first wife were elaborately set forth, and then it was recorded how the second wife admirably took up the position and duties of the first, and carried them out with an equal, if not greater amount of success ; it was droll ; I have read a great many effusions of the kind, but this one very much disturbed my gravity during the service. And here I would leave this great manufacturing centre, but as we are close to the Hagley Road, Edgbaston, in which stands the oratory of St. Philip Neri where Dr. Newman spent the last forty years of his life, it would not do to pass over a spot so interesting to English Churchmen ; for as we assuredly value much the record of Dr. Newman's life and work in the English Church, most ably told in the earlier chapters of his *Apologia*, **and** in his **letters** so wisely entrusted by him **to Miss Mozley, the two** volumes of which all English **Churchmen may prize, so** the rest of his life after he left us, **and the** place where he spent it will have their own special attraction. The Oratory **is a large** pile of buildings of no architectural pretensions, covers a good deal of ground, is built chiefly **of red** brick and consists **of** the church with residences for the Fathers of the Order, and a large school for the education of sons **of the** Roman Catholic gentry. The large school-room, or rather, the one side wall of it, is the chief object to be seen as you pass **by** in the road, and **in** that room were given the school entertainments, Greek plays and music, at which up to **the** last Dr. Newman was almost always to be seen. The entrance **gate** is quite plain, **and** brings you into **a long corridor** leading to the church, a fairly **spacious one, but** with no pretensions to beauty, architecturally or otherwise, and with no great amount of ornament; Dr. Newman had been made a Cardinal just before one of my visits, and his throne and canopy looked painfully new. **The** various altars were of interest, especially the **one at** which the Cardinal **daily** celebrated. **In** the corridor were white marble tablets commemorating the departed Fathers, and one felt much at home with the names of those, such as St. John, Dalgairns, Faber, Caswell, etc. **The** secretary to Dr. Newman kindly showed us over, and in him we recognised an English clergyman, once

vicar of a suburban London **parish,** twice married, now
a priest and a Father of the Oratory.   It is curious that
the Fathers in **1852** should **have** fixed themselves in
Birmingham **of all towns in** the land, and still more
curious to see the friendly and cordial welcome given to
the Oratorians by the **Unitarian** town **and** its chief
residents; showing them much attention, **and** even, on
occasions, special recognition ; but in no religious sense
could the Oratorians **be** called **a** power or influence in
Birmingham.

CHAPTER XI.

IF an apology is needed for the rambling, not to say
random nature of these recollections I most willingly
make it. We will return to Oxford, the home to
which the hearts of many Englishmen turned as the
birthplace of the "Oxford Movement," and indeed
there was a magic in the very name of that city for
some twenty or thirty years. It witnessed the steady
earnestness and industry of the Tract writers, the brilliant
scholarship of such men as Newman, Keble, Froude,
Pusey, Marriott, Mozley, Palmer, Morris, and others,
the enormous labour of writing, translating, editing,
collating; a perfect bibliography of the Movement has
yet to be made, and may justify the wonder and admiration, which the very name of Oxford raised all
over the country, extending to India, America, and
indeed all the Colonies. The practical results too in
Oxford itself may claim some attention. Many of the
Tractarian clergy were parish priests also, and their
work was felt in their several parishes. In the early
days of Newman at St. Mary's he was a working parish
priest as well as a man of deep piety and astonishing
genius; after him came C. P. Eden, editor of one of the

Anglo-Catholic Library series, and then Charles Marriott.
Bishop Hobhouse, Denison and Hamilton at St. Peter's-
in-the-East **were** model parish priests; of this last
named vicar Canon Liddon tells us so much in **his**
short memoir, of his fervent preaching, reverence **and**
wise-heartedness, giving impressions of religious earnestness to all around him. After him came William
Adams **author of** *The Shadow of the Cross*, etc., who,
had **he lived**, might **have** even excelled his two pre-
decessors; the memory of these three pervaded the
parish up to the early **fifties**. As to other parish work
we read of **Mrs.** Pusey, while health lasted, under **her**
parish clergyman visiting in St. Aldate's and St. Ebbe's,
and in Dr. Acland's report **of** the cholera time under
the **self-sacrificing Charles** Marriott, of Miss Hughes
and Miss Skene visiting the cholera patients in their
homes and **in the temporary** hospitals. Later on St.
Paul's was built **by Mr.** Combe, and Mr. Hackman,
chaplain **of** Christchurch, 1837, a famous preacher, was
vicar—the parish being taken out **of** St. Thomas's.
St. Barnabas is an off-shoot **of** St. Paul's and was
also built **by Mr. Combe**; the vicar was appointed
under the advice of the late Dean Butler then Vicar
of Wantage; St. Philip and St. James's was built about
1864. The story **of St.** Thomas's, Oxford, and its remarkable vicar, forms a record **in itself** of the practical
side of the **Church Movement and its** influence in
parochial **work** there. **Mr.** Chamberlain, student of

Christ Church and afterwards **honorary** canon, a man of scholarship and ability, of courage, determination and untiring energy, selected this **parish,** neglected for years, **poor, and** once the haunt **of thieves and harlots, for the work of** his life; **and for nearly** fifty years with curates, one of whom was Bishop Forbes of Brechin, **Sisters of** Mercy, and all **the helps** of frequent services, through **abuse and** persecution, wrought a change that must be **seen to be realised.** He **was also one of** the most active writers and editors in that **part** of Church literature which treated **of** simple dogmatic teaching, manuals and guides **to** devotion and **doctrine,** and much scriptural instruction. **On his death in** 1892, a solid block of granite with a **cross was a** most appropriate **monument** to **this** brave and determined vicar. **At daily** service and weekly Communion **one** well-known **figure was** that of Philip Edward Pusey, Dr. Pusey's only son, **who, though** debarred **by** great bodily infirmity from Holy Orders, worked **well** with his pen for the Church Movement, editing the works of Cyril of Alexandria for the library of the fathers, **always** bravely cheerful **under his** life-long suffering. **Of the** surrounding parishes not much can **be said in** the early **times** if we except Yarnton, under Vaughan Thomas **and Islip under F.** Trench.

In the county **must** be named Cuddesdon with its college and **excellent** parish **work, Cowley** with the preaching fathers **and** daily **services and frequent**

Communions, Burford, Cropredy, Henley, Iffley, Banbury, and **Bloxham.**

In Berkshire, Boyne Hill **was** the scene of **Mr.** Gresley's latest labours. Wantage, for years under Dean Butler, **a** centre whence came the working sisterhoods ; **Cosby** White, Mr. **Mackonochie and Canon** Liddon having been sometime curates. Radley College **under Dr. Sewell, and its still** successful wardens. **Bradfield was** also **a Church** College, founded by Mr. **Stevens, the** vicar **of the** parish. Cranborne under Conyngham Ellis, author of *From the Font to the Altar;* Lambourne under R. Milman afterwards Bishop of Calcutta; Clewer, with its **long** record of parish work and Sisterhoods, **under the** Rev. **T. T.** Carter the great spiritual writer of **the Movement—and** parish work **could be told of at Abingdon, Reading,** Hungerford, **and Newbury.**

In Buckinghamshire were Aylesbury and Colnbrook ; Little Marlow under the Rev. J. Baines already named ; **Aston Clinton and** Hambledon, long the vicarage of **the Rev. W. H.** Ridley, author **of** one of the earliest and most useful **manuals** for Holy Communion, a man **of the working** school of parish **priests,** and no **doubt fully in** accord with the chief resident in his parish, the late Right Hon. **W.** H. Smith, the record of **whose active** and beautiful life **has** been so ably **written for us by** Sir Herbert Maxwell.

To pass on northwards in Suffolk, Barsham, Claydon,

and Elmswell had daily services; at St. Matthew's, Ipswich, **Mr.** Gay (of Archbishop Tenison's Chapel) was working; and at **St.** Mary le **Tower,** Mr. St. Leger. In Norfolk, East Dereham, Heigham, and Ditchingham may be named, especially the latter where the Rev. **W. E.** Scudamore had one of the earliest houses of mercy and sisterhoods. He was also the author of *Steps to the Altar*, **1846,** one **of the** most widely **used** manuals.

Lincolnshire had many parish **priests** working on the lines of the Movement at Gainsborough, Kelsey, Lea; Edmund Huff, a scholar and prizeman of Cambridge, was vicar of little Cawthorpe in this county from 1853. Another model parish parson also **was** the Rev. J. R. **West,** Rector of Wrawby by Brigg **and** Canon of Lincoln, lately called **to** his rest. **He** worked in his **parish for** nearly sixty years, a Cambridge man of the highest order of genius and learning, author of *Tracts on Church Principles*, and many sermons; he has been truly described as **one with a** firm grasp of principles, clearness of judgment and unselfish consideration for others. In Derbyshire the Rev. B. Webb was at Sheen, the friend of Dr. Neale and Mr. Beresford Hope; at Derby Mr. Hope, **at** Bakewell Mr. Cornish, at Morley Samuel Fox, an industrious writer in the cause, author of *Monks and Monasteries*, the *Noble Army of Martyrs;* he also published an abridged edition of Markland's *Reverence Due to Holy Places*. When speaking **of**

Birmingham the great parish work done for years by Dr. Claughton at Kidderminster should have been **named.** In Staffordshire there were many working **centres,** such as Walsall, Aldridge, West Bromwich, Denstone, Handsworth, Rugeley, Willenhall, Wednesbury, **where** Mr. Trigg worked, and last but by no means least, Elford, the parish where the Rev. F. E. Paget was **rector from 1835. To him** (as to Mr. Gresley) is due **an** immense influence over thousands of young church **people by** means **of his** bright interesting tales and stories full of point and wit, bearing on many forgotten and neglected points of Church doctrine and practice, **such** as : *Tales of the Village ; St. Antholins, or Old Churches and* **New ;** **The** *Warden of Berkinghall, or Rich* **and Poor ;** *Tales of the Village Children ; The Christian's Day; Sursum Corda, and other Books of Devotion; Sermons on the duties of daily life ; The Burial Service ; Saints Days,* etc. Mr. Paget was said to have given an **adverse** opinion of the principle of Tract 90 which he afterwards regretted.

In Liverpool early work was done under Cecil Wray, Vicar of St. Martin's ; at St. James the Less by Revs. Bramah, Parnell, and George Chapman, and later on **at St.** Margaret's. Daily services and frequent com- **munions** at Atherton, Barrow-in-Furness, Kirkham, Leigh, etc. ; at Manchester, St. Alban's, St. George's, Holy Trinity, St. John Baptist's, under workers like Mr. Sedgwick and others.

In Yorkshire the **work** at Leeds has been well told in the lives of Dr. Hook and Dr. Pusey; in the county, Roystone where W. H. Teale, author of many excellent biographies and other works, was vicar; the influence of the Movement was extending to many other parishes, Baldersby, Barnsley, Halifax, Doncaster, Middlesborough, **Coatham**, Burley-in-Wharfdale, Bradford. The example and splendid **work of** the venerable Vicar **of Horbury,** near **Wakefield, spread about** the county the best **of** influences. **He was** ordained **in** that eventful year 1833, and in 1834 went to Horbury where he is working still. With his schools, orphanages, sisterhoods and house **of** mercy, **he has** fostered a revival of faith, and **a renewal of living** energy and practice. **In** Scotland the Movement went forward **from** many important foundations and centres: Cumbrae College, Glenalmond, St. Columba's College, Edinburgh, Crieff College, and Orphans' Home; in the lives and work **of** eminent laymen such as Lord Glasgow, Lord **Forbes, Sir** Archibald Edmonstone, G. R. J. Gordon of Ellon; of such bishops as Jolly, **Words**worth, Forbes, Eden, Cotterill and others; of clergy such as Dean Torry (whose biography **was** written by Dr. Neale), Fortescue, Moir, Pirie, **C.** Wagstaff, Comper, Canon Humble, and Patrick Cheyne, who at St. John's, Aberdeen, went through much trial and persecution in his forty years ministry, remaining as has been said ever devoted to **every part** of his calling—frequent and reverent services, unfailing attention to the poor, a watchful interest over the young; of quiet, retiring habits, during the time of his prohibition he was chiefly to be found at work in his schools. In a very large proportion of the churches in Scotland there was daily service and weekly Communion.

Even in Ireland the Movement was felt, and much improvement in the churches and services might be recorded. Such names as Archer Butler, J. H. Todd, Mr. Maturin of Grangegorman, Woodward of Fethard, Dawson, Travers, Smith, etc., are still had in remembrance.

The record of missionary bishops, most of whom were in accord with the main principles of the Tractarian Movement would form a noble history of work; Heber, Selwyn, Patteson, Abraham, Nixon, Medley, Armstrong, Mackenzie, Tozer, Steere, and very many others.

CHAPTER XII.

I WOULD wish to point out that although in these sketches and recollections necessarily the clergy of the various places have chiefly been named, one must by no means fall in with the notion that the Church Movement with its new life and earnestness, and its advance in all that was good, fine, and beautiful in devotion and worship, was merely a clerical movement; nothing can be farther from the truth, and to represent the clergy as pressing ceremonial on an unwilling laity is simply most untrue to facts. Certainly, the clergy set themselves to teach and preach the great but much forgotten truths, the faith and practice: and not only by preaching, but by every outward act and gesture did they teach reverence and care in all parts of divine service; but they had with them ever a large body of laymen, who were ready not only to follow, but constantly to take the lead in the many outward expressions of revived religion shown in the beautiful churches, services and ritual, in schools, sisterhoods, hospitals, homes, refuges, etc.

I will now try to tell more fully of the laymen's share in the Church Movement. There was, as we have seen, much opposition to the Movement from the popular evangelical preachers, such as Dean Close, Hugh Stowell, Hugh MacNeile, and a host of others, and the opposing laity were also numerous and powerful. There was Lord John Russell's famous letter to the Bishop of Durham, on the new Roman Catholic hierarchy just then established in England, which was made the medium of attack on the Tractarian claims for the Church and hierarchy of England. And with Lord John Russell in principle were Lord Shaftesbury (then Lord Ashley), Mr. Baring, Mr. Bevan, Mr. Whalley and others. It was quite a common saying that Lord John Russell and Lord Ashley had some voice in the appointment of the bishops in Lord Palmerston's time, and it was acknowledged that their selections were not always a success; one of *Punch's* cartoons represented these two as penitent Puritans, confessing to each other that they had made a mess of it ; and there was one cartoon of Lord John Russell having his fortune told by a gipsy, and among other things she says, "Beware of aprons, little gentleman, specially silk 'uns".

About 1850 the papers for the most part were in fierce opposition to the Tractarian Movement, and for months *Punch*, following in the wake of *The Times*, caricatured the clergy, their dress, vestments, ornaments, etc., to its heart's content. Huge meetings were held, and there was abundance of denunciations, the chief laymen of the opposing party doing their utmost to convert the anti-papal excitement of the day into popular indignation against the High Church party, gaining a cheap popularity with the rest of the world who had not taken the trouble to ascertain what the real opinions of that party were. In one of the speeches, alluding to St. Barnabas's, Pimlico, Lord Ashley announced his preference to "worship with Lydia on the banks of the riverside rather than with hundreds of surpliced priests in the temple of St. Barnabas". This sentence was clearly considered the gem of the meeting, as on its repetition the whole meeting rose with loud and prolonged cheering.

The Church Movement had many learned, intelligent laymen; and we cannot take a brighter example, or one more worthy to be mentioned first, than A. J. B. Beresford Hope, of Bedgbury Park, a man of great wealth, who devoted that and his talents to the cause of the Church; a thorough champion on all points, ready to speak and write on her behalf. He was at Trinity College, Cambridge, in 1841, and was heart and soul with Neale, Webb and the Ecclesiological Society: in archæology and architecture he was an authority. In his place in Parliament his voice, in his slow, rather harsh, but very impressive way, would be raised on every Church question; he recorded his undying, undeviating, and unmitigated opposition to the Deceased Wife's Sister Bill. He purchased and rebuilt St. Augustine's, Canterbury, as **a** Missionary **College**; had much to do with All Saints, Margaret **Street, and** St. Andrew's, **Wells Street**; rebuilt Sheen **Church** on his **estate** in Staffordshire, where he appointed the Rev. B. Webb as incumbent. He, with **a few others,** founded the *Saturday Review.* **His works and** articles were numerous : the chief were, *On the Greek and Roman Writers;* *The Church Cause* **and the** *Church Party;* *English Cathedrals;* *Worship in the Church* **of** *England.* **Not** only **was** he **a writer, but** he **was a** thoroughly earnest worker in the Church Movement. **His** *Letters on Church Matters,* **by D.C.L.,** to the *Morning Chronicle,* were an **exhaustive** popular defence **on** the **chief points of debate in** public speeches and meetings **about** 1850. **I will** reproduce a **passage of** his on **Lord** Ashley's **speech** about Lydia, alluded to just now :—

"**Lord** Ashley's magnanimous resolve **was simply a** piece of sonorous nonsense founded upon ignorance of **the Greek original,** which **I hope** it is not Popery to **prefer to the Authorised** Version. The noble orator **read** in the latter that **St.** Paul worshipped with Lydia **by a riverside, 'where** prayer was wont to be made'; **and his imagination at** once **pictured to** him the spectacle of something like **what we never** see in these **days, except at a** Primitive Methodist revival—and with a very safe forethought he closed with this, rather than with the worship of the Church or 'temple' of St. Barnabas. Permit me to assert that his lordship cannot have read, or if he has read must have forgotten, what St. Luke really wrote, which was, 'where there was a customary προσευχή,' that is a house or station of prayer or oratory : so that instead of having bound himself to turn out upon the river's bank where he listed, his lordship only asserted his preference for frequenting some stated house of prayer by the waterside, which might be less gorgeous than St. Barnabas's and might be more so."

The whole of these letters to the *Morning Chronicle* form a fair reply to objections on the most crucial points in dispute at that exciting time. Mr. Beresford Hope was a D.C.L. of Cambridge, and a Privy Councillor.

Lord Addington (formerly J. G. Hubbard), the munificent founder of St. Alban's, Holborn, was another staunch Churchman, and, though not a writer or author, was a speaker ever ready in the Church's cause, a most kind and generous friend to all in need of a friend, and especially to the clergy. Mrs. Hubbard, was also known to be a ready help to very many in substantial ways, especially the poorer curates. On one occasion a friend was complaining to her of the very long sermons preached by a curate. "Yes, I know," was her reply, "the good man evidently tries to bring the whole Gospel into every sermon ; no wonder he never knows when to stop." At Addington, Bucks, where the Rev. T. W. Perry was long time curate under Mr. Baker, Mr. Hubbard rebuilt the church in 1859, and, though a financier and first-rate man of business, he was seen at his best at his own place in the country. At the consecration of his church at Addington, his speech **was a model of what good** landlords and land proprietors should say and feel. **He** tells how he had but done his duty ; **that** he would have felt no sort of satisfaction, night or morning, with **what** God had given him if he had built his own house and left God's house in **ruins. As a** contrast **to the** general **com-**promise of **Church** principles displayed on the hustings, Mr. Hubbard's speech on his nomination to Bucking-ham was **a most** manly, plain, **and** straightforward statement. **Parts of** it would be interesting, especially **where he speaks of being** High Church, when he says : " Is the Church **not high ?** high in its glorious mission, **high in** the motives **it** sets before **us,** high **in** the objects **to** which it leads, high **in** its Divine Head and Founder ? " **Then** he spoke out admirably as to the popular use of **the** word Protestant.

Sir Archibald Edmonstone, who died **in** 1871, was a Churchman of the type displayed in his own book, *The Christian Gentleman's Daily Walk.* In the quiet life of the **true** gentleman he was one of the fruits of the Church Movement, unobtrusive, and but little heard **or talked** of. Some of his other works were :

*Family Lectures for Holy Seasons and Saints' Days;
Portions of the Psalms selected and arranged for Devotional Purposes; **Devotional Reflections in Verse,** arranged in accordance with the Church Calendar.* The Christian Gentleman was a practical book, presenting a course of Christian conduct in the higher walks of life.

In early days Mr. J. W. Henley was looked up to as a true Churchman and gentleman. Squire of Waterperry, Oxfordshire, he was a Magdalen College man, and spent a long and active life in many positions of trust and importance. He was President of the Board of Trade under Lord Derby.

Baron Alderson was for years not only a lawyer of high repute, but also a staunch Churchman. He will be remembered by many of the regular congregation of St. Mary Magdalen's, Munster Square, of which church he laid the foundation stone in 1849. He was a Cambridge man, and was in frequent consultation and correspondence with the most active Churchmen of the Movement, and from his high standing as a lawyer was ever ready to help and advise in all cases of doubt and difficulty. He wrote a learned pamphlet on the meaning and scope of the Royal Supremacy. A memoir of this eminent and Christian lawyer was published by J. W. Parker, in 1859, with extracts from his Charges :—it tells of his care for juvenile criminals, and, indeed, for all who were the subjects of his office. One of the most touching things in the memoir is a letter written to a younger brother, a scholar of Charterhouse, during his last illness.

Lord John Manners, now the Duke of Rutland, who was a statesman and a poet, was looked up to by many as almost a knight of chivalry and orthodoxy. His life was a very practical and busy one. He was for some time Chief Commissioner for Public Works, but found time to write a good deal ; among other works, *A Plea for Public Holidays.* So now he might heartily join in the plea for the revived observance of the day of our patron saint, St. George. In 1841 he wrote *England's Trust*, and in 1850 *English Ballads.*

Sidney Herbert (first Lord Herbert of Lea) well deserves mention in the record of the Church Movement. When Mr. Thomas Mozley was Fellow of Oriel, he described Sidney Herbert, at the gentlemen commoners' side of the high table, as the grandest and most interesting historic figure then at Oxford,—one not to be forgotten ; very tall, with large soft eyes, a gentle expression, and an unmistakable likeness to George Herbert, the sainted poet of Bemerton ; few would have thought then that he was the man to perform an important part in the administration of a great war, under most difficult circumstances, as Secretary for War, in 1852. He was devoted to his work, and his early death in 1861 was a national loss. The subject of dwellings for the poor and other plans for their comfort and benefit had his active help. He built Wilton Church at a cost of £30,000, and another church at Sandymount, Dublin.

Sir Stephen Glynne, of Hawarden, was a Churchman and an antiquary, a learned archæologist and historian, leaving notes and details of many thousand churches; a man of singular refinement and remarkable industry. At his death Hawarden became the property of a son of Mr. Gladstone.

Colonel Short, of Odiham in Hampshire, who died in 1857, was one of the most active and hardworking of laymen; so indefatigable was he in promoting all works of charity and religion which came within his reach that he might almost be called a public man. To all who were honestly fighting under the banner of the Church of England, Colonel Short's ready sympathy and, whenever possible, his energetic assistance, were never wanting; it was esteemed a happiness to enjoy his friendship. He was the son of Charles Short, Esq., of Woodlands, Hants. In 1814 he joined the Coldstream Guards as an ensign; was present at Quatre Bras in June, 1815, and at Waterloo on the 18th, and went through the whole of the campaign. After he had retired from active military life he still worked for his chosen profession, and published several works on military subjects and duties. From 1837 Colonel Short was actively engaged, and was a director of the Royal Mail Steam Packet Company. He lived in

Queen Square, Westminster, and was mainly instrumental in substituting the handsome church of Christchurch, Broadway, for the little chapel that stood on that site, and helped the clergy and the poor around. In 1847 the **House of** Charity, Soho, was founded; Colonel Short **was on** the Council, and by his indefatigable **work** helped largely to its success, and worked **for it up** to the time of his death. In 1852 he settled **at Odiham,** and there, too, the church was his care; **the high** wooden pews disappeared, the chantry was **put in** order, and **the** almshouses rebuilt. Colonel **Short** was brother to the revered Bishop Short, of Adelaide.

Of Mr. J. D. Chambers, Recorder **of** Salisbury, it **will be known to** many of **our readers** that, both **as a learned** lawyer and as a liturgiologist, **his** best services have been, and are still, given to the Church; and many handsome volumes testify **to his** research **and** industry, **among others** translations of the **old** Latin Hymns. **Mr.** Chambers **was on** the council of the *Union* newspaper, and was one of the chief members of the Society for promoting the Unity of Christendom, **an** object all Christians must approve of; **if** union **is** strength, disunion must be weakness. (His death has been recorded since these pages were first written.)

Sir **Perceval** Heywood's zeal and **work** for the Church will be fresh in the minds and hearts of many, as patron of St. John's, Miles Platting, and as munificent donor and helper to the **St. Nicholas'** College Schools at Denstone and elsewhere. **Speaking of** these schools **and the immense benefit they have been to** the rising generation, **we well remember** that **the** support **and** assistance **of the** Marquis **of** Salisbury, **when** Lord Robert Cecil, was heartily given to them : of this family **Viscount Cranborne (who** was blind) wrote a *History of France for Children,* **in a** series of letters, which was published **by** Mr. Masters.

Mr. F. H. Dickinson, **of** Kingweston, Somersetshire, should **be** mentioned **as a** scholar **and** Churchman. Among his publications were *Convocation and the Laity, 1857*; **and** *A **List** of old Service **Books, according** to the **Uses** of the Anglican Church, with the Possessors.*

Alderman Bennett, **of Manchester,** was a courageous and eloquent champion in **all** Church matters, and one **who** gave **of his** substance most liberally in church **building, etc.**

J. H. Markland, of Bath, whither he retired in **1841, was a most** active and learned lawyer, **anti-**quarian and Churchman, valued by many friends and entrusted with important interests and large charitable funds. **In 1849 he was** made D.C.L. of Oxford. **He** died in 1864, **and a** window in Bath Abbey Church **was erected to his** memory. **He was** the author of **many** valuable archæological **works** : *Remarks on English Churches; Reverence due to Holy Places;* and *Ken's Prayers for Persons coming* **to the** *Baths of Bath.*

Of Mr. Henry Tritton and Mr. Henry Hoare, the
two bankers of London, it would be difficult to say
much; for their quiet, unobtrusive lives and splendid
munificence were, as was intended, little known **to** the
outside world.

Earl Beauchamp's years of work are still fresh in
the minds of **most of us.** From his early days, as the
Honourable Frederick Lygon, he was first and foremost
in every excellent work, founding, building, and en-
dowing; and such a monument as the College at Newland, Malvern, with many another—Keble College, the
Pusey Memorial, etc.—will testify to generations
of this nobleman's piety **and** devotion. **He** published
several most useful devotional works, especially the
Day Hours of the Church of England, of value to the
numerous sisterhoods and religious foundations, pub-
lished, too, at a price that brings it within the means
of every one. He also edited *Liber Regalis* for the
Roxburgh Club.

I have already mentioned General Gomm and
Colonel Moorsom, and to them we must add the names
of Sir Alfred Slade, Colonel Shaw-Hellyer, and of
Colonel Errington, who printed **a** *Book of Prayer for
Soldiers*, with texts referring to the soldier's office,
morning and evening prayers and psalms, prayers for
the eve of battle, when wounded, on a march, at
sea, etc.

Henry Styleman Lestrange, of an old Norfolk family,

must be included in our record. An Eton and Christ-
Church man, he was most enthusiastic in all that
concerned religious art and architecture. He painted
the roof of Ely Cathedral, which took him four years ;
and he was two years decorating in St. Alban's,
Holborn, under Mr. Butterfield. Mr. Lestrange was
thoroughly at home in the work of the Church Movement.

Among good Churchmen, who were also good landlords and masters, the name of Mr. Eliot Warburton,
of Arley, Northwich, Cheshire, should be recorded.
The noble chapel he built there was an architectural
gem, and it was afterwards enlarged to take in the
tenants and labourers on the estate.

Mr. Gambier Parry, of Highnam Court, Gloucester,
must be mentioned as a zealous Churchman. He built
the beautiful church there, and with his own hands
helped to paint the roof of Ely Cathedral.

The late Earl of Fife built a private chapel at Innes
House, Aberdeenshire ; and on the birthday of Lord
Macduff, the present earl (now Duke of Fife), the
father and son presented the petition for consecration ;
the chapel was well and correctly ordered, and evidently
the chaplain's office there was a reality, and not a mere
title, as it had so often been.

On special occasions laymen were found who were
ready to lift up their voices in the cause of truth and
purity ; and in 1858 Mr. Holman Hunt, the painter of

the " Light of the **World**," etc., exposed some sad mis-
doings in the case **of a** Christian convert and an Arab
at Jerusalem; Mr. Hunt deserves many thanks for his
courage and trouble in the good cause.

Another religious painter, and perhaps *the* great
devotional painter of the time, was William Dyce, **the**
Royal Academician. **He was said** to be the originator
here of the pre-Raphaelite school. Overbeck and other
German painters about 1828 much approved of the
young artist's work **on** principles they had long been
working for. Dyce became director of the Government
School of Design, and Professor of Fine **Arts** at King's
College; **he gave lectures, and** painted. The **late
Prince Consort purchased** his beautiful " Madonna
and Child" in 1846, which was engraved in the *Art
Journal*; **he** was selected to paint some of the frescoes
in the new Houses of Parliament. But as a religious
artist and Churchman we are chiefly speaking of him,
and most of us well remember his charming picture in
the Academy of George Herbert at Bemerton. **As a**
church musician, too, he takes a very high place; **as
one of the** founders of the Motett Society in connection
with the Ecclesiological Society, and as compiler and
editor of the two beautiful volumes of the Prayer-Book
with **the** ancient musical notation superbly printed in
black letter with borders. Lastly, we must record
his defence of Church principles in his forcible reply to
Mr. Ruskin's *Construction of Sheepfolds*: it was a

valuable controversial **pamphlet** entitled, *Shepherd and Sheep*, and was a **full reply to Mr.** Ruskin, whose Puritan training had then landed **him in a system where the idea of a** living, teaching, **historical** church was **entirely lost sight of, and** with Mr. **Dyce, as** with **all** the Tractarian **writers, this** idea, or rather the revival of this great principle, was an essential.

Of Mr. Brett, **the** noble and beloved doctor of whom we have spoken before, there is much more to be told. The wondrous influence he exercised **on** all who knew and valued him reached far and wide, **in the** years after his death **on even** to the present **time. Of** his profession **Dr. Crawford** and **Dr.** Golding Bird were Churchmen.

One layman whom we **have already** mentioned, Mr. **John L.** Anderdon, **well** deserves to be remembered **in** further **detail. Mr.** Anderdon resided **for** many years at Chiselhurst, where his daughter was the wife of the vicar, the Rev. F. H. Murray, and there he will perhaps still be remembered. My first recollection of him was in the early years of the fifties, when he was partner **in** the firm of Manning & Anderdon, **West** India merchants, of **New** Bank Buildings; **his partner** was Mr. Charles Manning, brother **to** Cardinal Manning. **At that** time Mr. **Anderdon was the** very model of a **refined** English gentleman—tall, **thin,** with fine features, and brilliant eyes, **with a** most gentle and winning expression; to those who had the privilege of knowing him, his courtesy and unvarying kindness were simply impressive ; an unobtrusive, most consistent Churchman in every way, never altering or varying, staunch and true throughout his life, a friend to be depended on, generous, strong, and unfailing ; a gentleman and man of business, he was also a scholar, and, though a layman, he was almost a divine ; as a Churchman, he was of the **school of** George Herbert, **Izaac** Walton, and Bishop **Ken ;** to the memory of the latter he was indeed devoted, and one of his chief works was **a** *Life of Bishop Ken,* first in one large octavo volume with engraved portrait, and a second edition in two volumes ; several handsome editions of Ken's Prayers, Hymns, **and** his *Approach to the Altar* (the latter still, **I** think, **in** print) ; he also wrote a work entitled *The Messiah,* a devotional and practical **life** of our Blessed Lord. A lover of beauty in Nature and Art, he published in earlier days *The River Dove,* and other similar works. In the **City Mr.** Anderdon was for years **a** well-known presence, and a characteristic story of his love of the beautiful in Art may be told here. In his walks down Cheapside he was frequently attracted by some small water-colour sketches, many of which he purchased, and after a while was curious to know the painter and his address. On arriving at the address, he asked for Mr. Leitch, and as he was scene-painting at the Victoria Theatre, Mr. Anderdon went there and found him at work, and soon after arranged to send the artist abroad for some years to **study and paint**; he became the famous artist, W. L. Leitch, who taught the Queen, and whose works still live and **are** valued. As a memorial **of** his kindness, Mr. Anderdon accepted some of the artist's beautiful drawings, though he was not a collector like his brother of Upper Grosvenor Street, **known as** the donor **to** our National Gallery of Hogarth's wonderful picture of " Sigismunda ".

Arthur H. Dyke Acland, one of a family of excellent Churchmen, friends **of** Bishop Jebb, Alexander Knox, etc., must not be forgotten. He was the compiler of *Liturgia Domestica*, a most useful book of household devotion, **and** of the *Hours of Prayers*, with an introduction and a most pathetic dedication, **at the** end of which was reproduced, in a woodcut, the well-known **seal of** Bishop Ken, the crucifix as **an anchor.**

Sir Charles Anderson, of Broughton, Lincolnshire, was a typical English **country** gentleman, taking a leading part in all the affairs of the county, and universally looked up to; he was educated at Oriel College, and was known to Newman (going with him on a tour to Egypt), Keble, **and** the great leaders; but it was Keble who made **a** deep and life-long impression on him, and whose firm grasp of the position of the English Church he always thoroughly retained. He was an accomplished archæologist, the author of a work called *Ancient Models*, containing hints on church building, with illustrations, published by Burns; a staunch supporter of his parish priest, a regular worshipper at all Church functions and kindred gatherings, most free from cant or unreality. He was a great friend of the late **Sir** George Prevost, and his daughter is the wife of the present baronet.

A great friend of Sir Charles Anderson was Mr. **Curtis Hayward,** also an Oriel man, of Quedgeley, in Gloucestershire—and **in that** county he occupied **a very** similar position—a model squire and a thorough staunch and energetic Churchman ; he married a sister of Archdeacon Harrison, **one of** the writers **of the** *Tracts for the Times*, the great friend of Pusey and Newman. On **succeeding to** the estate, he at once **took measures to** convert the living **of which** he **was patron into a rectory, at a** very considerable sacrifice of **yearly income to** himself. **Mr.** Hayward's brother **married a** daughter **of the late Canon Wade, of** Gloucester.

Other names could be added, such **as Mr.** Wilbraham, **of Rode** Hall, Cheshire, whose daughter, Frances M. Wilbraham, wrote some useful tales on Church lines ; *The Loyal Heart* **and** other tales, translated from the **German** ; also **a** history **of** the Kingdom **of Judah,** from **the death** of Solomon **to the** Babylonish captivity.

A list of the working **women of the** Church Movement could **be made :** of such **were Miss** Byron, Miss **Sellon, Lady Elizabeth** Clements, Lady Gomm, Mrs. **Pusey,** Lady Emily Pusey and **others.**

A few living Church laymen **must** not be omitted, Mr. **Henry H. Gibbs, of** the family of the founders **of** Keble College, **Lord** Nelson, Richard Foster, G. **A.** Spottiswoode, Manley Hopkins, the Hawaiian Consul, and **Lord Forbes, who** himself wrote **an** admirable treatise on the Holy Eucharist ; **he** and the late **Lord** Forbes, his father, **were** both **for** some time resident **at** Brighton, and are remembered with much respect and affection by very many there, as always most kind and courteous and ready to help in every good Church work.   There were hundreds of other excellent **laymen throughout the nation,** all helping on the **revival heartily.**

CHAPTER XIII.

A VERY slight account of the publications of the Movement may enable those of the present day to estimate
the labour and industry of the chief writers, and also
of the publishers of the literature which, both directly
and indirectly, was one result of the Tractarian Movement; it may serve also to give some idea of the
influence and spread of knowledge on these particular
lines, from the octavo volume of essays, sermons, or
treatises down to the small penny tract, brightly and
vigorously written. Some one compared these tracts to
the "small arms of the Church Militant". Take any
popular book on any subject of which ten thousand
copies are sold, and read; it leaves an impression and
influence on a great many who read it carefully and
who remember what they read. This may be said of
any one ordinary single book; and the literature of
the Church Movement consisted of thousands of books,
large and small, the object being to raise the English
Church to the height of her own standard; claiming
for her a place as a true part of Catholic Christendom.
This was the foundation of all that was written and
attempted.

The literature of the Church Movement included the chief publications of four publishing houses—Messrs. Rivington, Parker, **Mozley and Masters**; the catalogues by the beginning of 1850 contained many hundreds of publications, and were often pamphlets of fifty or sixty pages. Some **early** works chiefly by Mr. Gresley and **Mr.** Paget were published by James of Rugeley, afterwards by J. T. Walters, who was ordained and retired to a country living. The name of Mr. Lomax, of Lichfield, appeared on some few of the title-pages. In London, Mr. Burns had much of the early Tractarian publications: a **vast number of** children's books, **tales,** allegories, tracts **on** Christian doctrine and practice; Bishop (then Archdeacon) Wilberforce's sermons; allegories, charges, letters, etc., works by Robert Anderson of Brighton, **and Mr.** Dodsworth: the *Baptismal Offices, Illustrated from the Uses of Salisbury, Cologne,* etc., by T. M. Fallow, **first** Incumbent of St. Andrew's, Wells Street; reprints of R. Nelson, Bishop Jolly, Lawrence, Hacket, Ken, etc.; the *Fairy Bower* and *Lost Brooch,* by Mrs. Thomas Mozley, Dr. Newman's sister; treatises, sermons, etc. by the older divines **and** fathers. For some time the *Magazine for the Young,* **edited** by Mrs. T. Mozley, and the *Englishman's Magazine,* were two useful serials.

Mr. Burns, originally, I think, a Presbyterian, was one of the regular congregation of **old Margaret Chapel,**

and was a man of some learning and great taste, which he displayed in his publications ; borders were engraved on wood, with head and tail pieces of artistic designs ; his book, *Poems and Pictures*, with poetry and drawings after Selous, Harvey, etc., was almost the earliest of those guinea table books, which became, for a few years, quite a feature with many publishers. One of the most successful of his books, the *Eucharistica*, was **entirely compiled by Mr.** Burns himself, the Bishop **of** Oxford writing the introduction **only :** this work had a sale of some hundreds of thousands ; the companion volume, *Horæ Sacræ*, was compiled in the same way, with a preface by the Rev. T. Chandler, of Witley. When Mr. Burns seceded from the Church, the greater **number of his** publications were continued by Mr. **Masters.**

Mr. Cleaver, of Baker Street, published for the Rev. **W. J. E.** Bennett, when he was at Portman Chapel. Mr. **Toovey,** then **of St. James Street,** published for Mr. Oakeley **at** Margaret Chapel, his Psalter, *Bonaventura's Life of Christ*, Sermons, Devotions for Holy Communion, etc. The late Mr. J. T. Hayes, started in what is now called South Eaton Place, and published **for Mr. Bennett of** St. Paul's, Knightsbridge, Rev. R. M. Benson, and many other clergy ; he was long time a worshipper at St. Paul's, Knightsbridge, and St. Barnabas's. Mr. Hodges, who came from Frome, made a **small** business in London. Many distinctly Church writers had their own publishing houses. The Rev. J. J. Blunt of Cambridge, author of *Sermons; The Parish Priest; The Early Fathers; Undesigned Coincidences;* etc., published through Mr. Murray. Mr. Macmillan published later on for Miss Yonge; Archer Butler's most valuable Sermons, Philosophy, and reply to Dr. Newman's *Theory of Development;* also for Mr. Hardwick and Mr. Proctor as well as for some Cambridge churchmen of note; Mayor's *Churchmen of the Seventeenth Century,* Ferrar, etc. Messrs. Bell and Daldy were also publishers for some of the well-known writers; Rev. W. Denton's Commentaries, Mrs. Gatty's Parables, and some standard Church poets like Miss Proctor; also Prebendary Sadler's works, some of the most valuable contributions to Church literature, viz., *The Second Adam,* or *New Birth in Baptism,* and his *Church Doctrine Bible Truth,* a book that has perhaps done better service than any later work we know of, written to prove that the distinct system of teaching found throughout the Prayer Book is exactly in accord with the dogmatic system found in the Gospels and Epistles of the New Testament; it is remarkable, too, that no attempt to reply to this work has ever been made by those who so constantly plead for the Bible and the Bible only, and condemn Church teaching as unscriptural; his *One Offering* is a complete treatise on the Holy Communion, its doctrine and ceremonial, in relation to the Atonement; Mr. Bell also published church music, hymns, canticles, etc. Mr. Ollivier, at 59 Pall **Mall,** published **the** *Parish Choir*, and **a** few Church **tales.** Mr. Mowbray at Oxford was a Church publisher later on.

The house of Rivington **was** always known as publishing on the old orthodox lines, and, indeed, for very **many** years had reprints and editions of standard **Church** writers, such as Nelson, Ken, Law, Jeremy **Taylor; the works of** such pioneers as R. Wilson **Evans,** author **of the** *Rectory of Valehead ;* Bishop Jebb, Alex. Knox, Bowdler, etc.; publishing *The Whole Duty of* **Man,** *Week's Preparation,* the *British Critic* for many years, and starting the *Church Review* **as** a quarterly on the same principles. They were the projectors of the Theological Library, edited by Hugh James Rose, **and** to which the Rev. C. Webb Le Bas **contributed.** Some of R. Wilson Evans' works appeared in this library ; some books which appeared separately, **such as** Newman's *Arians,* were originally proposed for this library ; they published the *Tracts for the Times,* **and Newman's Sermons,** Dr. Pusey's Sermons, Dr. Hook's, Manning's, James Mozley's, and most of the works of the great writers and preachers ; **Dr.** Words-worth's *Commentary,* the *Plain Sermons* by contributors **to** the *Tracts for the Times,* Mr. Isaac Williams' *Sermons and Commentaries,* and the *Treasury of Devotion ;* and, later on, the sermons of the greatest preacher **of our own** times, Henry Parry Liddon, the one who had such power and influence, whose preaching will **live on.**

Mr. John Henry Parker, the Oxford publisher, a learned archæologist and student of architecture, was a prominent figure in the Tractarian Movement, and issued its great publications, libraries, and series of **works.** The reprints alone from most of the best Church divines made quite a library in themselves, all printed in excellent style. Church literature for the million was also done in cheaper forms for general **cir**culation ; cheap reward books, tales for the young men and women of England on social **and** religious subjects, sacred prints and cottage pictures, private prayers, family prayers, books and tracts on the Prayer-Book, the seasons, public worship, etc. ; also the *Penny Post,* a popular monthly periodical, *Keble's Christian Year,* issued in various editions, all shapes and sizes, thousands and tens of thousands year after year. Mr. James Parker, his son and successor, has rendered service to the Church in historical works on her liturgy and ritual.

Mr. Mozley, the father of that talented family who took such an active part **in** the Tractarian **Movement,** was a well-known printer and publisher **at Derby, at** first chiefly of standard useful books. His sons, John and Charles, carried on and developed the business ; printing and publishing the *Christian Remembrancer* (successor to the earlier *British Magazine,* and *British Critic,* which latter Dr. Newman and Thomas Mozley

had edited); this for many years held a very high place
as *the* Church Quarterly Review, edited by William
Scott, of Christ Church, Hoxton, and contributed to by
such men as Dr. Neale, James B. Mozley, Robert Wilberforce, and others. Among their publications were
Robert Wilberforce on *Holy Baptism, The Holy Eucharist,* and *The Incarnation;* works by Mr. Rickards,
Canon Trevor, Caswall; the *Practical Christian's
Library, Lives of Englishmen,* Herbert, Walton, Kettlewell, Hooker, etc., Jackson's *Stories on the Collects,*
several Hymnals, Church Poetry, the *Lyra Apostolica;*
small popular tales—*Bessie Gray, The Conceited Pig,*
and *Michael the Chorister.* The *Monthly Packet* had a
special value of its own, under its well-known editor,
Miss Yonge.

The rapid growth of the Movement may be imagined
from a short sketch of the rise and progress of another pub-
lishing house, that of Mr. Masters in Aldersgate Street.
Mr. Masters was a Staffordshire man, apprenticed to
Mr. Lomax, of Lichfield; he came to London, about 1827,
to a small house on the west side of Aldersgate Street,
from which he moved in 1838 to No. 33 on the other
side, with printing offices later on in Bartholomew
Close. His first publications were quite general ones:
Throne Crick's *Commercial Traveller,* Miss Bunbury's
Rides in the Pyrenees, etc. His connection with
Staffordshire brought Mr. Gresley and Mr. Paget, two
of the ablest writers of sermons, tales, allegories, etc.,

there were sixty or seventy works **by these** two authors **alone.** On Mr. Burns' secession the Church work came on **Mr.** Masters like a flood, and taxed his resources and powers to the utmost: but his energy **and** practical knowledge stood him in good stead ; and about 1856-60 **his** catalogue **was a book** of 140 pages, a **thousand** volumes and pamphlets, some of them large and **im**portant **books, such as,** Badger's *Nestorians,* Neale's *Eastern Church,* etc., works by W. Heygate, Dr. Irons, **Bishop of** Brechin, **T. T. Carter, T.** Chamberlain, Denison, Helmore, Dr. Gauntlett, Cope and Stretton's *Visitatio Infirmorum,* Miss Yonge, S. C. **Malan, Dr. Mill,** Bishop Milman, E. Monro, Henry Newland, **G. A. Poole,** R. Redhead, Robt. Brett, Alex. **Watson,** Bishop Woodford, etc. **Mr. Masters'** energy was unfailing, and he **was** devoted to **his work,** with a real **love for it** ; he had excellent helpers, the head of the printing office, **Mr.** Essex ; his **reader, Mr.** Wright, **an** admirable scholar ; **Mr.** Phillips, and Mr. Stokes ; **as** well as a partner who took much of the literary editing work and preparation of MSS. from **1848 to** 1863. Dr. Neale **records,** in his early diary, **when** Mr. Masters had just undertaken *Spelman on Sacrilege,* and some larger works, **that** " Masters **is** working away like a young elephant ". Mr. Brett **and** the Rev. T. Chamberlain were ever ready to help in the editing and arrangement of small works on Church doctrine, practice and devotion, such as *Pocket Manual of Prayers, What*

to Believe, Simple Prayers, etc. Of serial works, there
were *The Juvenile Englishman's Library, The Juvenile
Englishman's Historical Library,* London Parochial
Tracts, Parish Tracts, The Church and the Million,
Tracts for Working People, The Poor Churchman's
Friend, The Churchman's Companion, from 1847 **to**
1883; *The Ecclesiastic,* a theological monthly, 1846
to 1868, mainly edited by the Rev. Thomas Chamber-
lain; among the contributors were **H. J.** Coleridge,
E. A. Freeman, Beresford Hope, **J.** G. Cazenove,
Dr. Neale, Robert Wilberforce, Bishop Forbes, Jus-
tice Coleridge, **Lord** Campden, Lord John Manners,
N. Pocock, W. J. Irons, J. Baines, H. N. Oxenham,
H. Newland, W. Denton, T. W. Perry, and Dr. Littledale.

The *Ecclesiologist,* 1845 to 1868, published under the
superintendence of the Ecclesiological (late Cambridge
Camden) Society, was a complete record of the improvement in church architecture, new churches, restorations,
works of art, art societies, church music, etc. Some
of the contributors were Rev. B. Webb, A. J. B. Beres-
ford Hope, Dr. Neale, G. E. Street, W. Scott, Sir
Stephen **Glynne, F. H.** Dickinson, J. **D.** Chambers,
etc.

Of the *Hymns for Little Children,* by Mrs. Alexander
(Miss Humphry), wife **of** the Bishop of Derry, first
published in 1848 — four sizes on sale — sixty-nine
editions have been published, or nearly 700,000 copies;

of her *Moral Songs*, thirteen editions, **or** over 70,000 copies.

The *Churchman's Diary*, commenced **in** 1845 with 2000, has a circulation of nearly 10,000.

Many diaries, almanacs and calendars were compiled ; one **was** an Ecclesiastical Almanac of 1845, without authority but compiled from authentic sources, published by **Mr.** J. Leslie, of Great Queen Street, Lincoln's Inn Fields.

Of newspapers, the *Morning Chronicle* and the *Morning Post* were favourable, as were the *Day* newspaper, 1861, the *John Bull*, and the *English Churchman*, for the early years **of** its **life.** **The** *Guardian* **was projected in** 1846 **in** the chambers of Mr. T. **H.** Hadden, an Oxford double-first (brother to Mr. Arthur **H.** Hadden, the historian), Mr. Sharpe, the banker, and others assisting; it was, as now, the family Church newspaper, ably conducted for very many years by the late Mr. Martin Sharpe. The *Union* newspaper flourished **for** a time ; and the *Church Times*, which took its bold and firm stand under Mr. G. J. Palmer, deserves special mention. The *Church Review*, under the English Church Union, too, holds on its orthodox way.

One can only hint at **the** various guilds and associations, sisterhoods, unions, confraternities, such as **the** English Church Union, originally called the Church of England Protection Society, the Guild of St. Alban, and hundreds of kindred societies, all doing special work for the Church, the poor and afflicted, and all aiming at a **rule of** life and devotion higher and more ennobling.

One of the earliest of these guilds was founded in Oxford, on the Wednesday before Christmas, 1844, called the Guild or Brotherhood of St. Mary the Virgin; **its original** purpose was the study of ecclesiastical art, **to which** were afterwards added certain religious and **charitable** objects. **The** resolutions were:—1. To rise **early.** 2. To be moderate in food. **3.** To devote **some time** each day to serious reading. 4. To speak evil **of no man,** especially those in authority. **5. To** avoid **places** of dissipation, and aim at recollectedness. **6. To** repeat the "Gloria Patri" morning and evening. **7. To pray** daily for **the unity** of the Church, the conversion of sinners, the advancement of the faithful and for each **other as brethren.** The title was after a time altered to the Brotherhood of the Holy Trinity, with a Master **(a priest), an** Almoner (a deacon), and an Amanuensis. In addition to the other rules there were special ones, *viz.,* never **to** quote Holy Scripture except for a religious **end; when** in company never to drink in all above **three** glasses of wine; to observe simplicity **in** dress. **Their manual** had forms **of** prayer for special occasions.

I will add, at the risk of some repetition, a list of the chief writers, classified as far as possible.

Theologians and Dogmatic Writers.—J. H. Newman, E. B. Pusey, **R. J.** Wilberforce, R. Owen, **J. J.** Blunt, **W. E. Scudamore, W. H.** Mill, Archer Butler, **J. B.**

Mozley, **W. J. Irons, H. J.** Rose, **Bishop** Forbes, R. H.
Froude, William Sewell, **J. B. Morris, W.** Bright, Thos.
Chamberlain, H. P. Liddon, F. **M. Sadler.**

Sermon Writers and Preachers.—J. **H. Newman, E.**
B. Pusey, Archdeacon Manning, John Keble, **Thomas
Keble,** Isaac Williams, W. Gresley, F. E. Paget, J. B.
Mozley, E. Blencowe, S. Rickards, Bishop Armstrong,
Dr. Neale, G. R. Prynne, W. J. E. Bennett, Jas. Skinner,
Bishop Woodford, H. Newland, H. P. Liddon, etc.

Historians.—S. R. Maitland, W. Palmer, E. Churton,
W. F. Hook, A. W. Haddan, **Bishop Stubbs, Henry**
Caswall, Canon Ashwell, etc.

Devotional Writers and Commentators.—E. B. **Pusey,**
J. M. Neale, Isaac Williams, R. Brett, **W. E.** Scuda-
more, **T.** T. Carter, C. Wordsworth, R. **C. Trench, Dean**
Goulburn, Chas. Marriott, **Dr. Littledale, etc.**

Poets and Hymn Writers.—R. W. Evans, J. H. **New-**
man, J. Keble, Isaac Williams, **Aubrey De** Vere, R. S.
Hawker, J. M. Neale, **F. W. Faber, J.** Chandler, R. C.
Trench, **H.** Caswell, W. J. Copeland, W. J. **Blew,**
H. Collins, W. J. Irons, Mrs. Alexander, Miss **Proctor,**
F. G. Lee, J. Fuller Russell, Dr. Monsell, Miss Inge-
low, Miss Rossetti, and others.

Stories and Allegories.—W. Gresley, F. E. Paget, J. **M.**
Neale, **S.** Wilberforce, **W.** Adams, **W.** E. Heygate,
Bishop Milman, Miss Yonge, Miss Sewell, the author
of *Tales of Kirkbeck,* etc., Miss Ingelow, Miss Skene.

On Law, Ritual, and Liturgiology.—W. **Maskell,**

Canon Trevor, J. Fuller Russell, W. J. Blew, T. W. Perry, C. Grueber, Dr. Littledale, J. D. Chambers, James Parker.

Controversialists in Defence.—Bishop Philpotts, E. B. Pusey, W. J. E. Bennett, J. H. Newman, W. Maskell, W. B. Barter, T. W. Allies, W. J. Irons, G. A. Denison, C. Grueber, **T. W. Perry,** Dr. Littledale, Canon MacColl.

On Art and Architecture.—A. J. B. Beresford Hope, A. W. Pugin, F. A. Paley, J. M. **Neale, B.** Webb, G. A. **Poole,** E. A. Freeman, **G. G.** Scott, G. E. Street, **J. H.** Parker, J. Carpenter, **W.** Burges, **G.** Truefitt, W. Butter-field, J. W. Hallam, Edmond Sedding, **W.** Dyce, **and** others.*

Church Music.—W. Dyce, Dr. Druitt, Sir F. Ouseley, Sir Henry Baker, Rev. J. **W.** Rumsay, **Dr.** Gauntlett, R. Redhead, **T. Helmore, W. S. Rockstro, Dr.** Dykes, A. H. Brown.

Foremost in the revival of church music was the *Parish Choir*; the name of the originator and editor was Dr. Robert Druitt; like his namesake Robert Brett, **Dr.** Druitt for love of the Church gave much valuable

* Benjamin Ferray, who died in August, 1880, deserves good mention as a church architect, eminent in the **early** days of the Gothic revival; as an authority **on** church planning and propor-tions he had scarcely a rival. The builder of St. Stephen's, West-minster, the restorer of Wells Cathedral and Lady Chapel, author of the *Antiquities of the Priory of Christ Church, Hants,* writer of *Recollections of A. Welby Pugin,* whose pupil he was. He was also one of the most perfect draughtsmen of his day; a thorough Church-man, who also gave much help in the revival of church music.

time to editing and writing in the *Parish Choir* and other such works. **Sir** W. Cope, **Mr.** Helmore, W. J. **E.** Bennett, W. **H.** Monk were also contributors up to 1844, as Dr. Druitt points out **in** his *Popular Tract on Church Music, with Remarks on its Moral and Political Importance.* The musical part of Divine Service **in** most parish churches is well known to have been most wretched; and **as in art and** architecture by the Arundel Society and Ecclesiological Society, so in the **sister** art of music the **Church** Movement brought great changes. Pamphlets and sermons were issued on the subject; the choir of the Motett **Society, connected with the** Ecclesiological **Society,** chiefly **promoted by** Mr. Dyce, held its **concerts at** the Architectural **Rooms in** Conduit Street; and here, for some years, the very **best** music **was** to be heard; motetts, madrigals, masses, services from the ancient Mechlin, and other **office** books, from Palestrina, Cherubini; carols and chorales, the " Vexilla Regis," the " Passion Music" of Bach, the works of Ravenscroft, and volumes of anthems and services from these best sources were published. The " Concordia " concerts **were** given **at** this **time,** and the interest in all this musical revival **led to** more care **in** the performance of the musical **parts** of Divine **Service**; and church after church felt the influence, **helped by the** works **of** Mr. Helmore, Mr. Redhead, Dr. Gauntlett and others.

. Bishop Hamilton, when first he went to Salisbury as

canon, and afterwards as precentor, set a good example, selecting **chants** and anthems, making the music, as **far as** might be, illustrate the Church's seasons and teaching; he was well seconded in his efforts to elevate the lives of the lay vicars and choristers to a higher estimate of their work by Dean Lear, the Rev. W. B. Heathcote and others. So cathedral after cathedral carried on **the work** of improvement in careful reverence; and the record now given **of** the work of our cathedrals on all **sides is** much due to the stirring times of the Church Revival. But of all parts of church music revived, that of the hymns of the Church was **by** far the most important. He was a wise man who said, " Let me make the ballads, and who will may make the laws ". The **enormous influence of** hymn singing in every religious **body speaks** for itself. Though at first Tate and Brady were sung in Old Margaret Chapel, leaflets with special **hymns for festivals, etc., were** used very soon, and in **a few** years, some dozens of pioneers to *Hymns Ancient and Modern* led the way. Small hymnals, compiled by various clergy **for** the use of their congregations, were published **by** Dr. Irons, Dr. Oldknow and others. **One of** the principal works **used more** or less in every collection was the translations **by Dr.** Neale of the old **hymns** of the Church in the *Hymnal Noted*, set **to** the old notation by Mr. Helmore, published by Novello. **One of the earliest of these** hymnals was compiled by Mr. Keble and Earl **Nelson,** at the request of Bishop

Hamilton of Salisbury, called the *Salisbury Hymnal*. The old evangelical hymns of Wesley, Toplady and others were used, care being taken to give them an orthodox tone, by adding the "Gloria" at the end of each hymn. Mr. Roundell Palmer's (Lord Selborne) book was a great help to the exact form of most of these hymns. Almost all these hymnals were, in the course of a few years, merged in *Hymns Ancient and Modern*, compiled by the Rev. Sir Henry Baker and others, under the musical editorship of the late Mr. W. H. Monk, assisted by Dr. Stainer, Dr. Dykes and others. No hymnal has yet been so widely adopted, or been felt to encourage so well the love of hymn singing most natural to every phase of religion. Some hundreds of tunes written expressly for this work have made the hymns familiar far and wide. There is very much in a tune, too (the compilers of hymns A and M took care to retain all the grand old tunes, such as St. Anne and St. James); and it is said that when Dr. Dykes, who wrote the music to "Lead, kindly Light," was introduced to the author at the Oratory, Birmingham, Dr. Newman said, "Your tune has been quite the making of my hymn".

This revival of music in Divine service was not confined to the Church. Many Dissenting congregations improved their music on the same lines. Dr. Gauntlett taught the Islington and other Dissenters to chant the "Te Deum," the Bible Psalms, and Canticles.

I would wish in conclusion to point out the thoroughly *English* character of **the** literature : **the** Movement was essentially in and **of** the Church of England, and in all **this** vast amount **of** learning and writing there is little from foreign sources and still less that accords with the modern decrees, recent articles, and definitions of faith of the **Roman** Church as we see her now.

To prove the English character of the Movement we **need** but glance at **the** reprints made by the principal Tractarians: they **were** from Laud, Andrewes, Sutton, Hammond, Sherlock, **Ken,** Nelson, Wilson, Kettlewell, Taylor, Sparkes, Cosin, Lake, Beveridge, Bull, **Butler,** etc., etc., most of them truly Catholic, referring, **as our** Book of Common Prayer does, **to** ancient times **and** precedents.